W9-DIA-798

The Perfect Sister

ALSO BY MARCIA MILLMAN

The Seven Stories of Love:
How to Recognize Your Own Pattern
of Love—and Choose Your Happy Ending

Warm Hearts and Cold Cash:
The Intimate Dynamics of Families and Money

Such a Pretty Face:
Being Fat in America

The Unkindest Cut:
Life in the Backrooms of Medicine

The Perfect Sister

What Draws Us Together,
What Drives Us Apart

MARCIA MILLMAN

Harcourt, Inc.

ORLANDO   AUSTIN   NEW YORK
SAN DIEGO   TORONTO   LONDON

Copyright © 2004 by Marcia Millman

All rights reserved. No part of this publication may be reproduced or
transmitted in any form or by any means, electronic or mechanical,
including photocopy, recording, or any information storage and retrieval
system, without permission in writing from the publisher.

Requests for permission to make copies of any part of the work should be
mailed to the following address: Permissions Department, Harcourt, Inc.,
6277 Sea Harbor Drive, Orlando, Florida 32887-6777.

www.HarcourtBooks.com

Library of Congress Cataloging-in-Publication Data
Millman, Marcia.
The perfect sister: what draws us together, what drives us apart/
Marcia Millman.—1st ed.
p.   cm.
ISBN 0-15-100895-7
1. Sisters—Psychology. 2. Sisters—Case studies. I. Title.
HQ759.96.M55 2004
306.875'4—dc22   2003019812

Text set in Minion
Designed by Lydia D'moch

Printed in the United States of America

First edition
A C E G I K J H F D B

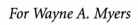

For Wayne A. Myers

Contents

Introduction

MANY OF US HAVE an image of the perfect sister. She understands you intuitively because she had the same parents and shared your childhood. She laughed and cried with you through all your early adventures: family outings and holidays, summers at the beach, shopping expeditions, getting through school, experiments with haircuts and makeup, surviving first loves and losses.

She accepts and supports you even when she would choose a different path. Although you started out as big or little sister, you evolved into equal friends. She never complains that your parents gave you more and that's why your life turned out better. She is always there for you in moments of crisis, knowing what you need without being told.

She can listen to you without offering advice when you just want a sympathetic ear. She was your ally in childhood who helped you deal with your parents, and later, she was your partner in coping with their illnesses. She gives you what no one else in the world can give you—a lasting connection to your childhood and family. Your sister shares your memories of all the important people and events in your life even after everyone else is gone. She's the one person you have for your entire life.

Some women are actually blessed with that perfect sister, and they can't imagine life without her. But for most of us, the reality doesn't always live up to the ideal. Some adult sisters feel they have nothing in common. They say their sister isn't someone they would have picked for a friend. There are sisters who have close relationships, but they keep having the same upsetting conflicts or disappointments. Others wonder why their sister relationships don't match their expectations or the cultural ideal. And hardest of all, there are the women who feel great pain when the sister they've always loved starts to act like a stranger.

I began to wonder how women deal with the gap between the sister they wish for and the complex relationships that actually exist. I wondered why some sisters are able to stay close and loving while others become divided and can't find a way to resolve their problems. Having a sister myself and listening to my friends, I know that sisters play a huge role in our childhood and identities. Sisters are often our first role models, allies, and friends. Sisterhood is also a bond that usually lasts forever. Most women I know feel deeply connected to their sister whether she's perfect or flawed. No matter what kind of relationship they have, they would like to find a way to make it even better.

In my professional life, I'm a sociologist with a speciality in social psychology. I've spent many years studying family interactions and relationships, and I've noticed that most of the attention has been focused on couples and parent-child relationships. Psychologists have looked at sibling bonds in childhood but have tended to see sibling relationships mainly as reflections of parent-child relationships even though siblings have powerful relationships in their own right. In the past two decades, several surveys have tried to evaluate whether adult siblings are a source of social support late in life. But these studies are limited in what they can tell us about sisterhood and its larger significance. For one thing, most of the studies haven't focused on sister-sister bonds, even though all the research suggests adult sisters are closer than brothers or mixed-sibling pairs. The studies also focus on either the beginning or end of life and neglect everything in between. For the most part they are surveys, so they don't probe very deeply into why sisters become close or divided, or whether their relationships change over the years. Most importantly, what's missing from existing research is an inquiry into the emotional attachments and feelings between sisters. What do these relationships mean to women, and how do they evolve?

It seemed likely to me that many of the common events of the middle years—raising children; dealing with the loss or the aging of parents; seeing children move away and establish separate lives; facing illness, divorce, or realizing that one might not have children or a permanent partner in the future—all these events might intensify a woman's wish or need to have a good relationship with her sister. Sisterhood is one of the few bonds that give us a sense of continuity from childhood to old age. When other familial attachments are lost, our bonds with our sisters may become a great deal more significant.

What does this mean for how one should go about studying sisterhood? It's true that sister relationships are initially formed in the context of our original families. You can't understand your relationship with your sister without recognizing how it originally fit into the bigger picture of your family. But relationships change as life circumstances evolve—and we need to relate to our sister in her current life, as well as to understand the legacy from the past.

I decided to undertake a study to learn how sisters actually relate in adulthood and find out what brings them closer or drives them apart. During the past two and a half years, I've interviewed one hundred women in long, open-ended interviews, investigating how their sister bonds have evolved throughout their lives. I didn't want to use a standardized questionnaire or do a survey of how often one thing or another would be reported. Rather, my aim was to go deep—to discover the different sisterhoods and to identify the major sister archetypes and the characteristic forces behind them.

The women I interviewed ranged in age from twenty-five to eighty-two, with the greatest concentration in their forties and fifties. They came from all sections of the country and had diverse class and ethnic backgrounds. They included a woman who had lived in a homeless shelter and a woman who had held a high political office.

Because I don't believe there's any one "truth" in a family or relationship, I was willing to interview any individual sister and accept her account as the reality she experienced. When it was possible, I would interview (separately) both or all of the sisters who grew up together, in order to hear about one family from different perspectives. My highest priority was to allow my subjects to speak fully and honestly, and I decided this required not using their real names and changing some biographical details.

A number of women I interviewed offered to ask their sisters if they would participate in the study because they thought (and I agreed) it would be fascinating to know and read about a relationship from different points of view. In the end, almost a third of my sample was composed of two or three related sisters.

One of the women I interviewed joked that she feared I might like her sister better! Her remark reminded me that it takes tremendous courage and trust to let your sister talk about you and have her account of your relationship stand alongside your own. But the ability to recognize that people in a relationship experience and remember things differently is the key to getting along.

I did find it illuminating to compare the different accounts of sisters who grew up together. Hearing more than one version of a family history is a powerful reminder that sisters may live in the same house but they live in different families. There are several reasons why: Sisters have different talents and characteristics, and they elicit different responses from their parents. They also occupy different roles and birth-order positions, and they're different ages at every point of the family history. Their positions may not only be different, but unequal.

Although sisters usually reported many of the same events, they often saw them very differently. This didn't surprise me but the conflicting perceptions also made me interested in the distortions of perception, which are often evident even in one-sided accounts. Our memories are never entirely accurate, but what we remember is the reality we live in. I did pay close attention to obvious or likely distortions of perception. They don't invalidate an account—in fact, they offer especially valuable information because they suggest when the speaker is driven primarily by wishes and illusions, which is crucial to understanding anyone's behavior.

For example, when someone describes how she was repeatedly hurt and surprised by her sister's behavior, it suggests she has expectations that are unrealistic, given what's described of her sister or the nature of their relationship. It suggests her expectations of her sister are driven by wishes rather than realistic appraisals.

I have noticed that sisters who come from happy families tend to remember events more similarly than sisters who come from unhappy families. Part of the reason for this may be that they have talked to each other more and have influenced each other's perceptions and memories. Through their conversation they built up a shared reality. But more importantly, children who aren't well cared for are often engaged in relationships that are driven by wishes or projections (on both sides) rather than accurate perceptions of people and situations. They relate to Imagined Sisters as well as to clearly seen ones. I'm reminded of the famous first line from Leo Tolstoy's novel *Anna Karenina*, "All happy families are alike but an unhappy family is unhappy after its own fashion." I don't agree, but I would propose instead that happy families are more likely to be remembered the same way by their members while unhappy families are not.

What I found in my research defies some of the common assumptions about sisters and what makes them close. Many sisters who were close as children drifted apart as adults. Sisters who barely spoke as children often became best friends as adults, frequently after having children of their own. The age gap between sisters didn't necessarily determine how close their adult relationship was, and financial differences in adulthood mattered less than I had expected.

In fact, I found most of the events that are commonly considered to be sources of tension between sisters—marriages, deaths, divorces, having children, caring for sick parents—actually brought sisters closer together as often as they drove sisters apart. It was the way that sisters related to these events that had real significance for their bond. Any major turning point in life can change our perspective and this often changes our relationships with our sisters.

I found that sisters are often divided because of the way their parents treat them: favoring one child over the other, requiring a child to assume adult responsibilities like being surrogate parents to their younger sisters and showing their children so little empathy that the children don't develop the capacity for empathy themselves. When sisters had loving and happy parents they were usually spared from some of the childhood sources of sister conflicts in adulthood. On the other hand, many of the strongest sister bonds I heard about were between sisters who'd received very little attention from parents. As children, they took care of each other in order to fill the void. They did what their parents couldn't do, and they did it with astonishing sensitivity and generosity. They often grew up to have happy lives, and their attachment to each other remained very loving and strong. Children often create their own shared worlds, apart from the world of their parents. They do so in both happy and unhappy families, but it's a world that's often overlooked by adults.

We know that it usually takes effort and thought to have good relationships with partners and children. But women often assume their relationship with their sister is intrinsically good or bad, or they can't figure out how to make it stronger. What I've learned from my research is that we need to radically shift the way we think about our sister relationships.

First, we must realize our sister relationship was originally formed in the larger context of our childhood family. In order to understand our sister bond we need to take in the whole picture and see how our relationship fit into the other family dynamics.

Second, we need to recognize that as an adult we do have the power to radically change our relationship with our sister. And it starts with getting a clearer view of her.

I discovered there is one primary difference between sisters who have good relationships and sisters with troubled ones: seeing or failing to see the person who is actually there. By this, I mean that most of us relate to an Imagined Sister, as well as to our Real Sister, and that relating too much to the Imagined Sister can get a person into trouble and so can mixing them up. We need to be able to recognize both figures and separate them. And we need to be relating to our Real Sister most of the time.

Who is this Imagined Sister? She's the one we created out of our needs and wishes, the same wishes that often keep us from seeing the person who's really there. This doesn't mean we are "imagining" things when our sisters leave us feeling angry or hurt. Many women I interviewed described their sister's actual behavior very accurately. But despite what they clearly observed, they held on to expectations that didn't fit with the real person—and so they were repeatedly disappointed, angry, or hurt. If we relate to the sister we wish for, or the one we perceived in our childhood rather than the one who exists today, we need to discover the feelings and needs that are making us relate to this created figure. This process happens in both directions, so we also need to understand what's going on when our sister isn't relating to us but to her own Imagined Sister.

And who is the Real Sister? She might be a wonderful person or a terrible one. Usually she has both good qualities and limitations. And most importantly, she's different from us. We can't expect her to think or act the way we do just because she's our sister. I found that women who could fully see and accept that their sister was different and that she had different needs were usually able to see their Real Sisters. Women who remembered that their sister did not have the same experience they did growing up in their family were usually relating to their Real Sister. And I also learned that the ability to recognize the real person is something we can gain at any point in life.

Some sisters relate primarily to their Real Sister from childhood. Others only learn to do so as adults. When it happens later, it's usually because some change in life circumstance has encouraged a greater empathy or altered the need for an illusion that obscured a clearer vision.

For example, many women told me they first got to really know and appreciate their sisters when they both became mothers. They loved bringing up their children together and especially doing mother-daughter things with their sisters and nieces. When I asked them why having children brought them closer, several women said they wanted their children to have an extended family. Others said that becoming mothers had given them something in common with their sisters. Some of them noticed that having children made formerly unequal sisters become equals. Others said that when they became mothers, their sisters offered them the help and support they had never gotten from their own mothers.

I realized that all these explanations share a common thread: They all involve shifting perspectives and/or a change in roles. When women become mothers they often try to give their children a better experience than the one they had. So they're already poised to reexamine and change familial patterns from their past. It can be even more satisfying to do this in the company of the person who was your witness as a child, the person who shared your childhood, even if her experience of it wasn't the same as yours. With everything else changing, you are no longer so locked into your childhood roles. Becoming a mother often makes a woman see her own mother and childhood differently. This change in perspective also allows her to look at her sister in a fresh way. One major conclusion I drew from my research is that our feelings for our sisters are often connected to the feelings we have toward our mother and the way she related to each of us. The sister relationship is part of a web of mother-daughter relations and the family constellation as a whole.

Sisters frequently serve as mother surrogates to one another when their mothers are unavailable, missing, or incompetent. Even in adulthood, sisters sometimes unconsciously project needs for a mother to one another.

One finding that surprised me enormously was how often my interviewees complained about their mothers. Though most loved their mothers, a majority described them as difficult: controlling, critical, depressed, withdrawn, guilt-inducing, or unaccepting of them. Much more often, they remembered their fathers as a much greater source of love and warmth and understanding.

I had no idea so many women found their mothers to be critical and controlling and their fathers so sympathetic. It may be that daughters who had conflicts with controlling mothers tended to view their fathers as fellow sufferers. More than one woman I interviewed said that her father had been banished to the garage—a kind of human doghouse. One recalled her mother wouldn't let her father smoke in the house, so he spent nearly all his time in his "Cinderella Corner" in the garage, with his radio and ashtray. She joked that at night you could walk down her parents' street and you wouldn't believe how many men were out there in their garages.

I was surprised by this sympathy for fathers and the anger at mothers. The women I interviewed have lived through the age of feminism, which has taught us how mothers (and women, in general) are frequently blamed, while men are more likely to be idealized and admired. Some of the women I spoke with could even relate their mother's difficult behavior to social constraints, remarking that as they became older they often had a more realistic view of the challenges their mothers faced. But interestingly, they still described their fathers with greater affection.

It may be that their mothers were doing more of the supervisory work of parenting, while the fun times were with their fathers. More importantly, I suspect the identification between mothers and daughters draws the attention of each to the other one's flaws. We tend to react sharply when we see something we don't like about ourselves expressed in a person we feel closely identified with. Mothers don't want their daughters to repeat their mistakes, so they often criticize behavior that strikes a chord. In adolescence, daughters often have a harder time separating from their mothers than their fathers, and so they scrutinize their mothers' defects.

On a related note, I noticed that women were often aware when their mother had divided them from their sisters or put their own needs first. Fathers, also, may set up their daughters to be rivals. But the women I interviewed almost never perceived this. They were aware of competing with their sisters for their father's love— but it rarely occurred to them that their father might have encouraged the rivalry to serve his own needs.

In most cases, it seemed that brothers did not loom as large in their emotional landscapes as sisters. Most women didn't compare themselves to their brothers in the same way they did to their sisters. They felt it would be like comparing apples and oranges. The greater intimacy and involvement, or disappointment, was in the sister bond. In adulthood, too, women were usually less emotionally involved with their brothers. Several believed their married brothers had just withdrawn from their families and had become resocialized into the families of their wives.

Another unexpected theme that impressed me was how often these women's lives were deeply affected by unplanned pregnancies. A very frequent theme in these stories is that my interviewee or her mother or sister became pregnant before abortions were available or acceptable, and having a baby before they were ready was especially destructive to the women who wound up marrying men they didn't love.

MANY WOMEN I interviewed would say, with anger or resignation, that they couldn't understand their sisters. They didn't know how someone who grew up in the same house and was raised by the same parents could possibly act the way their sisters did. The reason sisters often can't understand each other is precisely because they think they grew up in the same family, when they didn't. The differences between sisters and what they elicit from parents, their often-dichotomized roles and positions in the family, and different ages all mean they live in a different family even if they spend sixteen years sharing a bedroom. If you want to understand your sister, you need to learn about her family, which isn't the same as yours.

If you are puzzled by the conflicts between you and your sister, it helps to think about these questions: What did your sister get in childhood and what was she never given? What does she believe she got and what does she think you got? And equally important, ask these very same questions of yourself. You need to figure out the baggage that both of you are carrying. Also ask yourself what happened (or failed to happen) to each of you later in life that either one of you attributes in some way to your childhood. This is the key to understanding your sister, because you really didn't get the same things, no matter how fair your parents tried to be. Timing, position, and different talents all create inequalities that are almost inevitable.

Sisters often argue about whose perceptions of family relationships is correct. It is useful information to learn how another person experiences your family or your relationship, but arguing over who is right or wrong is beside the point. You need to understand that your sister's different experience was, and is, just as real for her as yours is for you. It's not just a matter of different perceptions but different experiences. Until you truly accept this you can't recognize or respond to each other's needs.

Looking at what you and your sister were given and what was withheld from either of you includes clearly seeing everything that might affect her feeling for you. Your appearance and intellectual and social skills were different. Your mother and father responded to those differences and projected their own feelings of pride or shame. They made different demands of you and you received different rewards, no matter how fair they tried to be. One of you may have received more love, acceptance, recognition, attention. Your mother may have felt closer or confided more in one of you at any given time (usually the older sister, initially). One of you was probably your father's favorite. One of you might have been designated as the one who would be a great wife and mother, and the other might have felt closed out of the circle of women. Your parents may have had more time or more money to spend at different times in their lives. They may have been happier with each other when the older child was growing up; the younger one may have been exposed to more of their anger or depression or vice versa.

Unfortunately, it's very common for sisters to be placed in split, or dichotomized, roles like good/bad, pretty/smart, easygoing/ difficult. Even more divisive (and common) is when one daughter is chosen as the special confidante of their mother. This often disrupts the possibility for an alliance between sisters because the chosen confidante has become her mother's peer rather than her sister's. Not only do these roles exaggerate our differences and divide us, but they become extremely destructive whenever a sister feels too defeated to compete along any desirable dimension.

Sisters often resent each other because they think their disappointments in life are due to what the other sister got and they didn't get from their parents. This may not be self-deception at all, because it's often true. The only thing wrong with the reasoning is blaming your sister for what your parents did. You need to understand the nature of rivalry in your family and where it came from—your parents' negative and positive projections, as well as the innate differences between you. Sisters who get along understand that their parents might have preferred one of them not because they were really better, but because of their own needs.

Although my study was about sisters, understanding the context of their relationships required examining their families more generally. Sister relationships are one lens for seeing the intricate workings of family life. Some of the things I've learned about sisters might apply to relationships between brothers or between sisters and brothers.

———

SOMETIMES IT'S EASIER to recognize our patterns of relating when we can look at them in someone else. I couldn't include the stories of all the interesting sisters I interviewed in this book. I chose those that express the range of common experiences and that helped me to understand the recurrent themes that appeared in my research.

I start with stories of women who do relate to their Real Sisters, for the most part, and who also played primary nurturing roles to each other at some point in life. In part II, I examine archetypes of "problem" sisters and explore troubled sister relationships. These are the stories of women who relate to an Imagined Sister, though some of them come to recognize their Real Sister. I want to stress that although some of my informants used the interview to vent their frustrations or disappointments, it was obvious that most of them also loved their sisters and were deeply attached to them. I wasn't surprised they would end a long complaint by saying, "But I really love my sister" or add that they really enjoyed being with her most of the time.

The disappointments or hurt that surface in an interview may coexist with a generally pleasant and caring day-to-day relationship, as it does with any close bond. It took a lot of courage for them to talk about painful feelings that many people would not be willing to face, let alone share with others.

In the final section, I tell the stories of sisters who were able, relatively late in life, to create loving relationships with their fully recognized sisters, sometimes after years of having unequal or distant relationships. This brought them a great and unexpected gift as adults, because their tie to their sister also gave them a positive connection to their past. Sisters can help us feel a vital connection to our childhood and our parents and therefore help us deal with loss. It's one of the unique blessings of having a sister. But in the best relationships, sisters don't just reminisce. They move beyond loss and relate to their current sister—not just the sister of their past.

PART ONE

The Real Sister

CHAPTER I

Identical Twins
and Their Husbands

NOW THAT SHE'S in her sixties and starting to think about mortality, Ellie told me she worries about who will die first, her identical twin sister, Emma, or herself: "I'd rather go together." If one of them were widowed first, they'd want to live near each other—which might require moving away from her grandchildren. "I would rather be with my sister than with my grandchildren," she admits. "We have the same interests, and we shouldn't set our lives aside for the grandchildren, although I wouldn't like leaving them."

Ellie's fears of losing her twin triggered a memory from my early childhood, one that I'd always tried to push out of my mind. I grew up in Manhattan, and a pair of identical twin girls lived in our apartment building. I would always see them with their mother in our elevator. As a small child, I was fascinated by these duplicate girls. We weren't quite the same age, and I didn't know their names. I knew them only as the twins. They were always dressed in identical outfits. I can still picture them in their plaid dresses, blond bangs, and ponytails.

One day, my mother and I got into the elevator, and I was surprised to see only one twin with her mother. "Where's the other twin?" I asked, because I'd never seen them apart. Either the mother or the child—I can no longer remember which one—immediately burst into tears, and no one answered my question. My mother yanked me out of the elevator when the door opened, and as soon as we were alone, she told me I should never ask them that question again. She explained that one of the twins had run into the street and had been killed by a car.

Not long after that, the family of the twins moved away, but whenever I've thought of them, I've always felt dreadfully guilty about my question, and I've never forgotten the image of that mournful little girl staring at me. Even as a child, I understood that this was an unspeakable tragedy. I'd never known any other child who had died, and I'm sure I thought the surviving twin was now only half a person.

Reminded of this tragedy by Ellie's concern about one twin dying before the other, I felt a new pang of guilt for my insensitive question. Why was I feeling so guilty? I began to wonder if I'd really known the answer before I asked the question—did I feel guilty because I'd been purposely cruel? Then I started to wonder how old I was when this happened. Had I been old enough to know better than to ask?

I immediately called up my sister, Sandra, to ask if she remembered the twins and if she knew what had happened to them. As usual, she remembered many more of the details than I did. My sister is two and a half years older than I, so she was usually better informed whenever anything like this happened.

She remembered that the twins fell between us in age, which is why they weren't our playmates or classmates. Much to my relief, she said the girl died around the age of six or seven, so I would have been about five or six. Too young, I thought, to have been malicious in asking the question. My sister assured me that no one in our family would have talked about it or warned me not to ask about the absent twin.

I probably have always felt horribly guilty about this incident because I'd obviously upset my mother (who rarely criticized me) as well as upsetting the twin and her mother. And I'd often been told that I asked too many questions. Or maybe I always felt guilty because I had a sister, and here was a child whose sister had died.

My sister and I pooled our memories of this event: The twin had been hit by the car on the street just behind our apartment building—a street that was supposed to be closed to traffic during the daytime. It was where all the children in my building would roller-skate or jump rope or play with marbles. My sister remembered that one of the twins was named Iris, which rang a bell in my mind, and Sandra remembered, as I did, that the family disappeared not long after the accident. We decided the family must have moved because staying where the twin was killed would have been unbearable.

One reason I go into this personal digression is because, like so many women I interviewed, I find it comforting to have a sister who can remember all the mundane and dramatic things that happened around us as children. I always find it uniquely reassuring to discuss childhood memories with my sister. She's my connection to my past, the only person who can help me remember what happened.

The memory of this event also helped me to understand what Ellie was saying about her attachment to her twin sister and why it would be harder for her to adjust to losing her sister than to losing her husband.

Ellie is a pretty and vivacious woman who looks much younger than her nearly seventy years. She began our interview by talking about her inauspicious beginnings. Her mother was unmarried and living in a small Midwestern farming town when she became pregnant with Ellie and Emma. At the time their mother became pregnant, she belonged to a religious Catholic family and community. Becoming an unwed mother was certainly not acceptable in their mother's world, and neither was an abortion. So she decided to move to Chicago in order to have the baby in secret and give it up for adoption.

She told everyone, including her family, that she was leaving town to get away from an engagement that hadn't worked out. In fact, her boyfriend had more or less broken off their engagement when she told him she was pregnant. When they'd gone to a priest for counseling, her boyfriend had agreed to marry her but said he didn't love her. The only other person she confided in was her older sister, Anne, who went with her to Chicago. Ellie continued the story:

I learned all this, secondhand, fifty years later, from my aunt Anne. My mother had agreed to give her baby up for adoption. But when she gave birth to two instead of one, she wanted to keep us. My aunt Anne stayed with her, and they lived in Chicago. One of them worked nights as a telephone operator, and the other had a job during the day as a secretary, so someone would always be with the babies. We were almost a year old before her family found out about our existence. My aunt was never able to have children, but throughout her life she took in every niece and nephew whenever her sisters needed help—one child who had tuberculosis and another when his parents divorced.

My grandmother came to see my mother in Chicago and told her she didn't care what people thought, she was bringing us home. So we lived with my grandmother until my mother met my father when we were two and a half. My mother was selling shoes at the time, and she came home from the movies one night, all excited. She'd met Bill Blake, a professional musician who played the organ and piano in movie theaters, churches, orchestras, and skating rinks—he moved around a lot, wherever he got work. He asked her for a date, and she fell head over heels with him. They eloped because his family was strict Lutheran (his father was a minister), and they wouldn't have approved of his marrying a poor Catholic woman who was five years older and who had two illegitimate children.

Once they got married, the Blakes wanted my parents to keep our birth history a secret, and my mother's family agreed. So we grew up believing that Bill was our father. We never learned the truth until after my mother died. We always questioned her about what it was like to have twins, but she never wanted to talk about the events surrounding our birth. Our father said he went away to college and that's why he was away when we were very young, but it never added up to us—how could he go to college when she had babies? Since she was five years older than our father, we just decided that she didn't want to talk about it because she was sensitive about her age, or we thought that maybe she'd had to get married.

We moved away from Wisconsin in 1940, when we were seven, and stopped for six weeks in Ohio and then moved on to Georgia, where my father played in a small trio and worked in a piano bar. For five years we stayed in Georgia while my father worked in different cities around the state. During the second grade, we went to three different schools and we always lived in hotels. In 1945 we moved again when my father got a job in Florida and we settled there. We cried our eyes out because we didn't want to leave Georgia and our friends.

Their marriage wasn't happy. My father was a nice-looking man, and he was out every night, working in bars. He'd play poker through the night, and I know he had at least one long affair. My parents would get separated, and get back together. Their quarrels were very traumatic to us. He'd be out drinking and then my mother would drink and stew. We got up and made breakfast for ourselves and went to school. We'd walk home and make our own lunch and walk back to school. At night, we stayed home and did our homework or we'd go to the movies. My mother let us do what we wanted. She didn't keep track of us, and my father wasn't around much.

When we were thirteen, my mother got so fed up with him she told us about his affairs. She'd found love letters that a woman had been writing to him for two years, and she threw the letters on the floor and said, "Look at this." By then, the affair was over, but she always kept bringing it up.

In 1952, when my father was thirty-eight, he had surgery for an ulcer; and he stayed in the hospital for three weeks, fighting an infection. We got a call that he was running a very high temperature, and we had to rush to the hospital from home. I was with him before he died, and he told me, "I'm scared." I was nineteen and I'd just finished business school, and my sister was a nursing student.

Fifty years later, Ellie still has recurrent dreams about her father's death. Remarkably, her twin sister has very similar dreams— always about being abandoned by their father. The twins rarely dream about their mother.

In my dreams, my father appears; and I always say, "You died, and now you are here. You lied to us—you didn't really die." Or I'll dream that because they had a difficult marriage, he left, and I said, "Why did you go away?" He shows up and I'm angry that he left.

He died young, and my parents were always on the verge of breaking up. Their fights made us very anxious, and I think the dreams come from the anxiety that's left over from when we were kids. My sister has even more anxiety dreams—many more than I do. We talk about it. It's an outlet for the anxiety that goes back to our childhood—the instability of our parents' marriage and moving around as we did.

My father was very loving, but he was strict and the disciplinarian—he'd been raised by a minister. He'd just give us a look across the table, and we'd cry. Then he'd talk to us, and say, "Why are you crying? I didn't hit you."

His death was a real shock, and we'd never had anyone close to us die. It took us a year or more to realize he was really gone because he'd been gone so much when we were growing up. Because of his jobs, he'd been away for six months once, and one time for a year. When he died it didn't sink in for a long time because it was almost like he would be back.

My mother was very upset when my father died. They had an argument just before he went to the hospital, and she felt guilty. She started drinking too much and was depressed for two or three years. She would go into her room and sleep for days. She'd come out and make a meal and go back to sleep. We just kept up our own routine.

When Ellie shifts from memories of her parents to memories of growing up with her sister, the picture really brightens.

We were always close. We slept in the same double bed, and we never had any serious conflicts. We never didn't like being twins. We always had each other when we had to start a new school. We were always in the same class, and we wore identical clothes. People made a fuss over us—relatives and friends. They'd tell us to stand up together, so they could compare us. My father wanted us to get up and sing and perform on the stage, but we never wanted to.

Our friends could differentiate between us—I was a little more animated and outgoing, and Emma was more serious. Our parents never made any comparisons. Our teachers could tell us apart. Our grades were usually the same—I recall one year I got a B– and she got a C. But we usually had pretty much the same grades.

My mother made all our clothes until the end of the Depression, and she always made us identical outfits. She made us three dresses to start every school year. There was always a plaid dress with a white Peter Pan collar and two others. People in our neighborhood used to watch us every day, to see what we were wearing.

Once, we had two identical outfits that had ruffles layered in three colors: pink, white, and green. We looked like a pair of triple ice-cream cones walking down the street. We said we didn't want to wear that dress and have to walk down the street. People were very friendly; they'd come up to ask us about being twins.

In our ninth-grade graduation picture, we're wearing identical outfits that my mother sewed for us. But after the Depression, we bought most of our clothes in a dress shop in town. We learned we had to order our clothes before we needed them, because they usually carried only one dress or blouse in each size, and we had to have the same thing. If we saw something we liked, the lady would have to order another one, and we'd have to wait until it came before we could wear them.

There's an attitude now that parents should make their twin children become individuals—that they shouldn't dress them alike, or put them in the same class. I think it was in the 1950s or '60s that this new attitude came into fashion. But when we were children it was different. The only time we were ever separated from each other was when my sister had a burst appendix when we were ten.

She'd had three attacks of abdominal pain, two of them after we'd spent the night with friends. So my mother thought at first it was from eating too much candy. We were in Georgia then, during the war years. The third time, she was so bent over—her appendix had burst—they had to put her in an ambulance and she went to the hospital. She was actually on the critical list for seventy-two hours, but they didn't tell me until later. The night after she left, I had abdominal pains, too. My mother called the doctor, but mine were sympathy pains.

She was in the hospital for ten days, and at that time they didn't allow children to be visitors. But they let me go up to her room and visit her because we were twins and we'd never been apart. Sulfa drugs had just come out during the war, so they were able to save her, and they drained her infection. It was the only time we were ever separated until we were adults. I went to see her every day, and they also let me bring a friend. We shared all our friends—we never had separate friends as children.

We did everything together. We both worked in the same gift shop when we got our first jobs, but we had to work on different shifts because they only needed one cashier. We worked as movie usherettes together.

Ellie tells me that after high school, they gradually started to lead separate lives. Emma entered a four-year nurse training program at a Catholic hospital in Florida. Ellie stayed home for the next two years, going to business school. When Emma moved from home to live at the nursing school, Ellie really missed her. "I'd go to visit her on Friday nights, but they were very strict and didn't allow overnight guests. I'd wear her coat and sneak in, right by the Mother, and we'd both sleep in her bed."

The major break in their joined identity came when Ellie's sister met her husband, Paul, and married at age twenty-two. Her husband was in the navy, and they moved to California where he'd been posted.

She'd had a boyfriend the year before, but it only really hit me when she got married and was moving to California. I started crying. I always thought we'd live in the same area, and this going off, cross-country, really hit me. I knew this was it. Our relationship would never be the same again. I was jealous of her getting married and having a man in her life.

Ellie met her husband and married two years later.

I was doing dictation in a medical office, and my husband was a patient. He was cute and talkative, and he asked me to a movie and later we went dancing. We've been married forty-six years, and my sister's been married forty-eight years. My brother-in-law was transferred back to Florida after I got married, so for most of this time we've lived a few hundred miles apart. What has been good for us is that we've never lived in the same city since we married.

We visit each other every three months; one of us will drive up or down the coast. We always spend our birthday and anniversaries together. Our husbands get along very well: We play golf or bridge, and we've traveled a lot together. Both of them were in the service. Paul worked in banks most of his life and my husband was an investment analyst for thirty years.

Our husbands are very good about the twin thing. In the summers our two families used to rent a big house together in Maine. Emma's husband, Paul, liked it—he has a lot of fun with the twin thing, he'd say, Let's switch and see if we can fool somebody.

Ellie told me a story about her brother-in-law that illustrated what makes her such a loving sister. At the start of our interview, she'd said that she never knew about the circumstances of her birth until she was forty-nine.

After Mom died and my grandmother died, I organized a surprise party for the forty-fifth wedding anniversary of my aunt Anne and Uncle Jim. Jim was an old friend of my father's—he'd met Anne through my parents. For some reason, Uncle Jim chose that time to announce that Bill wasn't really our father. We've had many family gatherings with people drinking, and this had never gotten out. I later learned that he waited until after my grandmother died, because she'd stopped him from telling us and told him to let it be. I wasn't angry that everyone had kept the secret. We found out at an age when we were mature. In our younger years we might have been more upset, and as teenagers we would have been judgmental. There's no right time to give this news if you haven't told children as early as possible. It just gets harder and harder.

This happened in April of 1984. In July, I got a call from my brother-in-law Paul telling me to come. Then he dropped the bombshell on my sister and me.

After Paul found out that Bill Blake wasn't our father, he started to dig into our past. He'd found our birth certificate and the court records of our mother's attempts to get child support. He got all the records. The three of us had gone out for breakfast and he just presented all the documents to us.

He'd also tracked down our biological father—his name was in the court records—and he'd talked to the man's daughter. The daughter told him not to call anymore, because it was upsetting her father. Fifty years had gone by, and the man was in his eighties. But Paul didn't give up. He told his son, my nephew, to make a trip to the man's house and knock on the door and introduce himself as his grandson. Our father wouldn't let him come into the house and just talked to him for a few minutes on the porch.

I hadn't been interested in finding this man. We felt so accepted by my father's family that I hadn't wanted to look for my real father. My sister was very upset that Paul had done this without our consent. He thought he was doing a wonderful thing. He thought it was fascinating, and he didn't realize that we might not be fascinated. Emma told him she had the weirdest feeling, and she was incredibly upset. I didn't say anything because I knew he had meant well, and he already knew Emma was upset.

When he realized how upset we were, my brother-in-law just said he would take off for a long walk down the road, and he'd wait on a bench by a rest stop. If we wanted to meet him, we'd know where to find him. After he left, I told Emma it bothered me, but I made up my mind not to make it a big issue because she was already upset. Paul meant well, and he felt terrible when he realized that we were upset.

We just figured how long it would take Paul to walk to the turnout, and we drove there and met him. We had breakfast and were very quiet. Paul and Emma talked about it together, and I thought, it's between them, and it's already done. The biggest issue was really between them, so I felt I didn't have to put in my two cents.

I asked Ellie how she could exercise such self-control, and she answered that having grown up with parents who quarreled all the time, she didn't like conflict. Because of that, she'd never argued around her children, and she'd learned to hold her tongue.

I looked at the court records with my sister. The birth certificate shows that my mother was in such turmoil. She made up a fake name for the father, and first she'd put a check next to where it said "legitimate." Then she'd scratched that out and checked "illegitimate" and wrote in her family name.

I realize now she was going through all this anguish—she'd made up this story and then changed it. My aunt told me that after we were born my mother was crying and said, "I can't give them up." The woman who had been arranging the adoption and who had given them a place to live was very upset when she changed her mind.

I realized that if we had been adopted, I might have been separated from my twin sister, and all my life, I might have felt something was missing. I've read this happens to twins who are separated—they feel something missing in their psyche and then they find out there's a twin. I didn't think that much about what could have happened until I saw the records.

I bless our mother for bringing us into the world and for keeping us together. I didn't realize until after she died that she'd suffered from depression over the years because she was afraid we'd be told what happened. I feel sad I didn't understand what she was going through when she was alive. She was so scared of rejection. She'd been rejected by the man who was our biological father, and she felt she'd be rejected by her community.

Ellie's response to her brother-in-law's meddling taught me something about sisters who are very caring. She was upset, but she immediately forgave him because she knew he meant no harm and she also didn't want to add to her sister's distress. Ellie also is a person who tries to look at the positive side of things. The revelation upset her mainly because she realized how much her mother suffered and that she hadn't understood her mother before she died. But she turned that regret into gratitude. Only now does she realize how close she came to losing Emma—she shudders at the thought that she would have been separated from her sister if their mother had put them up for adoption.

When their mother was dying of lung cancer, Ellie's sister provided most of the care because she lived closer to her than Ellie did and she was trained as a nurse. Their mother lived for a year between her diagnosis and death, and Emma never expressed feeling burdened by having to care for her nor did it cause any tension between the twins. Ellie and Emma are instinctively generous toward one another.

I think our marriages would have been more difficult if we lived in the same place. My husband, Art, is less enthusiastic about the twin thing than my brother-in-law, Paul. Art's a little envious of my sister, and when we're all together, he'll complain that I talk to my sister all day. My husband didn't come from a close family—they didn't communicate. I'm closer to my sister in that we can just talk about anything—our emotions, whatever is bothering us. My husband's a man, and he's not as open.

Now that I'm almost seventy, I'm thinking of mortality and about who will die first, my sister or me. I never thought about it until a few years ago. I think about how we would handle it. I'd rather go together. But we both have made a lot of friends, I have a great support system of women friends. It might be harder on my sister. We've talked about it.

It would be a bigger adjustment for me to lose my twin than to lose my husband. My brother-in-law had a heart attack ten years ago—it wasn't serious even though he had angioplasty. My husband is in very good health. If at some point we lose our husbands, would we move in together? It would mean being away from our grandchildren, and my children don't like the idea. But I would rather be with my sister. I have an idea that if we should become widows, we'd live together or our husbands would be supportive if one of us lived very near.

I find that after my sister and I spend time together—like a week—I'm in a funk when we leave. I feel depressed for at least a day. There's a famous pair of twins who live in San Francisco. They're about eighty years old. I read about them in a magazine. They dress exactly alike, down to the gloves. I think that's too much. They won't let anyone else into their life. They never married, and they walk around all dressed up.

I wouldn't want to be that kind of twin. It's not healthy. My sister and I haven't dressed alike since high school. But we pretty much like the same clothes. Our taste is the same—we both like a certain style of sweater and pants. We have the same hairstyles. When we color our hair, we try to get the same color—we want to be in the same color range. At one point I let my gray grow out and she didn't. I could see the difference when I looked at her, and I went back to coloring. Our taste in food is very similar. In restaurants we usually order the same thing.

A number of women I interviewed said they might live with their sisters after their husbands died, but I never heard anyone else say she hoped she and her sister would die together because she couldn't imagine either one of them living without the other. In her deliberations about her preference to be with her sister and her reference to the San Francisco twins, I can see that Ellie is struggling to feel she's earned the right to go back to the person whose company she enjoys the most.

A few things she told me hint that the twins still have a partly merged identity and that this brings them great pleasure. Several times Ellie mentions that, although their daughters don't look at all alike, she and her sister see common features in their sons. "Our sons are really half brothers, not cousins." She told me this a number of times. I asked her what she meant, and she told me the boys have the same DNA from their mothers. The implication is that she and her sister are one and the same. I thought to myself, yes, they have the same DNA from their mothers, but they weren't raised by the same mother.

Obviously Ellie thinks their undifferentiated identity isn't limited to the genes they contributed. She mentioned that her sister and brother-in-law were more successful as parents and had an easier time raising their children. She assumes (probably cor-

rectly) that the X factor is their husbands rather than any difference between herself and her twin.

> Paul's style of parenting is different from Art's. Art is stricter,
> and Paul is more communicative. Art's a lecturer. He had big
> disagreements with our kids when they became teenagers. And
> he never would talk about it. It was never the right time. There
> were problems that never got solved until the last two years. I
> became more vocal and now he's listening. My sister and her
> husband never had that problem. My husband came from a
> family that wasn't close, so there's a difference there, but Art has
> learned to accept closeness.

I can't recall any other woman who volunteered so freely that
her sister and brother-in-law did a better job of parenting. But it's
easier for Ellie to be uncompetitive as a mother because she thinks
of her twin and herself as the constant factor—so she can easily
blame her children's problems on her husband. Ellie is so likeable,
I find it hard to resist her reasoning. But children's personalities
are not like simple science projects in which you can keep everything constant and manipulate only one factor.

Her pleasure in feeling they have a shared identity was also expressed in Ellie's account of their growing ESP. She's heard that
other twins have ESP, and she thinks it's increasing between them
now that they're not so busy raising families.

> The ESP has gotten stronger as we've gotten older. Last Decem-
> ber I picked out a group of cards from Costco—and my sister
> and I sent each other the very same Christmas card. On our
> fiftieth birthday we both picked out pearl pendants and earrings

to give to each other as gifts. We sent each other the same present that we chose from a catalogue. When the phone rings, I do know when it's Emma.

I noted Ellie's conviction that their ESP has been growing since they're not so busy raising children. Recalling her admission that she wants to spend her old age with her sister and her wish that they could die together, it strikes me that, because she's been a devoted wife, mother, and grandmother for nearly fifty years, Emma feels she has earned the right to go back to her first relationship. She's had a good marriage, but the relationship with her sister has been ideal. They've never argued or had any deep disagreements or felt resentful or competitive. They understand each other perfectly. In fact, they are the perfect sisters that many of us wish we had. Today, "merged identities" are often assumed to be a common problem for identical twins. In fact, one of the current stereotypes of twins is that they have a hard time establishing separate identities or that their bond gets in the way of their marriages.

If anything, Ellie and Emma exemplify the positive image of twins—siblings who are best friends from childhood and have an understanding of each other that is uniquely profound and loyal. Ellie mentioned how attitudes have changed since her childhood and that child-rearing experts now encourage parents to separate their twin children more. Merged identity often has a pathological connotation. One thinks of people who are psychotic, who don't know where they stop and the other person begins. But it strikes me that a deep mutual identification with someone else isn't necessarily a problem. Thinking you share a common identity with your twin would only create problems if it gets in the way of your life—for example, if you choose a partner who wants to be the only person you feel really close to. Emma and Ellie put some geographic distance between themselves and chose husbands who could deal with it—Paul because he actually enjoyed the "twin thing," and Art because he apparently didn't demand that much intimacy himself.

I wonder why "merging" is viewed as a problem for twins, but not for partners. In marriages it's considered acceptable, if not desirable. People often merge some of their identities with their spouses, and some feel very happy and unembarrassed about doing so.

"I'm looking for my other half!" I recently heard an elderly woman remark on an airplane as she crossed the forbidden line between first class and coach, where her husband was seated (only one had been given an upgrade). "Where's your better half?" is a line I always used to hear from an older generation. Merged identity in marriage isn't necessarily frowned upon—to the contrary, merged spouses are often portrayed as having found their perfect match.

I'd initially felt a little skeptical when Ellie told me she thought she might have spent the rest of her life feeling incomplete if she and her twin had been separated at birth. I know there have been many reports of this sort, but how could someone miss what they never knew they had? Some have argued that twins relate to each other in the womb. So they might have "known" each other before parting at birth.

While I was writing this, a story of twins who were separated at birth and mysteriously reunited appeared on the front page of the *New York Times*. As if to confirm Ellie's worst fears, the twins had been put up for adoption in Mexico when they were born, and they went to different families. By some incomprehensible coincidence, both twins had been adopted by families that now live near each other in New York, and the girls went to nearby colleges and wound up having mutual friends. Neither had known about the existence of the other, but when their friends and acquaintances started greeting them by each other's name, they learned they had a twin.

These twins had not felt that a part of them was missing. In fact, one was initially reluctant to meet her sister. But it turned out there were other mysterious coincidences in their lives. The media were filled with the story of the twins. There are few things as satisfying as a miraculous reunion, and people felt that there might be some mysterious force that tries to reunite those who were meant to be together.

I think stories like these have universal appeal because they're the ultimate example of undoing a loss. A reunion restores some part of ourselves and our past. It undoes the intervening years—denying aging, separation, and death. It's like the comforting notion that your mother or father or someone you loved and lost will be waiting for you when you die to bring you to heaven. I understand why Ellie would want to leave this world with her twin rather than with anyone else.

CHAPTER 2

Life Savers:
Sisters Who Mother
Each Other

I MET SEVERAL SISTERS who bonded closely as children, attaching to each other to fill a vacuum left by absent parents. Their mothers had either died or were too depressed or overwhelmed by other problems to respond to them, and their fathers weren't around very much. These children were basically left to fend for themselves, and they built an alliance to take care of each other.

These relationships were different from those described by sisters who were forced to become a mother's "helper" and were saddled with unwanted responsibility for raising a younger child. Unwilling babysitters often saw their baby sisters as a drag on their lives and competition for their parents' attention. In contrast, the sisters I talk about here were closer to each other than they were to their parents. Their sister relationship was their primary bond, and they carried that attachment forward into their adult lives. As a rule, these sisters rarely fought and were less overtly competitive because they depended on each other and they weren't competing over their parents. For several women, the major challenge of their relationship was separating from one another and balancing their sister attachment with their marriages and the families they created. One reason I begin with these sisters is because they illuminate the separation problems that are common even among sisters who are well cared for by parents. They also show how some sisters serve as allies, role models, mentors, and surrogate mothers for one another, and the power and significance of these roles.

Charlotte and Lizzie Bender formed their own small world in childhood because their mother died and their father couldn't fill the void. They bonded closely in the absence of competent adults who could care for them. Because Charlotte was nearly three years older, she was also something of the "mother" in this relationship, and Lizzie was the "child," although they also related as peers a lot of the time. The older-younger division is an aspect of sisterhood that's nearly universal, and these sisters illuminate the struggle to evolve into equals. Because Charlotte and Lizzie didn't have a mother, their relationship probably had more lasting mother-child overtones. The Bender sisters weren't left unscarred by their mother's death. A vulnerability to loss has always been a big theme in their lives. But as adults, they also displayed the strengths I've frequently seen among sisters who overcame early adversity—generosity and sensitivity, traits they developed as children in relation to each other.

Losing their mother was clearly the event that defined Charlotte and Lizzie Bender's lives. She died at thirty-one when Charlotte was six years old and Lizzie was nearly four. Lizzie is now a fifty-three-year-old literature professor who also writes poetry; she lives in Cambridge, Massachusetts. Charlotte went to medical school and works for an international agency concerned with giving aid to malnourished children. She lives in Amsterdam.

I spoke to Lizzie first, who began her story with the death of her mother. Her memories were obviously mixed with things she'd heard from her sister and others. Like Charlotte, she created a perfect image of her mother to fill a large void. Both sisters built their young lives around this fleeting and romantic figure and the bond they formed in her absence.

I was born in 1950 and spent the first twelve years of my life in Dorchester, on the south side of Boston. I was the youngest of three children. My brother Carl is six years older, and my sister Charlotte was two and a half when I was born. My mother was an aspiring writer, and my parents named all their children after literary characters they liked.

She was the perfect mother, the saint who became more saintly after she died. She got sick with bone cancer when I was six months old. At first, the cancer appeared in her right arm, and her arm was amputated—the doctors told my parents the cancer hadn't spread so my mother agreed to let them take it. But soon after they cut off her arm, the cancer reappeared in her hip.

My brother had been my mother's favorite child—he was brilliant, and she let him run wild because she didn't want to inhibit him. My father never got along with Carl—he resented how my mother doted on him, and he thought my brother was difficult. When my sister Charlotte was born, she became my father's favorite—"Oh, Charlotte is Sam's favorite," everyone always said. When we were children, she was always the "good" girl . . . she took care of my father as well as me.

My brother was very traumatized by the amputation of my mother's arm, and he never recovered from her death. He's a very damaged person. He rarely talks about my mother, but he told me she died for him when they cut off her arm. My mother died on June 29, and Carl's tenth birthday was on July 3. My mother had planned a birthday party for him, to be held in her hospital room. He prayed to God to let her live until his birthday, but she died a few days before. Right after the funeral, my sister and I were sent off to live with my aunts for the summer. My father later explained he needed time alone to pull himself together. But my brother was considered so wild that none of the relatives wanted to take him, so he was sent off to camp. My father always tells us how Carl begged to be with us—"Please don't send me to camp—let me be with my sisters." This is the centerpiece of the family dysfunction: my father's guilt for sending him off alone.

My sister and I would cling to each other. Everyone says they'd never seen sisters who were so close—we were unusual in that we never fought. We were clinging to each other because we had such a sense of loneliness and abandonment. I could feel what she was feeling; we became so connected. While my brother was at camp, the counselors sent my father letters saying, "Your son won't let anyone touch him or come near him."

I have a certain guilt around my relationship with my sister because we always had each other and my brother was the outside person and he had nobody. So my closeness with my sister had a certain tainted quality because it meant someone was rejected in the midst of our closeness. My sister and brother weren't close because he resented her when she was born— until then, he'd been the only child.

Lizzie has only a few hazy memories of her mother, but in her thirties she fell in love with an older man who was a distant cousin of her mother's and who had shared childhood summers in the country with her mother. When I asked Lizzie if this connection added to Howard's appeal, she denied it, but she did admit she felt a little embarrassed about marrying a distant relative. While not discounting Howard's other merits, I find it hard to believe that Lizzie wasn't drawn by her husband's connection to her mother. By knowing her mother, he gave Lizzie a connection to her past.

Howard remembers how wonderful my mother was: nurturing, loving, generous, strong. He remembers how she was always reading poetry and she was an early feminist, a bohemian. She wrote children's stories and played the piano. I attribute the best parts of me to those first few years I had with my mother, as opposed to what I got from my stepmother. I don't remember my mother, but I've always aspired to be like her.

Everyone always talks about how wonderful she was. Even when she was dying in the cancer ward in Massachusetts General Hospital, she wouldn't talk about herself, but she'd ask people how they were. They'd wheel her into the children's ward, and she'd read to the kids who were sick. I have only a few vague memories of her. Walking down the street with her once. Mainly I remember sitting in bed with her.

And I remember the last time I saw her. The ambulance came to take her to the hospital. She was carried out on a stretcher, and we were saying good-bye. My sister remembers my maternal grandmother was there, and when we looked out the window and saw my mother being put in the ambulance, my grandmother said, "She's never coming back. You'll never see her again."

My sister and I both thought we murdered our mother because she had fallen and for some reason we thought she had slipped on a pencil that we'd left on the floor. We thought she hurt her hip when she fell and that's why she died of cancer. I realize now she must have fallen because she had cancer in her hip, but that's what we thought when we were children. My brother also thought he murdered her. He was on a trolley car with her, and the door closed on my mother's arm. He thought it was his fault my mother's arm was amputated because he hadn't stopped the door from hitting her arm.

When I met Charlotte I asked her what she remembered of her mother and of these events.

I don't remember much of my childhood at all. It's hard to know what's my memory and what other people told me. The earliest thing that feels like a memory to me is Lizzie as a baby and helping to feed her. Soon after Lizzie was born, my mother was sick. I remember my mother lying on the bed, holding her. I don't have any images of her arm being cut off or how she was able to hold Lizzie or take care of me. I know she was right-handed, and after they amputated her right arm, she taught herself to write with her left hand. I remember trying to learn how to write with my left arm, in case something happened to my right arm. I always assumed I would die young.

Charlotte and I talk about how trauma can wipe out memories, and later, Charlotte notes that her brother has almost no memories of their mother even though he was ten years old when she died. She reflects:

That's what trauma does to you. I think the memories are there— it's just the connections that are lost. Because if you recover the memories, you recover the loss, and the pain is too much.

When Charlotte was about forty, she went through a period of wanting to learn more about her mother. This was around the time her first marriage was breaking up, and I imagine her search for her mother was prompted by her most recent loss. I suspect every loss in her life must reverberate from the original one.

Charlotte had only little bits and pieces to start with: Her father had burned everything personal—like the letters her mother had written and the manuscript she was working on at the time of her death. She told me her father found it too painful to keep any of these items. Apparently, it never occurred to him that someday his children might have wanted to have something that would make them feel connected to their mother.

I do have one letter that she wrote to me from the hospital—I found it years later in a box, and I'd forgotten all about it. It's really lovely—it gave me a sense of what a lovely mother she must have been. It's about braiding my hair. We also had some children's stories she had written. I had a notebook she'd kept. She had glued in things she liked—reproductions of paintings she'd seen and poems.

A woman who had been a teenage friend of my mother's had seen Lizzie's name on a poem she had published, and she'd written a letter to Lizzie to ask if she was related. Lizzie never responded but she gave the letter to my father, and he gave it to me. I tracked her down, and before she died, we met her, and she gave me a photocopy of a book of poems my mother had written for her on her sixteenth birthday. She told me my mother's favorite songs and about how they used to go to Cambridge when they were teenagers, hoping to meet boys.

Whenever we'd go to family weddings or bar mitzvahs, there was a distant cousin, an older man, who would say that he had home movies of my mother. I don't think we really believed him. After he died, Howard was able to get the home movies converted to videotape, and my mother did appear on them for just about one minute.

She was exactly the way I remembered her. Somewhere, inside your body, you remember. The way she smiled and moved, and how she related to people. She was eating an apple and putting her arm around someone. She was sensual, warm, loving, funny. She looked like she had a sense of humor. She was laughing—she just had an amused look about people and life. A fond amusement on her face. This movie was taken before I was born—Carl was already born. It confirmed my nice view of her.

Charlotte also confirmed Lizzie's story that their grandmother proclaimed, "She's never coming back," as their mother was taken to the hospital. She remembers her grandmother was very depressed about losing her daughter and therefore oblivious to the children's feelings. She also remembers what her father did the night her mother died—another snapshot that captures how little thought he gave to how his children might absorb or be affected by his comments and behavior.

I shared a room with Lizzie, and when my mother died, my father woke us up in the middle of the night. We both started to cry when he told us the news, and he said, "You can't cry. You have to help me tell Carl."

It was clear, right then, that my role in the family was to take care of everybody and make everything all right. So when he'd come home and ask how everything was, I'd say everything was fine. I could have said, "Oh the house burned down, and Lizzie was trapped inside," and he wouldn't have heard us. He'd just have said, "Fine."

Their father worked at three jobs, and he was hardly ever home. When they returned home after the summer their mother died, the children were left in the care of a series of awful housekeepers. One was always drunk, another was slightly sadistic. But the children never complained to their father because he wouldn't have heard. "We didn't tell our father anything. They were awful, but he wanted everything to be okay."

I asked Charlotte about Lizzie's memories of feeling responsible for their mother's death and also about Lizzie's report that their brother believed he murdered their mother. Charlotte laughed:

> No, that was my memory on the trolley car, and I don't remember my brother being there. We were in a trolley car, and my mother got off first. I don't remember if she had Lizzie in her arms. My mother was reaching up for us, and the trolley door closed on her arms, and I thought that's why she got sick after her arm was amputated. It must have been before she got sick, because she had arms to reach up and to get hit.

It's a haunting memory, not only in recalling a child's effort to understand her mother's illness, but the image itself—of being separated, of her mother reaching up to take her in her arms and the doors closing shut. According to Charlotte, they weren't actually separated—the doors closed only momentarily—but I'm not surprised that this is one of the few images burned into her memory. It's also interesting that Charlotte's memory becomes Lizzie's story, which she projects to her brother. Pooling memories is one of the ways that sisters shape each other's past.

And what about that lethal pencil, I asked Charlotte. Charlotte remembered this well and laughed at how that childhood memory was retrieved. Right after finishing college, she was working at the copy desk of a newspaper.

> It was a relaxed atmosphere, and the ceiling was made of this material that if you threw pencils up into air, they would stick there, and eventually they would fall down. The writers and editors were always throwing pencils up at the ceiling. I found myself compulsively picking up the pencils from the floor—and then I had a Proustian memory of my mother falling in the hallway of our apartment. And for some reason, we thought she had tripped on a pencil and fallen, and that's why she got cancer on her hip. We felt responsible for most things.

Why would a child be so ready to blame herself for her mother's death or share in that guilt just from hearing the story from an older sibling? Children often blame themselves for their parents' deaths because guilt is less overwhelming than losing your sense of illusion of control. If you think you caused your mother's death, then the event is under your power, and it means you can do things differently and make the outcome better at some point in the future.

The sisters' need to restore a sense of control is evident in Charlotte's recollection of the game she and Lizzie invented and played to master their perpetual anxiety that something awful was about to happen. They called their favorite game Hyena!

One of them would start the game at some unexpected moment by leaping up into the air and yelling HYENA! and chasing the other. Just as the victim was cornered and was about to be attacked, she could yell out HYENA!—reversing the roles of the attacker and the prey—and proceed to chase after the original aggressor. In this way, they would run back and forth, chasing each other around their apartment.

> You'd be terrified, never knowing when you'd be attacked. This stimulated our anxiety that something awful would happen to us, but it gave us the feeling we could control the anxiety by yelling, "HYENA," and becoming the chaser and not the victim. We played this game ourselves; our brother wasn't part of it.

The sisters took comfort in the private world they created. Charlotte remembers her little sister was always following her around and was sometimes a pain, but she remembers enjoying Lizzie.

> She was cute. We had bunk beds—and I really liked sharing our room. I slept on top and Lizzie on the bottom. Both of us were anxiety-ridden. I'd be worrying the bed would collapse and I'd crush her. Lizzie would worry my bed would fall down. But we also had fun and created a world of our own. On Sunday mornings, when we didn't have to go to school, I'd drop the covers from the top bed over the opening so the bottom seemed like a tent or a cave, and we'd play inside for hours. We also both read a lot, and I'd be reading up in my bed while Lizzie read down below.

Lizzie also had fond memories of sharing a room with her older sister. She recalls that one time they stayed up half the night waiting for Charlotte's favorite song to come on the radio—"Twilight Time" by the Platters. They had lots of friends in their apartment building and the immediate neighborhood. They played street games—stoopball, red light/green light—with children who were a mix of both their ages. Their grandmother married a man whose adult daughters had grown up and moved out and left behind dozens of shoes. Charlotte recalls how she and Lizzie would play "shoe store" whenever they visited.

Lizzie also remembers the relationship wasn't really equal—typical of younger-older sister relationships in childhood. She adored her older sister and always followed Charlotte around—a pattern that continued into their adult years:

> I would do anything for my sister. I adored her. And she was always there for me in the important ways. But it wasn't equal. I accommodated to her. We were supposed to take turns going to a grocery store that was a block away, and I would go with her when it was her turn, just to be with her. But she never came with me when it was my turn. I'd have to trudge to the store by myself. Many years later, when I worked in an office, it was always such a powerful thing for me when a friend was willing to walk me to the corner for lunch or walk me to the vending machines, just to be with me. Because my sister wouldn't do it. But we were the most important person in each other's lives; she was my lifeline.

On the day of their mother's funeral, the children weren't allowed to go to the service so they spent the day with the family of Charlotte's best friend from first grade, Jackie. Many years later, Jackie's father told Charlotte he remembered that day and how she and Lizzie were walking up and down the beach, holding hands.

Lizzie remembered that in these early years Charlotte displayed her depression more obviously than she did. She showed me a photograph taken behind their apartment building with a smiling Lizzie and a blank stare on Charlotte's face. There's a stark look to the photo—two little girls standing against a backdrop of concrete, wearing roller skates clamped on their shoes. Lizzie recalls that Charlotte would sit for hours on the stairs to their apartment building when their housekeeper forced her to go outside to play.

Lizzie also recalled acting more like the cheerful one when they were very young because she kept hearing from adults that she was less affected than her older siblings were by their mother's death. Everyone assumed she was less traumatized because she was too young to remember her mother. If anything, Lizzie's loss was greater because she had even less time with her mother to establish the basic sense of trust that's needed to have healthy relationships.

When Lizzie was seven and Charlotte was nine, their father remarried—to a very young flight attendant (she was twenty-three and he was thirty-eight) who came from a small town in the Midwest. Both sisters remember trying to impress her the first time she came to their home. They wanted a mother so they could be like the other children they knew and have someone to love them. Lizzie recalls:

> We brought out all our toys and the masks we had made from paper bags, trying to make her like us. We were like little dogs in the pound who wanted to be adopted. He dumped us on her, and she had no idea how to be a mother.

They called this young woman "Mom" right away and always referred to her as their mother from the day she arrived. It was part of the family's general denial—denial that these children had lost their mother and that they needed to grieve. But although they now had a "mother," the stepmother didn't fit in with their expectations or those of the neighbors. For one thing, she didn't look or act like any other parent they knew. She was a young mid-western farm girl, just twelve years older than their brother. All the other mothers in the neighborhood were older and wore house-dresses while their stepmother wore jeans and attracted the curiosity of the neighbors. Charlotte recalls an old lady stopping her on the street and offering her a piece of candy in order to pump her with questions about what was going on at home.

The sisters agree their stepmother wasn't physically affectionate or comfortable with the expression of emotions. "I felt a mixture of hostility toward her," said Charlotte. "She wasn't like our mother. I really wanted a mother in order to be loved and to be like other kids. But she came from an entirely different culture. I was used to affection and touching. I remember I'd want to hold her hand when we walked down the street, and she didn't like being touched. I don't remember her ever hugging me." Charlotte feels more sympathetic toward her stepmother now because she herself became a stepmother later in life and discovered the diffi-culty of the role.

Lizzie is angrier because she became the stepmother's desig-nated "child." Since Lizzie was the youngest, her stepmother felt she could make Lizzie more of "her" child, and Lizzie also felt more obliged to take care of her stepmother's needs. According to Lizzie, her stepmother was no more aware of their feelings than their father was. "There was a terrible competition between my stepmother and Charlotte for the love of my father because my sister had always been his favorite child, and my sister was trying to be the mother to the family, and my stepmother was threatened. I hated being thought of as my stepmother's favorite, but I got stuck with her. My sister was a caretaker to me, and I became our stepmother's caretaker." Lizzie also feels the stepmother joined the others in denying her feelings and her need to grieve. "People would say my mother's death wouldn't matter to me. 'She's too young to understand.' My feelings of grief weren't accepted; I was told I didn't have them."

The marriage was not successful. Their father was always sexually unfaithful; he'd been unfaithful to their mother as well. Charlotte later learned that her parents also had been on the verge of divorce when her mother was diagnosed with cancer. Soon their father was staying out all night, and the children were witnesses to terrible fights.

Their stepmother was always complaining, "We need money, we need money." More than anything, she wanted the family to move to a more desirable neighborhood. There was no way they could afford the prime Boston Beacon Hill neighborhood she aspired to. But at her insistence, when the girls were twelve and fourteen, they moved to Brookline, where they found a barely affordable apartment. In school, the girls were both excellent students, but Charlotte got A pluses while Lizzie got As. Lizzie says she feared outdoing her sister.

> I adored her, and I was afraid to compete with her. I felt I didn't deserve to do as well... I'd made an unconscious deal never to compete with her, never to do anything to outshine her. She was always in the top five of her class, and I was always in the top ten. We had the same teachers, and they always made comparisons in Charlotte's favor. Charlotte was the good one, the serene one, and by now, I'd given up the cheerful act and I'd become the sullen one. I wasn't happy in high school—I wanted to go away.

Perhaps one reason why Lizzie became depressed in high school was the departure of her sister, her lifesaver. Charlotte had moved to California, to get away from home and to be in a challenging college that appealed to bright, serious students. Three years later, Lizzie followed Charlotte across the country to the very same school.

In college, both sisters let their academic records slide a bit in favor of intense, stormy relationships with troubled boyfriends who absorbed all their time and attention. This became their pattern for many years. After graduating from college, Lizzie decided she loved poetry and earned a Ph.D. in literature.

Charlotte moved back to Boston, where she led a life that seemed very glamorous to Lizzie. After a few years of working in journalism, Charlotte went to medical school, although her career has been more political than clinical. She has worked for international organizations devoted to helping children who are threatened by starvation and infectious diseases.

From Lizzie's admiring perspective, Charlotte had one exciting boyfriend after another. When I asked Charlotte about those times, she doesn't recall a glamorous life. She just remembers trying to find someone to love her.

During the years they lived on opposite coasts, the sisters didn't see each other that often, but Lizzie would call Charlotte for support whenever she felt lonely or her love affairs were failing—something that happened regularly because she always picked men who weren't available: out-of-town men she could see only once every three months, or men who weren't that interested in her. And then she would suffer when they left.

"I never was able to end a relationship, even when I no longer wanted to be in it—I had to wait until they broke it off," said Lizzie. I asked her if she got into painful relationships because of her early experience losing her mother. She said that she'd always assumed it had more to do with how her father treated her.

Charlotte also acknowledged that until she was in her forties, she could never leave an unrewarding relationship—and, like her sister, she was always the one who was ultimately left. She does feel that this is the legacy of her early loss.

I experience any separation as a death, so I'm always trying to avoid ending relationships with men. This is mother-related. Once the separation has occurred, I'm okay. It's just the process of doing it. For me, it's a matter of never giving up, of feeling that everything can be worked out—that you have to keep trying to work things out. You never give up voluntarily because it's too much like death.

During their twenties, the sisters' relationship was always close but not equal. Charlotte felt responsible for Lizzie and wanted to help her through her rough times. But the closeness she felt was more like protecting someone she regarded as almost a child, and she didn't want to confide her own worries or problems to her younger sister.

When Charlotte turned thirty-one (the age her mother was when she died), she decided that she was going to live and it was time to take her life more seriously. At this point, she also decided to marry someone she'd known from work—a man who had custody of his ten-year-old son and nine-year-old daughter. His children had been badly neglected and abandoned by their mother who'd been a product of foster care. For years these children had been shipped back and forth between a series of relatives in Puerto Rico and the United States, their lives constantly disrupted and their relationships severed. In that awful irony of repeating our most upsetting childhood experiences, Charlotte became a stepmother to traumatized children she believed she could save. But there was a big difference. These children were seriously disturbed and lacked the academic and emotional strengths—and the sister bond—that had helped Lizzie and Charlotte survive.

Even Charlotte's father could see this was not a promising situation, although Charlotte couldn't.

> My father took me for a walk when I decided to get married. He said, "I just want to make sure you know what you're doing."
>
> Something in me thought I could do a better job. It was the same as when we had to take care of ourselves in a way children shouldn't have to. Luis was very dedicated to his children, and we were going to be a happy family and make a difference to these children. I thought I could help them and make a difference. I loved him and he loved me.

Charlotte's first marriage was a turning point for all the siblings. Carl and Lizzie flew back to Boston for the wedding. Lizzie, who stood beside Charlotte during the ceremony, couldn't stop herself from sobbing. She felt she was losing her sister because now Charlotte's husband would be her sister's principal relationship, and she'd always thought of their bond as the primary relationship for both of them: "I was sobbing so loudly, and my sister's whole therapy group was there, staring at me sympathetically."

CARL, WHO HAD BEEN the most brilliant child of the three according to his sisters, had been deteriorating emotionally since his twenties. He'd been traumatized by the death of his mother, and after one relationship with a woman that ended when he was a young man, he'd never had a close relationship with anyone, including his family. After college he became a heavy user of LSD, and Charlotte and Lizzie speculate that the combination of his childhood loss and isolation made him fragile and vulnerable. Despite his brilliance, he'd never found a career that worked out. At the time of Charlotte's wedding, he'd been living on the West Coast. When he came for the ceremony, he stayed at his father's apartment, and after the wedding, he never left. He was back in his old room—the one he had as a teenager—and he wouldn't come out. He was to remain there, dependent on his father, for the next twenty-three years.

A few years after Charlotte married, Lizzie fell in love with Howard, the man she has been with ever since—someone totally different from her youthful choices. By now Lizzie had also returned to Boston, as a literature professor. She thinks she stopped picking rejecting men because Charlotte had married, which gave her permission to find a man who loved her. She'd also just lost her mother surrogate to marriage; perhaps she needed a new nurturing figure. When I had asked her if part of Howard's appeal was that he'd known and remembered her mother—and was therefore a link to her past—she denied the connection but made a comment that supported my suspicion. She said, "I tried all my life to escape from my family, and then I married into it, like Oedipus."

Lizzie was joking, but there are other connections to the myth. Oedipus didn't merely marry into his family. He also was abandoned as a child, unwittingly killed his father, and wound up marrying his mother. Lizzie didn't kill her mother, but as a child she had felt responsible for her mother's death, and she chose a man who'd known her mother before she was born.

She hadn't seen Howard since she was about seven and he was seventeen—and she'd had a little childhood crush on this older boy. She remembered that she and her sister had been taken to visit Howard's family, and an aunt had jokingly said that she and Charlotte would wind up marrying Howard and his brother.

They hadn't seen each other for twenty-five years, and then, after she moved back to Boston, she went to a bar mitzvah for the older son of the cousin that she and Howard have in common, and she ran into him. He'd married early—at eighteen—and raised two children who'd grown up. By the time Lizzie saw him at the bar mitzvah he was divorced.

Two years later, when her cousin gave another bar mitzvah for a younger son, Lizzie spotted Howard again, sitting at a table across the room. Her cousin encouraged her, "Go talk to him," and Lizzie did.

We went on a date, and we talked for seven hours. Then I didn't hear from him for two weeks. Then we went out a second time, and that was it. We've been together ever since. There was such a natural connection. We came from a similar background and had so many common interests. We have the same sense of humor.

We've been together for nineteen years, but it took us seventeen years to get married. We just got married a year and a half ago. I never really wanted to get married. Or when I was younger, I only wanted to marry the guys who didn't want to marry me. When I got involved with Howard, I thought, Who needs government interference—who needs the piece of paper—and I guess I was afraid of commitment because it terrified me. I thought I'd stay with him forever, but he did want to get married.

Two years ago, Howard had a severe heart attack, and for a while his survival was in question. He needed to have heart surgery and was treated at Massachusetts General Hospital, the hospital where my mother died. It brought back everything about my mother. He wound up spending a week in the intensive care unit because of complications from the surgery. It was a terrible experience, but it drew us closer.

Howard went to a support group for cardiac patients, which is not at all like him. People in his group would say, "I got sick and my wife left me." But he was able to say, "I got sick and my girlfriend married me."

We eloped, we did it privately, we didn't tell anyone. Of course my sister knew we were getting married. We drove north and got married by a justice of the peace. We had no witnesses, and we had to ask workmen who were working in the parking lot to be our witnesses.

He had always wanted to get married and used to be very upset that I wouldn't. By the time he got sick and we married, he felt secure in our relationship, so it didn't matter as much. But we got married because I wanted to bombard him with love, to keep him alive.

In our wedding pictures, I look very tense. I couldn't even smile. Even then, I felt a terrible fear of commitment. During the ceremony, I kept thinking, *Can I stop it now?* But I kept going, even though I was hyperventilating.

The next day I told my father and my cousin, and gradually I adjusted to it. I started to love wearing a wedding ring, and now I love saying, "my husband" instead of "my boyfriend."

Lizzie turned to Charlotte for help during the crises of Howard's heart attack and surgery, and Charlotte, as usual, was always there for her, though she was in need of some instruction. "At first she would give advice but pretty quickly she got the message that I just wanted her to listen, and she said all the right things," Lizzie said.

Charlotte's first marriage, which lasted for ten years, was troubled pretty early on. She'd thought she could help her husband's two children, but they were emotionally damaged from years of neglect and angry with their father for the years he had left them with relatives after their drug-addicted mother had given up custody. Charlotte was often angry with him, too, for not being the kind of father she thought he should be.

> I was very attracted to him, very excited about him, but the actual marriage had a lot to do with the children. When you have children with problems or disabilities, it takes its toll on a marriage. Those kids needed a full-time mother, and I wasn't prepared to do that. I wanted to be a physician and go to work. The boy eventually turned out okay but the girl's been in and out of prison for drug-related crimes. She's almost forty years old now, and in prison. She's been through a lot of drug rehab programs, but none of them worked. I haven't seen her for years.
>
> After the kids left home, I wanted to save our relationship, but Luis was very angry. He didn't want to go into therapy—he felt we'd had family therapy and that it hadn't helped. He felt we didn't have enough in common—our interests were too different, and at the end of the day, he was right. But for a long time I kept trying.

I wondered why neither of these sisters ever had children of her own since they are such nurturing and family-oriented women. It's not unusual for professional women to pass up having children in order to concentrate on demanding careers. When Charlotte and Lizzie were starting out, women had to work much harder to break into their professions, which were still largely restricted to men.

It was also common for politically active women to fear that motherhood could be a dangerous trap during the start of the feminist movement in the late 1960s and '70s. Certainly many women of that era felt they had to choose between children and careers. But I still found it interesting that neither sister became a mother, since they'd spent so much time and energy taking care of other people. Or, it may be that not having children gave them the freedom to be so generous to others.

When I asked Lizzie if she regretted not having children, she told me that she never had a strong desire to be a mother, that she cared more about her career as a professor and writer. But she also feared she'd be a terrible mother, like her stepmother. At another point, she said she always followed her sister, and as long as Charlotte didn't have a baby, she felt she couldn't either. She also feels that Charlotte's first husband kept her sister from having a baby at the point when Charlotte was ready to. It makes her furious that Luis did this to Charlotte after Charlotte spent so many years taking care of his messed-up children, and she also feels that since she couldn't let herself have anything her sister didn't have, Luis indirectly kept her from being a mother, too.

Charlotte didn't express anger toward Luis or blame him when I asked her about this, and she said she didn't have terrible regrets about not having children. "I was pregnant twice and had abortions because it wasn't the right time in either case. The first time, I was in college. The second time I was an intern just starting my medical career. I did want to have children later with Luis, but he'd already had two children, and he didn't want to have a child with me."

Motherhood isn't for everyone, and if Lizzie and Charlotte hadn't spent so much time and energy on unrewarding relationships with men and, in Charlotte's case, stepchildren, I would understand how their career demands would have been difficult to combine with raising children. But I also wonder if motherhood seemed too dangerous for Charlotte and Lizzie. Sometimes women whose mothers died when they were very young are afraid to become mothers because, subconsciously, they link becoming a mother with dying: They think of mothers as women who die. Both sisters had told me they always expected to die very young. Given their conscious identification with their mother's mortality and their fantasy that as children they killed their mother, why wouldn't they try to avoid their mother's fate?

AFTER CHARLOTTE'S FIRST MARRIAGE ended, the sisters' usual roles were reversed: Charlotte was alone, and Lizzie had settled into a satisfying relationship with Howard. Until this point, they'd been close, but Charlotte had always taken the role of the helper and had not confided her own problems. Charlotte recalled, as Lizzie did, that Lizzie pushed for a more reciprocal and equal relationship at this time. And Charlotte explained how they were able to change the way they related.

> When my first marriage broke up, our relationship changed because Lizzie was very insistent that she wanted to be there for me, and our relationship shifted to an equal one, where we were supportive of each other. We bring different strengths to the relationship.
>
> She's more direct if something upsets her, or if she needs something or thinks I need something and I'm not expressing it...Lizzie has always been able to express anger to me, and I find it hard to express anger, unless I get carried away, and then I can be awful. In therapy, I've started taking a risk, trying to ex-

press anger toward her. I'd get heart palpitations. I was very anxious that I'd devastate her. My therapist, who knew Lizzie— he'd met her—said that anger didn't bother Lizzie. He said, "It bothers you. She doesn't have a problem expressing anger. She can deal with it."

Increasingly, I could take a risk expressing myself, and Lizzie didn't dissolve into a pool. And Lizzie became insistent on my telling her things that were bothering me and not just brushing her off. Howard and Lizzie were both very kind to me after my first marriage ended. They always included me and invited me whenever they were going to a party or an event they thought I'd be interested in.

And then Lizzie did something that turned out to be fateful for Charlotte—she gave her sister the phone number of a man she thought Charlotte should meet, the man who turned out to be the right partner for Charlotte. But Lizzie also jokes this was her own undoing because Charlotte's second marriage carried her away to Amsterdam, where she's lived ever since.

When Charlotte moved to Amsterdam, Lizzie was devastated and wondered how she could have been the catalyst for her sister moving three thousand miles away. By the time Charlotte left, they'd both been living in Boston for ten years, and Lizzie missed her sister terribly. Finding lasting partners did raise a new problem for the sisters—namely how were they going to integrate their husbands into what had been their lifelong primary relationship with each other.

Lizzie and Howard decided to join Charlotte and her new husband, Carter, on their honeymoon in the south of France. Only afterward did they realize this was ill-advised. Charlotte should have known better because her first honeymoon with Luis had gotten off to a bad start when they stopped to visit Lizzie in California for a few days on their way to Hawaii. Too late, Charlotte remembered that Luis had felt very slighted because this was their honeymoon and he felt Charlotte was too focused on her sister.

This time, the fight erupted between Charlotte and Howard, and it was Howard who felt slighted, putting Lizzie in the middle of a feud between the two people she loved most. As Lizzie recalls, there was tension between Howard and Charlotte from the start of the trip over little things—a missed connection, a borrowed car. She thinks Charlotte was anxious about getting married and a bit grouchy and controlling about how things should be done, which got on Howard's nerves. Then Charlotte literally screamed at Howard and wouldn't apologize. Howard stopped talking to Charlotte completely, and then Lizzie started fighting with Howard because she thought her sister was partly right.

This continued for two awful weeks—neither Charlotte nor Howard would apologize or talk with the other about it. Charlotte felt that Howard had ruined her honeymoon, but a few months later, she wrote to him saying she was sorry for the way she had acted but she'd also been upset and she wanted the two of them to share the blame. Howard refused to accept any responsibility. It took a long time, but eventually they became friends again.

Charlotte had a slightly different perspective on the fight:

We'd been married a month, but this was my honeymoon. I should have learned my boundaries, but I yelled at Howard...I grew up with him, he was part of my family, which is why I felt free to express my anger to him. But he was feeling jealous because Lizzie didn't want to get married, and Carter and I had just gotten married.

Howard is Lizzie's primary relationship now, or we are coequal. But Howard would have been right in thinking at that time that I was the most important person in her life and legitimately feeling that as a grown woman she should feel he was the primary person. He also should have understood how much our relationship meant to us because of our mother's death.

Charlotte viewed the issue in terms of need and hurt, whereas Howard thought the conflict was over controlling behavior. I can't know who's right—probably there's something to be said for each view. But since then, the couples have patched things up and have taken several pleasant vacations together—which isn't that easy, considering how difficult travel can be. It's notable that Lizzie was included in both of Charlotte's honeymoons. Doing it once may be dismissed as poor judgment. Doing it twice is irrational, especially when the first instance was a mistake. I wondered if Charlotte felt guilty or worried about marrying and making her husband the primary person when she knew that Lizzie would feel abandoned. Did she feel she had no right to make any major change in her life without including her younger sister? Why could Charlotte yell at Howard when she always worried that her anger would make Lizzie dissolve?

It was Howard's illness, several years later, that was really devastating to Lizzie. So far, he's been doing well, but when he was sick, Lizzie was in despair over the fear he would die. For at least a year, every checkup or little pain would send her into a panic, and she'd call Charlotte, like the old days when she'd fall apart over a relationship ending. This was when she had to explain to Charlotte that she needed a sympathetic ear, not someone to offer advice.

She'd be very good, in a certain way, but one thing our family always does is try to make everything better. I just wanted her to listen to me, and for her to say, "It's terrible." I didn't want her advice. She tends to give me advice instead of just being with me in my pain. She'd tell me, Oh this will happen, or You can do this or that. A couple of times I felt this wasn't very helpful—I don't know if I told her so, but she got it. We've been open with each other ever since.

Charlotte did get the message.

It was so awful. Lizzie and I spoke frequently on the phone. She was suffering so much, and she was so worried for Howard. I'd feel bad for her and I wanted to know what I could do. She was good to say, It helps me so much if you just listen. It was not at all a burden to talk to her when she let me know I could help by just listening.

In Amsterdam, there's an ancient bridge called the Bridge of the Two Sisters. According to legend, it was built to reconnect two sisters who lived on the opposite shores of a river. Marriage had also separated Lizzie and Charlotte, but creating an equal relationship allowed them to have their sister bond again. They have made their own bridge because they value their relationship so much.

The one area where Lizzie still feels tension with Charlotte concerns their stepmother who has never stopped being in need of money and help. This forces the sisters to discuss her and try to agree on what to do. Their father and stepmother finally split up after Lizzie left for college, and her father married twice more— a brief third marriage to a woman with a bad drinking problem, then finally, twenty years ago, he met the right woman, his fourth wife, and they've been madly in love ever since. She's much younger than their father—she's a year younger than Lizzie—and both sisters adore her. They feel their father's good qualities blossomed after his need for love was finally met. But things have not gone well for their stepmother.

After the divorce, she'd followed Lizzie to California, which Lizzie did not appreciate, since she'd gone there to be with Charlotte and to get away from the rest of the family. When Lizzie was a child, her stepmother was constantly complaining that they needed more money, and she was always spending more than they had. This pattern never stopped, and as she grew older, she fell into increasingly dire straits. As always, she had aspirations that exceeded her means, and every foolish scheme she pursued only added to her downward spiral. For the past eighteen years, she's been a constant drain on Lizzie and Charlotte. She'd asked Lizzie to be the cosigner on her mortgage. "I went through the papers. And I just couldn't do it." Then she asked the two sisters to lend her nine thousand dollars. They talked about it and decided that if she'd agree to go to Debtors Anonymous, they would lend her the money. She didn't agree to their terms, but Lizzie felt sorry for her and gave her the money, which, of course, she never paid back. Lizzie discussed this situation with me.

The tension with my sister is that Charlotte is better at setting boundaries. She can say no more easily, but then we have to decide which one of us will call her. We bring her to Boston for Christmas when Charlotte is visiting and find a place for her to stay. But the last time we did this, in 2001, Charlotte became very ill and was worried about a friend who worked in the World Trade Center and was suffering from post-traumatic stress syndrome, and my stepmother didn't even notice. Nothing's ever enough for her. If you give her lunch, she's talking about dinner. She's insatiable. I still feel responsible because I can't stand the thought of her winding up on the street. Charlotte can handle her better. She irritates me so much, I can't have any fun when she's around.

Charlotte agrees she has a cooler relationship with their stepmother.

Lizzie was stuck with my stepmother more when we were kids, and my stepmother expects more from her. Lizzie tries to take care of her, and then, when she gets off the phone, she's angry at how much she has to give. I've put up a cold barrier between my stepmother and me, so I'm not so angry. In my last round of therapy I learned how to avoid getting so angry with her, and now we can actually laugh on the phone. I still find her neediness, her lack of directness, and her self-absorption really difficult. So I make sure I never call her before bedtime so she doesn't affect my sleep. I could be in the position to help more, because Carter says he's willing to help, and now he'll have a decent pension. I'll also investigate what she can get from state benefits.

She brought me up to date on their father, who lives in the same apartment their family moved to when Charlotte started high school in 1961. For decades the original owner tried to have Mr. Bender evicted because the apartment was rent-controlled, and he wanted to raise the rent. But scrappy little Mr. Bender—Charlotte compares him to a bantam rooster in a cockfight—has managed to prevail, though once he was actually removed from the apartment in handcuffs. Charlotte says that the forty-year battle to keep the underpriced apartment has probably kept her father alive. The original owner died several years ago, and now their father fights on with that man's son and daughter.

Things are even looking up for their brother, Carl. Two years ago, he got a job he enjoys in Arizona and he finally moved out of his father's apartment where he'd been living since 1978. Now he's living an independent life and has found a community of friends. He comes to Boston when Charlotte is visiting and then Charlotte tries to spend time with Carl alone because when everyone in the family is together, they all compete for attention. She wants to build a relationship with her brother, and it's easier for her to focus on him when they're alone. Lizzie is trying this approach, too.

Lizzie observes that the quality of her relationship with Charlotte has changed as they've both become happier. "We used to relate over sadness and talk about the sad things that happened. Now we plan a nice day together, and we have fun together."

This tells me, more than anything, how much they've achieved. Many sisters I interviewed resented being saddled with responsibilities they shouldn't have had—taking care of a younger sibling or a parent. Lizzie and Charlotte were both given too much responsibility, but they remained loyal to each other.

Their initial bond was created in loss. But like everything in life, sister relationships must go forward and not just look back. As Lizzie explained, life is more than loss and needing to nurture one another in pain. Maybe Lizzie and Howard didn't belong on Charlotte and Carter's honeymoon, but the impulse was good—to celebrate their happiness together and to bring their attachment forward into their new primary relationships.

Making the transition to being together as couples rather than just as sisters took some work. They regressed a bit, and initially Howard felt, perhaps justifiably, that Charlotte mattered more to Lizzie than he did. In the seventeen years since, they have worked things out, and the two couples have spent many good vacations together. The sisters also evolved into equals, which isn't always easy. They both succeeded in getting past loss and going forward together. If Lizzie and Charlotte could only share their past, they wouldn't have had that much. The past is never enough, and their past wasn't great to start with.

Charlotte thinks they are all in a better place now, though it's taken a long time. I ask her why she thinks she's been able to sustain such a good relationship with Lizzie over all the years, despite all the sadness of their childhood.

> We both continued to grow. We both had a lot of therapy, and we've been through relationships—not just through them, but with help, we learned things from these relationships. We've taken risks with each other.

At one point, Lizzie told me that one impact of losing her mother was her lifelong fear of taking risks. This connection makes sense. In order to take a risk, you need to believe that if something doesn't work out the way you had hoped, something else—just as good—will eventually happen. If you lose one relationship, you'll find another. Optimists have more confidence in the future, so they can roll with the punches.

A child whose mother died when she was three doesn't get another mother. All she's learned is that some losses last forever. But both sisters learned to take risks in love and in their relationship with each other. And, as Charlotte explains, they've continued to grow by working hard at their relationships and learning something from their mistakes with the help of therapy.

It's clear they admire each other. Charlotte always thought of Lizzie as the sibling who had the most impressive career (Lizzie says the same thing about her sister), but she no longer thinks of Lizzie as the child who needs protection.

She's become a much stronger person, so it allows me to ask for things, and let her give me things. She's an incredibly sensitive and thoughtful sister.

We still struggle. Our mother must have been a special person and given us a lot of love. We must have had a wonderful time when we were babies. And my father, for all his faults, is capable of love and has become a more concerned and interested parent. He got the love he needed from Sasha [his current wife]. As for Lizzie and me, aside from our mother dying and having to fend for ourselves and not having our needs met, we've had lucky lives. Now we're very fortunate in our lives. We do have loving relationships and we do have each other. We're not starving to death.

As Charlotte recounted all the ways that she and Lizzie have been lucky, I wondered, at first, if she was still being the good girl—never complaining and always saying that everything is okay as she was trained to do. In this, she and Lizzie are different, as they must be, having grown up in somewhat different circumstances. It strikes me that Lizzie is more willing to speak about the dark side of things. She sees her brother as damaged by his early losses, where Charlotte sees that he's doing much better.

And, of course, it's easier for Charlotte to feel they've all had a happy ending. Her husband is healthy, while Lizzie still worries about hers. Lizzie told me the last time Howard went for a checkup, his specialist cheerfully introduced him to the new resident, "Here's a man who wasn't supposed to be alive today." Despite what happened to her mother, Lizzie has learned to adopt the optimist's perspective on illness. She's learned that statistics on the odds—great or small—of surviving are meaningless. When it comes down to your individual case, the only thing that matters is whether your case turned out well. I would say this about the Bender sisters. The odds were against them, and they've turned out remarkably well.

I'm also left with the image of their young mother in that one-minute movie, laughing, full of life, putting her arm around someone. It reminds me how fragile and irreplaceable each person is. Her death was the defining moment in so many lives—and it took years of struggle for the sisters to undo the damage inflicted by that one tragic loss. But Lizzie and Charlotte kept doing that very hard work, and in the end, they did make good lives for themselves and gave a lot to others.

Their mother wanted to be a writer and to make the world a better place. Her daughters lived out her dreams. Lizzie told me that she and Charlotte avoided competition by fulfilling the different sides of their mother's desires—she became the creative writer and Charlotte became the advocate for social justice. Modeling themselves on their image of their mother's perfection, they each became the wonderful person they remembered.

CHAPTER 3

Guilt and Sharing Alike

ONE CHILDHOOD MEMORY sisters often describe is how they would divide a single cookie or a piece of pie between them. This was a challenge that demanded surgical precision. One sister would make the cut, and the other got to choose her half—a ritual to ensure each one got her fair share. For some sisters, this vigilance about being fair extends into adulthood and is now more about giving your fair share rather than splitting a treat.

It is common knowledge that one major source of tension between adult sisters is sharing the work of caring for aging parents. And sisters often wind up with unequal shares of that responsibility because of where they live, other life circumstances, or their different relationships with their parents. The aging of parents also evokes the specters of loss and guilt, which get played out between sisters. I found that women who had guilt-inducing mothers often had more difficulty taking care of them and that guilt sometimes created alliances between some sisters but more often divided them. Guilt is a factor in how much of a sacrifice a daughter will make for a mother who is hard to please, but sisters aren't equally susceptible to it. There are other factors, too, such as how much punishment each daughter had been given as a child.

Guilt is the basic glue in many families so it also affects sister relationships. We often do things not because we want to, but because we want to avoid guilt or because we want to be the "good" one. We all make decisions about how much we will do out of guilt, and then we naturally use our own choice as the standard by which we judge other people. This is unfortunate because there are different ways to meet the needs of a family and everyone shouldn't have to do it in the same way.

In my interviews, I heard many accounts of how hard it was to be the daughter of a depressed or excessively critical mother who pulled guilt trips. As children, these sisters were raised to respond to the call of guilt. It's threatening for children to acknowledge their mothers aren't emotionally equipped to take good care of them. Many children would rather blame themselves when their mother is angry rather than recognize their parent as the one who is inadequate. Because these children have already experienced so much loss, they fear it even more. So they try to be good and to do what their parent wants.

"If you don't do what I want, I'll die" is the basic message that gets implanted like a hook on a fishing line in children who already fear loss. They get reeled in any time the string is pulled. Some will grow up doing what their parents want in order to be good. Others will resist, but they often pay the price of guilt. Others resentfully do things they don't want to do because they fear their parents will die and they'll never get over the guilt of not having done something their parent wanted. Caring for parents who loved you well and didn't manipulate you in this way is not only much more pleasant and rewarding, but less likely to have problems that also get played out in sibling relationships.

When adult daughters are driven by guilt or fear of loss—when they're powerless to resist it—it generally makes them angry. It also makes them angry with their sisters who don't feel compelled to take their fair share of the burden—"fair" usually being an equal share of the sour pie that the guilt-ridden one is ready to swallow. The anger gets projected onto sisters not only because they want their perceived obligation to be shared, but also because they can't get angry with an impossible-to-please parent who might die, and it's safer to redirect that anger to the sister who isn't so easily controlled by guilt. That sister may think the parent hasn't earned her love, because not much was given to her when she was a child. Or she may perceive that any sacrifice will be pointless because she knows her overcritical parent will find fault with whatever she does.

There's always plenty of guilt to go around in a family, and it spreads across relationships and generations, as Lizzie Bender observed of her own family. They all felt guilty about the death of Lizzie's mother. Her father felt responsible for her brother's psychological problems and wound up being his adult son's caretaker. Lizzie felt guilty that she and her sister had each other while her brother had no one. As an adult, she felt too guilty to say no to her insatiable stepmother. And because she made sacrifices for her stepmother she wanted her sister to make them, too.

I also interviewed many women who had found a way to resist or resolve their feelings of guilt toward their mothers, or to prevent it from creating divisions between themselves and their sisters. They were able to perceive and relate to their Real Sisters, even through the heavy fog of guilt that permeated their childhood.

One woman I interviewed, Marlie, was the preferred child of both parents. Like her mother and father, she was academically oriented and did well in school. She shared their values and felt nurtured by her mother. But as an adult, she came to see that their mother didn't treat her sister, Tracy, very well. Now in their forties, the two sisters are best friends and adore each other. But it wouldn't have happened if Marlie hadn't acknowledged her sister's different experience.

> I remember when my paternal grandfather died—I was ten and my sister was thirteen. My sister wore a miniskirt to the funeral. All the way home from the funeral my mother was screaming at her, "You looked like a tramp at the funeral with that skirt and all that makeup."
>
> I remember asking my mother how I looked, and my mother said, "Oh *you* look fine, you always do." My mother should have said something to my sister before we went to the funeral instead of yelling at her later. I kept thinking *Why didn't she say something before?* But I didn't come to my sister's rescue. I didn't want my mother to yell at me so I didn't speak up. She didn't yell often so it was scary.

Around that time, Tracy swallowed a whole bottle of aspirin and had to be rushed to the hospital to have her stomach pumped. The next year, when she was only fourteen, she became pregnant and got married. The two sisters didn't become close friends until many years later when Marlie had children, and Tracy helped her out with them. Later, Tracy remarried and had a second family so the sisters wound up raising some of their children at the same time.

"My sister didn't have her needs met, and she didn't have needs that my mother wanted to meet. My mother couldn't relate to my sister." When their mother was dying, Marlie didn't resent the fact that her sister wasn't that involved in her care. "I understood it. Mother wasn't there for her."

Another woman I interviewed grew up with a critical, angry mother who'd always been unhappy because her marriage had uprooted her from her family and her world in Japan. Belle's mother became even worse after her most beloved child, Belle's younger brother, died tragically at the age of twelve in an automobile accident.

Belle was twenty-one years old and had just moved away from home to get away from her controlling and guilt-inducing mother. But when her brother died, her already depressed parents totally fell apart, and Belle moved back home for a year to try to help them out and to protect her younger sister. She wanted to encourage her sister to gain independence from the family as she had done herself. But her sister didn't share Belle's perception of their family and would always say, "Stop helping me."

A few years later, Belle married and gave birth to a baby boy. She dismissed her mother's warning not to bring him to a memorial service that was held at her brother's graveside on the third anniversary of his death because she didn't want to leave him in the care of a babysitter. Belle's mother still lived with the traditional beliefs she grew up with, and she'd warned Belle her son would be harmed by evil spirits if she brought him to the cemetery. Belle thought this was ridiculous. But soon after the service, her baby developed a life-threatening illness (which he survived), and Belle felt horribly guilty.

At this time, Belle's sister tended to echo their mother's attitudes and remarks. On one occasion, her mother and sister became hysterical when Belle told them she was thinking of moving to a town that would require driving a long distance on a dangerous highway in her daily commute to work. They accused her of being a bad mother for taking this risk, and Belle's sister actually snatched the baby from Belle's arms, in a gesture of trying to protect him. Belle adored her child, and it really upset her that her mother and sister could think she was a bad mother.

It was Belle's perceptive husband who helped her to understand what was going on. "Don't you see?" he told her. "Your mother is jealous that you have a son and she lost her son." This was something that had never occurred to Belle. Her husband also helped her to understand how devastating the loss of their brother had been to her sister. Her sister had always been closer to their brother because they were nearer in age and had always played together. Eventually Belle's sister married and had children of her own, and the two sisters became close friends. They adore each other's children, and Belle has decided she always wants to live near her sister, at least until their children are adults, because she wants their children to grow up with a close, extended family.

One pattern that showed up in my interviews was how sisters might transfer the feelings they had for their mothers to their sisters, especially after their mothers died. This was often true when a grown daughter couldn't separate from a guilt-inducing mother or remained dependent on her. After her mother's death the daughter might turn toward her sister as a surrogate mother and ask for the care she never got from her mother. Then the sister who struggled to break free from their unhappy mother had to deal with the guilt of not being able to make things better for her sister. I encountered a number of women who were perplexed about what to do with a dependent and dysfunctional sister. They worried about how much they should do to help, especially when all their efforts seemed futile.

This was the case of Arlene Dyson, who told me about her sister, Claire, who has lived a progressively withdrawn and narrowed existence. Arlene felt frustrated about being unable to help her sister, but mainly she felt sad for her rather than angry or manipulated. Her sister's withdrawal from the world is driven by anxiety and phobias. Arlene feels great sympathy toward her sister because they grew up in a very unhappy home with two depressed and anxious parents. She loved her sister when they were children, and she loves her as an adult. It took years for Arlene to recover from their guilt-inducing childhood while her sister never did. Although her sister never criticizes her the way their mother did and she doesn't try to make her feel guilty, Arlene gets very frustrated when her sister won't take any of the constructive actions Arlene suggests. But Arlene has never stopped loving her sister, because she's learned to establish limits, as she had to with their mother.

Arlene is now fifty-seven and Claire is fifty-five. They grew up in a working-class neighborhood in Pittsburgh, where their father worked as a waiter and handyman. As children, they liked each other and were close. They shared a room in their two- bedroom apartment and played together. When Arlene was in the fourth grade, the family moved to a wealthier neighborhood where life became harder for Arlene. They were the poorest kids in the area, and Arlene didn't fit in.

> I was nerdy and shy. They picked on me because they didn't like my clothes and because my father waited on tables. My sister handled the move better—maybe because she was younger. She always looked better and had lots of friends, and she had boyfriends at a younger age than I did.

At home things were difficult. Their parents fought constantly. Arlene's father was quiet and depressed, and their mother was angry and dominating.

My mother would hit me all the time. I was more questioning and mischievous than my sister, and I said what was on my mind. Claire was seen as the good one, and I was the bad one. I didn't obey authority, and my sister did. She was scared not to. She feels my mother stifled her personality because she was so afraid to get into trouble.

My father developed Alzheimer's when he was very young— in his mid fifties—and my mother tortured him and blamed him. But he'd been very withdrawn for years before. I think he suffered from post-traumatic stress syndrome during World War II. He was a medic in a combat unit, and his whole outfit was wiped out. He was missing in action for a while.

They'd been married for four years when he left for the war, and my mother told me he was a different man when he came back. He'd been very intelligent and verbal and wrote poetry. She showed me some letters he wrote to her when he was first in the army, and I couldn't believe my father had written them. I'd never seen that side of him. It must have been very disappointing for my mother. My mother's mother was also dying for two years while he was away, and my mother took care of her.

When Arlene was eighteen and a freshman at the local city college, she got pregnant.

We made some connections to have an abortion, but I was afraid to go to someone who wasn't a doctor, and I couldn't find a doctor. We didn't have enough money. So we decided to have the baby and then I had to tell my mother. We got married right away, by a judge. I've never felt terrible about what happened. I was only eighteen, and I would have had the abortion if they were legal. But we were practically engaged anyway, and I wanted to get out of the house. My parents were always fighting, and it wasn't a pleasant place to be.

My mother pulled a big guilt trip when she heard the news. It was terrible. She acted like I was doing this to her, and I was so afraid of her. I went into therapy for years because I was such a mess. I had no self-confidence. I thought I was worthless and wouldn't open my mouth, and it was mainly because my mother was so critical. She told me nobody would like me because of the way I behaved. She said I'd never hold on to a husband and I'd never have a friend.

After Arlene got married, her husband and mother actually became good friends. Arlene's husband had come from a family that was even worse than hers, so he gravitated to Arlene's family. "He was just as insecure as me." Claire was very supportive of Arlene's marriage. "She looked up to me, and still does."

Arlene dropped out of college for a year and then went back to school while a neighbor watched her baby. A few years later, she had another child. Claire also dropped out of college and married young to escape the turmoil at home after her father had become ill. But Claire was divorced just a year after she married, which also drew her mother's wrath.

Arlene recalls that when her sister turned thirty-five, her life started going downhill. After catching a virus, Claire developed allergies and a pain in her jaw, and she had to quit her job. "I don't know how much of this was real and how much psychosomatic," Arlene explained. "She became completely dependent on her second husband and started to withdraw from the world. She had no friends."

Their mother had moved to North Carolina after their father died, and Claire decided that North Carolina would be better for her allergies. So Claire and her second husband moved to the same town as her mother. Arlene thinks her sister really moved because she was attached to their mother, even though she complained about her. Claire claimed her allergies improved in North Carolina, but this doesn't make any sense to Arlene.

Arlene explains that Claire's second husband had fertility problems, but her sister tried artificial insemination only twice before giving up on trying to become pregnant. Arlene feels her sister gave up trying too easily and that she could have convinced her husband to adopt children.

> By the time Claire was forty, she thought her life was a waste. She had no career, no children. She felt she had nothing and got more and more depressed.

Several years ago, Arlene and her family moved to Oregon, and both she and her husband built very successful careers. Their kids were in great shape and happy. Then Arlene's mother developed Alzheimer's, and when she had a stroke, Claire was terrified their mother would die. She made Arlene cut short a holiday in Europe to come to North Carolina, insisting their mother's death was imminent, even though the doctors told Arlene she'd be okay.

> My sister was hysterical. She said it wasn't fair that I was away, and she needed me to be there. My daughter offered to stay with my sister in my place but my sister said she needed me.

It's significant that the only time Arlene could recall Claire using guilt as a leverage was when her sister was in a panic about losing their mother. During the ten years Arlene has lived in Oregon, her sister visited just once.

She said she got sick from the Oregon water, and she'll never come again. She thinks she has allergies, a stomach ailment, and a heart condition—she has a minor mitral valve prolapse, which isn't serious at all. She's also allergic to newsprint.

My kids have turned out really well, and my sister is crazy about them. They call her, but she never calls anyone but me since my mother died. She's been much more dependent on me since my mother died. She wants me to talk on the phone more than I have time for.

Arlene has visited Claire often; she used to go to North Carolina twice a year when her mother was alive and more often than that toward the end of her mother's life. She finds it more depressing to visit her sister than it was to see her mother in the nursing home.

I forgave my mother by the time she died. I knew she did the best she could. But Claire didn't forgive her. She's still angry at the horrible way my mother treated my father, and she identifies with my father while she sees me as being strong like my mother.

My mother died of Alzheimer's in her eighties, but my sister's life is a living death. I love my sister but it's hard for me to spend time with her. She won't leave her condo without her husband. She's glued to the television, watching CNN. When I went to visit her a few days before my husband arrived, she couldn't tear herself away from watching the coverage of the presidential election disputes. She watches CNN day and night, and when I tried to get her to go out, she got angry with me and said I was bothering her. By the time my husband arrived, I said, "Get me out of here." Then she was calling me on the cell phone to talk about the election. She grabs onto television news stories and can't even have a meal without watching the news. It takes her four hours to put on her makeup to go nowhere, and she has a television in the bathroom so she can watch CNN while she's putting on her makeup.

I said, "Why don't you join the local Democratic committee if you like politics?" She said she hates local politics. She has an excuse for everything.

I worry about my sister. What if anything happens to her husband? She can't take care of herself. She won't come to Oregon because the water makes her sick and she'd drive me crazy.

She doesn't cook or clean. Her husband does the laundry— he runs an office for a real estate company, but he takes care of the laundry. They eat out or buy take-out food. She'll even buy tuna fish salad ready-made from the deli. The less she does, she does even less. She's on antidepressants and tells me she feels calm.

After September 11, she was really bad. She wouldn't leave the house, and she cried all day. My daughter and her partner had a baby in October 2001. They'd just bought a beautiful new house near Washington, D.C. I went there to see my grandson, and my sister was so afraid. She begged me not to go there—she said I might not be able to leave if there was a smallpox epidemic and they had to quarantine the city. She wants me to visit her, but I told her I want to visit my daughter and my grandson whenever I have free time, and she should come up and visit us there. But she won't travel.

I love her, we are friends, but I feel sad for her. She has no friends because she won't leave the house without her husband and it takes her so long to get ready. The only place she goes to is the mall.

Besides watching CNN, all she does is shop—at the mall and on the cable television shopping channel QVC. My mother had to bail her out of debt about ten years ago because she'd spent so much money on jewelry on QVC—that's her thing. She doesn't drink alcohol. She's into jewelry. She has enough jewelry to wear something new every single day for a year. And she goes nowhere.

She's still very attractive, even with her depression. She doesn't eat much so she's thin, and she fixes her face all day. My husband is very understanding of her. Last Christmas I wanted to take a vacation in Hawaii, and he said, "You haven't seen your sister in over a year, and she needs to see you." He's known her since he was twenty, and she's the only family we have.

I see what happened to my father, and I wonder if my sister has what he had, but his depression was triggered by the war. My sister is weak and passive like my father. My mother worried that my sister was like my father.

My sister wasn't like this when we were kids; she was happy. I've always believed that if she had had children, this wouldn't have happened to her. She wouldn't have had time to focus so much on herself.

I wondered about Arlene's belief that not having children was at the heart of her sister's self-absorption. At no other time did Arlene express any stereotypical ideas about women. She didn't need to look any further than the example of her own mother—having children hadn't turned her mother into a happy person. But having a baby was the way that Arlene had escaped from her mother, and having children had been the source of great joy in her life. Loving her sister, she probably regretted that Claire had neither been able to separate from their mother nor gotten what she needed to be happy.

Other women I interviewed had similar histories—their mothers had been very controlling or guilt inducing, and their sisters had never achieved independence. After their mothers died, their sisters transferred their dependence to them. What makes Arlene's story different from some of the others is that she and Claire aren't angry with each other. Arlene admits that some of her sister's habits can drive her nuts, but there's a tone of affection and understanding that comes through, even when she describes her sister's most maddening behavior. Arlene is different from her sister, but she knows what it's like to feel anxious and depressed, and she's able to empathize with Claire. She learned how to separate herself from her mother without feeling guilty. Perhaps that's why she can also set the limits she needs when she's dealing with her sister. She can do this, she doesn't feel controlled by Claire. She's not driven by guilt to do things she doesn't really want to do, so she doesn't wind up feeling angry.

CHAPTER 4

Perfect Sisters: Little Women

I WAITED A LONG TIME to find someone who felt she had the perfect sister, and then I found someone who has three. Maureen Ryan's story of her inspiring father and four loving sisters reminded me of Louisa May Alcott's *Little Women,* the model of sisterhood that many of us were raised on. At times, I wondered if this ideal world could possibly be real. Maureen's family story makes you want to open their front door and step right into their life, and it's nice to see such families exist.

Maureen Ryan's mother is totally unlike the guilt-inducing mothers in the previous chapter. Mrs. Ryan receded so far into the background of Maureen's story that she almost wasn't there. She was supportive and sweet, but she had so little presence in the family, her daughters may have drawn together to make up for her reticence or lack of authority. She wasn't demanding, and she kept the household going, but as Maureen put it, her father was clearly the dominant parent. The Ryan daughters did feel very nurtured and cared for, and they had the full involvement of their father. Their mother presented no impediment to their sisterhood, and they could give each other whatever motherly wisdom they might have needed.

Maureen and her three sisters are now in their thirties (she's the youngest, at thirty-one). Three of the sisters still live in neighboring Rhode Island towns near where they grew up and where their parents still live. Together, the Ryans have created such a happy and complete world that none of the sisters ever wanted to leave. They've just added on their own children and their four husbands, who've all become close friends.

Most summer days, the Ryan sisters pack up their young children (collectively, six girls and six boys) and hang around the swimming pool in their parents' backyard—the same pool where Maureen and Cindy practiced their dives and gymnastics when they were young. Six years apart, they'd both shined as cheerleaders and captains of their high school diving teams. Maureen attributes her teenage glory and popularity to her father. He was the coach of several athletic teams at their high school, and all the boys she grew up with loved hanging around him. He was the dad to kids who didn't have one. Around town, people still refer to her father as Coach Ryan, even though he's now pushing seventy and his health isn't great.

When he was young, Coach Ryan had given up a promising baseball career to support his younger siblings when their father died, but sports continued to be a driving part of his life. The Ryan sisters like to joke that it was lucky their father had four daughters and no sons, because he wouldn't have been able to tolerate a son who wasn't athletic.

"A winner never quits, and a quitter never wins," Maureen recalls her father's favorite motto.

You'd be sleeping in the sun and he'd wake you up and make you swim laps. He made us do sports and pushed us to be competitive. From the time I was five or six he signed us up for the swim club. But he came to every swim meet and every basketball game we played in, and whenever we were in trouble he'd apologize and say he'd been too hard on us, and that he would try to mellow.

Maureen's recollections of her mother all involve traditional mother things: baking, making sandwiches, doing volunteer work. She made hot chocolate in the winters while the girls were out sledding with their father. She made hot cider, to welcome them home on Halloween night after their father had walked them for miles and miles around the neighborhood, trick-or-treating. Maureen is clear that her father was the focal point of the family and the dominant parent: "He made the rules." "Wait till Father gets home," her mother would say, whenever the girls got into trouble.

Today the grown-up Ryan sisters and the next generation spend the summers in their old backyard, by the swimming pool of their childhood. They gather every morning at eight sharp, and don't leave until nine P.M., when it's time to put the children to bed. Their old friends come by, and they all sit around telling wacky stories. Even Cindy, the one sister who moved to Texas because of her husband's military career, comes back for the summer ritual. When they married, her husband agreed she could take the children and return for three weeks every August.

Growing up, the Ryan sisters were the good girls in town. Maureen recalls how they'd dress up every Sunday morning and sit beside their parents in church "like ducks in a row." At Christmas, the Ryan sisters still keep all the family rituals and traditions they grew up with. They always spend Christmas Eve at their parents' house, sitting in a circle around their father while he reads "'Twas the night before Christmas." The only difference now is that the grandchildren sit in a second ring around their parents. During the reading, they always call Cindy in Texas using the speakerphone so she can be included.

The Ryan girls weren't all close as children. Some only became friends once they were teenagers or had children of their own. When Maureen was small, she admired and envied her oldest sister, Lynn, who is eight years older. Lynn got all As in school without any effort, while Maureen had to work for them. And Maureen felt hurt when Lynn established her independence from the family. She remembers crying when Lynn left for college. She didn't want anyone to leave. Then, after her freshman year, when Lynn didn't want to join the rest of the family for their annual vacation at Cape Cod, Maureen was very upset. "I saw her as not caring and didn't realize she was just older and needing to separate. I thought we have to be a family, and I wanted to have everyone around me."

Maureen also fought a lot with Dora, who is three years older and closest to her in age and with whom she shared a room. "The house was not huge, so the four girls and my parents all teamed up in pairs. The two older girls shared a room and they were complete opposites: one was messy and the other was very organized. Dora and I shared a room and we were always fighting over silly things. But at night, we would giggle and hold a make-believe school where she would teach me what she'd learned that day."

Growing up, Maureen was closest to her second-oldest sister, Cindy, who is six years older.

She was my idol in life—very nurturing, always there for me. She still is. She was a cheerleader and a gymnast and a diver. I wanted to be so much like her, I did everything she did.

The first time I got my period my mother was away visiting her mother, and I didn't know what to do. I was supposed to go to a swimathon, a walkathon, and a pool party that day [the pace obviously set by Coach Ryan]. I couldn't tell my father, and the only person I could tell was Cindy.

She was so amazing. I'd never had a really personal conversation about the body with anyone, and she brought me into the bathroom and explained what to do and held my hand. Then she told my father who called Mother.

I was lying in bed, crying. I didn't want the feeling of growing up. She was lying in bed with me, stroking my hair like your mother would do. Ever since then, we can talk about anything. She made me feel better than my mother could have. She made me laugh by telling me how embarrassing things slipped out of her purse, and she told me not to worry.

She told me I didn't have to go to the swimathon that day. I think I did do the walkathon and went to the pool party. She said, "Just call me if you feel sick and I'll come and pick you up." She's such a neat person. She helped me then and still does now. She's a gem. She's a teacher now, which is perfect for her.

When Cindy was getting her driver's license, she'd take me for a ride. Cindy was a junior in high school and I was in the seventh grade. We'd go and get a can of whipped cream and eat the whole thing. We'd drive by the houses of boys we liked and turn up the radio and then speed away. We'd do silly things like that.

During high school, it was Cindy that Maureen turned to for advice about boys and dating. Cindy was still around then because, like all the sisters, except Lynn, she'd chosen to stay close to home and attend a local college.

But Cindy was the first to marry and the only one to move

away. She fell in love with a boy who was attending West Point when she met him, and they moved to a military base in Texas. At the time, Maureen resented the separation and she still thinks Cindy misses the family, but Maureen's forgiven her brother-in-law. "He made her light up and they blended in so well, I can't hold it against him."

Before Cindy and Rick became engaged, Maureen remembers Rick asked her father for permission first, and called him sir.

Cindy came in with a ring on her finger and it was the first time I saw Dad cry—she was so happy, and he was happy for her. I did feel a sense of loss because she moved away. But we ran up the phone bills. Cindy, Dora, and I are very emotional. We can look at a Hallmark card and cry. My sister Lynn shines in a different way. She's a pediatric nurse, and we gravitate to her whenever anyone is sick and we have questions about what to do. She was so strong when my father got sick, probing my mother to get a second opinion, to make sure it would happen.

Several years ago, Maureen's father had a heart attack, and Maureen couldn't bear to see him in the hospital.

I couldn't go—I'd just cry and he'd feel upset. But Lynn held his hand and she would cry only after she left the room. Lynn gave birth to her first child when my father was still in a wheelchair. They wheeled him into her room and she told him she'd named her first child after him. We'd all expected she would give him her husband's name [juniors were the custom in his family], but she told my father, "This is how important you are to me."

By the time Cindy married, Maureen was turning to Dora for dating advice.

When I was dating my husband, Jim, I remember when our relationship was fizzling a bit. I told Dora I didn't know what was going to happen, and it was difficult because Jim and I worked in the same company. That day a beautiful arrangement of flowers arrived for me at work, with a card that said "Thinking of you." I thought Jim had sent it, but my sister called and asked, "Did you get the flowers? You have to thank Jim for the flowers. Trust me, this will help." So I thanked him and he said, "They're not from me." Not long after, we were engaged.

It's Dora that Maureen talks to every morning, as soon as their kids leave for school. If for some reason, they don't talk at 8:40, they talk at 4 P.M. Maureen told me the time they spend talking on the telephone is somewhat annoying to their husbands, but there's no way they would stop.

"Dora's amazing, she just gives and gives." Maureen described how her sister gets up at 4 A.M. to start baking children's birthday party cakes that she "sells" for the cost of ingredients. She needs to do this early, because she has four young children. "She makes things for everyone. Mom just had a birthday and everyone but my sister who lives in Texas was there. Dora made T-shirts that had pictures of Mom at all the stages of her life, and she made all the kids wear one." Some of Maureen's and Dora's children are the same age, and get along well. The two families rented a house for a week at the Cape this summer, where they used to go as children.

She's known Dora's husband, Steve, all her life: He was in her sister's class, although he came from a different social set. Steve's family was rich, and he had a reputation of being rowdy. "Dad wouldn't have let her date him." But Dora always had a crush on him and they met up years later at a high school reunion.

> He turned out to be a hardworking guy—he owns a construction company—and he'd do anything for anyone. One guy who was working for him was down on his luck and Steve gave him his car to use and said, "When you have enough money, give it back." When he hears someone can't get a job, he'll hire him.

In fact, after Coach Ryan had a heart attack, and the family decided he needed a less-stressful job than being a salesman, Steve convinced him to work in his construction business. He said he needed him to make sure no one was stealing the deliveries. Now that Maureen's father works in her brother-in-law's business, they can see him every day.

> We are always together. We would always be there for each other, especially Dora. If something happened to Jim and me, I'd want Dora and Steve to take our children. She'd just move them in—she'd have six children instead of four.
>
> I see that my sister embraces life—she gives her children opportunities and she's never negative with them. She encourages them to be everything they can. She does the stuff we did as kids. She never liked athletics, and she didn't like to swim, but my father encouraged her and she was so proud when she won a ribbon. My sister does this with kids. She makes cakes for them that say, "Congratulations—you did this." I see that, and that's what I need for my kids.

A few months ago, Maureen's father was diagnosed with cancer, but it was caught very early, and Maureen was told there's a 90 percent cure rate.

He's doing amazingly well. He goes in for radiation, and goes to baseball games right after. One of my sisters was crying and said, "We've been too lucky." But I feel nothing bad will happen. I'm an optimist.

After September 11, my sisters were the first ones I phoned, because Cindy's husband is in the military and he might get called. Rick is forty-three, he's far up in the ranks so he wouldn't be fighting, but he'd be in charge of a big operation. I asked Cindy if she was upset and she said, "No. You have to be strong for the kids. This affects them. You have to explain he's fighting for a cause."

Maureen felt this did help their kids, and it helped her.

The sisters have been looking out for one another for as long as Maureen can remember. She told me that when she began first grade, she was very fearful of the nun who was her teacher.

I was so frightened I threw up every day on the bus, and Dora had to sit next to me because the other children were mean, and she was the only one who would sit next to me.

She never complained to me. She walked me to the nurse's office and I got cleaned up and they let me go home. Now she teases me, "You better be nice to me; I sat next to you when you were throwing up on the bus."

Maureen's younger daughter is having the same problem.

When we started her in preschool, she'd throw up on the way to school. The first year, I pulled her out of school. When she started school the next year, she was throwing up again. We talked. I told her, "You need to be here. I'll bring extra clothes and if you get sick, you can change." She went two days a week, and for the first two months I sat in the waiting room, and eventually she got used to it.

My sister got me through this when I was in the first grade. She was there to help. When my daughter gets to the first grade, her sister will be in the third grade. She's very competitive with her sister, the way I was with Dora, but it will help her to have her sister there.

Maureen's family lives in the same town where her husband was raised; they live three streets away from his childhood home. Their kids are going to the same school her husband attended. Lynn, Maureen's oldest sister, lives in the town where the Ryan girls grew up, so her children are going to the high school that she and her sisters attended, where their father was the coach.

I drive by the high school and it looks exactly the same. I haven't been inside, but next week my niece has a volleyball game so we're all going to the old gym, even my mom. I see so many messed-up families. I look at my family and think how lucky we are. Look at what we have.

OF ALL THE SISTER STORIES I heard, Maureen Ryan's came closest to the traditional image of perfect sisters. Is there any price to having such a perfect family that you'd never want to leave? Maureen and her sisters have young children, and they've given priority to being mothers without any evidence of feeling bored. Maureen didn't talk very much about her own or her sisters' career aspirations, other than to say a teaching career was perfect for Cindy and they all appreciated Lynn's knowledge as a pediatric nurse. The Ryan girls had been the focus of their parents' lives, and Maureen seems content to be a full-time mother.

Among the women I interviewed, having and raising children together was the single most powerful factor in bringing sisters into a close adult relationship, regardless of whether they'd been close as children or worked outside the home. Even those who hadn't grown up in ideal families wanted to give their children a close extended family.

When Maureen told me that she and her younger daughter both vomited through their first years of school, I wondered if their home life had been so perfect that venturing into the outside world made them anxious. But it didn't seem that her problem was caused by an anxious or overprotective mother. It was Maureen's sister, not her mother, who helped her to get over her fear and many of the other challenges of growing up, and Maureen expected this would also be true for her daughters.

Maybe the Ryan sisters are unusual in that their family met all their needs so well, they had little interest or motivation to move away. One might argue they gave up the excitement of exploring what lay beyond their happy universe. Maureen and her sisters have managed to blend in their husbands and children instead of splitting up and breaking away. But who could argue with preserving what most people yearn to have?

The family reminded me of *Little Women,* the novel that has been a favorite children's story for over one hundred years. Generations of critics have reinterpreted Louisa May Alcott's nostalgic story about four loving sisters who live in Concord, Massachusetts, during the Civil War era. It's also been adapted several times for Hollywood feature films—each version changing the story to reflect the mood of the time. In the most recent adaptation, by the Australian director Gillian Armstrong, Winona Ryder plays the leading role of the independent Jo March, the sister who aspired to be a writer (apparently Louisa May Alcott's alter ego) and Susan Sarandon is the mother.

In the original novel, the heroine regrets how marriage has scattered her sisters and ended their youthful creative ambitions. In the Armstrong version, the story is altered by the director's feminist vision. The sisters aren't so willing to abandon their creative ambitions or their attachments to each other and their original home just to marry. Instead, they all return to Concord with their husbands and their artistic careers and form an extended family built around the sisters' bonds, which remain at the core.

This is also true of the Ryans, from Maureen's description. Maureen's attachment to her father, who has the love and admiration of all his daughters; their mother's supporting role; and the traditional values and choices of the daughters are what you see first.

From Maureen's description, all her sisters have happy marriages, and their husbands are strong and successful men. But it's also obvious their husbands had to accommodate to the sisterly bonds—those sisters are never going to get off the phone. Even the one husband who moved his wife to Texas because of his military career deferred to the Coach by asking him for his daughter's hand (and this was in the 1990s) and agreeing to let Cindy and their children return home for a month every summer. With the exception of Cindy, the Ryan sisters solved the problem of blending in their husbands to their core family by marrying men they'd grown up with in high school (this was true for Dora and Maureen) and who also came from families still living nearby.

Many of the women I've interviewed have described, if not articulated, one source of domestic power that's not always fully recognized; women often make their own families the main one their children get to know. (What was usually articulated was their complaint that their brothers became too absorbed into their wives' families and values.) More often, one hears grandparents expressing some concern over who will become the "chosen" ones—the ones their children will choose to live near and who will have the greatest contact with the grandchildren.

Maureen told me that neither she nor her husband had to give up their childhood families, and neither wanted to. This was possible because they grew up in neighboring towns. Maureen lives just a few streets away from the house where her husband was raised, and just a few miles from her parents' home. They spend every Christmas Eve circled around Coach Ryan, but they spend every Christmas Day with her husband's family. Her sister Dora also married someone from the neighborhood. They've all just managed to keep adding on, without giving anything up. It may not happen often, but the Hallmark family is still the one that many people are yearning for.

CHAPTER 5

The Sister
with a Secret

SOMETIMES A SISTER who is different from the norm is afraid she won't be loved if her family—including her sister—finds out who she really is. In her eyes, the difference is huge, while it may not be so big in the eyes of the others. This is a story of sisters, Kate and Patty, who have different sexual orientations. But what came between them was not the fact that one was heterosexual and one was a lesbian. What really came between them was Kate's insistence on keeping her sexuality a secret.

Kate is twenty-eight; Patty is nearly thirty. Their lifestyles could not be more different. Kate works as an administrator in a large legal firm. She recently moved to Manhattan to live with her partner in a lesbian and gay community. Patty lives in suburban Long Island, is married to a bond trader, and is a full-time mother to her three young children. But neither has ever felt judged by the other; in fact, they've always been very close. They grew up in a large, close Italian family with an older brother: Frank, who is thirty-five. I spoke with Kate first.

Patty and I grew up sharing a room, and we played all the time. We're just eighteen months apart, but she was two years ahead of me at school. She'd come home from school and be the teacher and teach me what she learned. She'd choreograph dances I had to dance and lead me in cheerleading. She was in control—she's bossy and dominant. We each had a best friend, but we lived in a remote area, about twenty minutes from school, so we played together at home.

I knew from the first grade that I was attracted to girls. Now I realize my mother and sister knew I was a lesbian the whole time. But when I was a kid, I accepted that I liked girls, so I thought I must be a boy. I used to pray I would wake up with a penis. Then I could like girls and it wouldn't be a problem.

Kate's sister, Patty, has similar memories of their relationship, but from a different perspective:

We shared a room, and we were always very close. If one of us was in trouble, the other would cry. We had tons of stuffed animals and made a village with them. I was probably more dominant, and as we got older, I dominated her more.

She'd want to play Monopoly, and I'd say yes, but only if she agreed to my rules: I got Boardwalk and Park Place and if she landed on them, she couldn't buy them. She was very sweet and easily manipulated by me. She'd feel bad if I told her she wasn't being a good sister. She always played into that. I'd tell her to go get me things and make her do stuff I wanted her to do.

When we were teenagers, we were close, but not how we were before. She was dealing with her sexuality. I had a feeling she was a lesbian, but she wouldn't talk about it.

Once she told my mother and me that she'd been hugging a

friend, and her friend's mother came into the room and accused them of being lesbians. My mother and I both asked, "Are you?"—because we felt she was, and she freaked out and bawled and said she wasn't. She left the room, crying. After that, we didn't talk about it. We couldn't push her; we didn't know.

She had a pattern of making a best friend, and then moving on. I didn't realize until later that stuff was actually happening between them. I just thought she had crushes.

In high school, Patty was "small, cute, and blond," and Kate recalls her older sister trying to make her look more feminine by applying makeup and curling her hair. Patty recalls this, too:

She was popular, but when she got to high school, I was concerned. We went to a Catholic high school with a lot of rich children, and you had to look a certain way to get along. I was worried she'd get teased. She was a tomboy—she wasn't like the other girls, but she was so likeable she did great.

She had very short hair in grade school, and she was constantly being mistaken for a boy in stores and restaurants. People would say "young man" to her, and she'd start to cry. This was when she was eight, nine, or ten. So I encouraged her to grow out her hair—to have a really long ponytail, so at least she wouldn't be mistaken for a guy.

I'd say, "Let me put makeup on you." NO. "Let's go shopping." NO. It was partly because I wanted her company, and partly because I wanted her to look more feminine. Finally I gave up.

When Kate went to college, my mom and I would talk about it, a lot. Neither of us knew for sure, but we felt we did know. It was harder for my mom to deal with it, because Kate's her daughter, and my mother is older. My mother was mainly concerned that life would be hard for her. I'd say, "Yes, but that's who she is." We accepted it.

Once I went to her house early in the morning, and her girlfriend was there. It was obvious she had spent the night there. Kate said to me, "She's working on my computer." I just got so sick of her lying.

No one in her family knew that Kate was really tormented by confusion. In college, she tended to fall for girls who would hurt her. She'd get involved with girls who cheated on her with boys to cover their reputation. "I liked straight girls and thought I should be a boy."

Patty was the catalyst in helping Kate to come out to her family.

When Kate was twenty-two, she went to a bar with Howie, her good friend and roommate, and she had several drinks. She'd arranged to meet Patty there, and when Patty saw her drinking and smoking a cigarette, she started yelling at her: "What are you doing? Dad just had a heart attack."

Kate was drunk enough to blurt out, "I have bigger problems. You don't know the pressure I'm under."

Patty answered, "Then tell me. What pressure?" She pulled Kate into a back room, and said, "I know you're a lesbian, just tell me."

Kate was drunk enough to blurt out that she wanted a sex-change operation.

"This was totally upsetting and shocking to me," Patty recalls. "I was prepared for her to tell me she was gay, but not that. We were both crying. 'Are you sure?' I asked her, 'Why do you feel you want that?'"

I didn't want to discourage her. But later we talked about the steps she'd have to go through, and she said she would need counseling and there were lots of steps before she would have surgery. That made me feel better—to hear that you couldn't just sign up for an operation.

I knew how hard it was for her to come out to me because we were so close, and I was twenty-four, and she was twenty-two. This was so late, and I had to drag it out of her. "I was afraid you wouldn't love me," she told me. I don't know how she could think that.

Around this time, Kate was meeting people who had varied identities: gay, lesbian, bisexual, and transgendered. This was a revelation. Since childhood, she'd always had the hope that all her problems could be solved and she could be a heterosexual if she just became a boy. "Now I realized that no matter what I did, I'd still be queer." Around this time, Kate was also involved with a girlfriend who helped her decide that she was a lesbian.

Kate knew that once she told Patty anything, it would be "like going on a broadcast system." She was right. Patty told their mother and brother (which made it easier for Kate), but no one told their father. He was not in good health and had become very emotional since he'd had a heart attack and had to retire. After Kate felt more comfortable about her sexuality her major fear in coming out to her family was that it might upset her father so much it would kill him or create a serious rift. Her mother may have contributed to her worries about her father's reaction. So they kept the secret from her father for a few more years. It became harder for her after she developed a happy and committed relationship with Carol, her partner, who is a biologist. Now Kate wanted Carol to meet her family.

I wanted to tell them, "This is my girlfriend." I was twenty-six, and Carol's been out to her family for a long time. I tried saying, "This is my friend." I think my mom didn't want me to tell my father because he'd be upset, and she was afraid he'd blame her. I talked to my sister about it, then to my brother Frank, and he said, "Dad's a smart guy. He's not living in a bubble."

When Kate and her mother and sister finally gathered the courage to tell her father the truth, after all those years of worrying, it turned out to be nothing. He told Patty, "I had an idea. She's twenty-seven and never had a boyfriend." He and Carol get along very well.

Coming out to her family was a major event in Kate's life and brought her closer to her sister again, the way they had been as children. Kate also gave Patty the courage to break up with a long-term boyfriend when she met the man she ultimately married.

My husband is quiet, and Kate's the one person who reaches out to him. I really appreciate it. I consider her my best friend. I know if I need to talk to someone or share something or get an opinion, the one person I want to talk to is her. I trust her opinion and value it, and she'll tell me the truth. She has a good view on the world, she's really levelheaded.

If I call Kate and say I'm tired, she's supportive and loving. She'll say, "What can I do to help?" She plays with my kids and helps me. She doesn't judge my life. She embraces it, and she loves my kids. All my friends love her, too.

Patty's daughter is named after Kate (it's her baby's middle name). "My sister was with me when I gave birth to my daughter,

along with my husband and my mother. My father wasn't there—
it would have been too embarrassing for him."

I asked Kate whether she felt excluded from conversations about
babies or being a mother in her big Italian family. She recalled one
gathering of the extended family, with a lot of fuss around her sister and her sister-in-law and their marriages and babies. "All these
pregnancies and kids, I felt left out. I went into the kitchen and
stayed there, washing dishes. It's easier now." She and Carol aren't
at the point of deciding whether to have children.

> I'm not out to my aunts and uncles or grandparents—they're
> idiots. They know, but I don't want to discuss it. They'll say,
> "Where's Kate's friend? When are we going to meet her?" Patty
> will say Carol is great, but I don't want them knowing anything
> about me. Patty asked me why. I feel my aunt is just snooping
> around; she always wants to know if my sister and I really get
> along—she thinks we're putting on a facade, because in her
> family everyone hates each other.

The one point of conflict between the sisters is Kate's annoy-
ance when Patty implies she is letting Carol dominate their relationship. When Kate was younger, she used to get involved with
women who controlled her, and Kate suspects Patty doesn't see
that her relationship with Carol is different.

> I've changed a lot in the last three years—I've worked on this—
> and I think about everything. Patty is protective of me, but she
> hasn't recognized how much I've changed. She was worried
> when I was the one who gave up my cottage to move in with
> Carol. But I wanted to live in the city anyway: I have friends

there, and I like the larger queer community there. I was ready
to move.

The real issue may be Patty's fear that Carol might get a job offer
in another part of the country. She would hate it if Kate moved far
away.

She's like my two closest friends, but a level above my best
friends. She's my sister. We know what each other is thinking.
We're so connected. When my family goes to the shore every
summer and we all spend a lot of time together, I feel like a kid
again with her. Swimming, dressing up, waking up in the same
house. We're all there together . . . I'd hate it if she moved out of
the state. I want my children to know her.

Patty told me she thinks her parents are great individuals, but
they haven't had the happiest marriage. She wonders if she and
Kate responded by learning to make their needs secondary in
order to create a happy place around them. She also offered another interesting view of why she and Kate have always gotten
along so well: "We were never competitive. She didn't see me as a
role model, because of her sexuality. We were just friends, so we
weren't competing. We didn't have to compete with our brother
because he was older and beyond competition."

When Patty said that Kate is her best friend, but even better, it
reminded me that the "perfect" sister is someone who helps you to
find your own identity. Sometimes a sister is able to do this more
easily than a parent because parents often feel any difference in
values that a child asserts represents a rejection of who they are, or
their failure as parents. Some children, like Kate, who adore their

parents might feel even more guilty about causing them any disappointment, real or imagined.

Adolescence is a time when young people separate themselves from the views and assumptions held by their parents and siblings. In this stage, a sister can be a confidante and helper or a rival who parrots a parent's critical judgments. As girls move from childhood to womanhood, their body image and sexual feelings are big concerns, and these get played out in relationship to sisters as well as parents. The competitive side—which sister is prettier or thinner or more popular—often gets played up in media images of teenage sisters. But some sisters actually help each other find and accept themselves.

Sisters who can't form an alliance at this point, when they should be separating from parents, may always have a problem, or at least as long as one sister identifies with her parents in a way that increases the exclusion of the other. Patty helped smooth the way for her parents to accept Kate's sexuality, and Kate reached out to Patty's husband.

Another lesbian I interviewed raised a related issue. Andrea told me that her heterosexual sister was the favored child (a feeling not expressed by Kate), and that as children they weren't close. Andrea did resent that Shelly was favored, but they had something in common—their hatred for their older brother. Their brother had tormented both of them, and when the sisters became teenagers they formed a lasting friendship. Several times in adulthood one would rescue the other, giving money or emotional support, and the devotion was mutual.

When Shelly fell in love and became engaged, Andrea accepted that her sister had another primary relationship. "I thought for a while she'd drop me. But it's nice for me that she has a partner.

She's been able to break out of her isolation and open her heart. I feel hope for myself, that I can do it, too."

But one thing did come between them. Andrea, unlike Shelly, had also been assaulted by their father, and this became a source of conflict with her sister.

I'd been asking her to believe me when I told her what my father did. This was a big challenge for her, because they had a different relationship. Last summer it came to a head. I was ready to walk away from the relationship if she didn't believe in my integrity when I told her what happened. All that stuff was very serious, and the ramifications were very serious. My father had been dead for thirteen years. I felt we would either upgrade our relationship or I wasn't interested in pretending we had a relationship.

She would say, "I believe you believe he did that to you." That wasn't enough for me. That's different from "Yes, I believe that happened to you, and that Dad was capable of that." We went through this for a week. Finally she said she believed me, but she didn't want to talk about it, it was too traumatizing for her. I could understand that. Both could be true. For her, hearing about those things that happened to me could be traumatic for her. So I decided, okay, I can live with that.

Andrea needed a real acknowledgment from her sister that their father had abused her. Not having that felt like her existence was being denied. She would have liked it if her sister was able to talk about it, but she was willing to compromise on getting just the acknowledgment because she accepted her sister's needs, too.

She goes about things in a different way than I do, and we respect each other. What's hard is letting go of the feeling that my way is right and your way is wrong. You know how in close relationships you quit trying to change the other person. Over time, we've grown to respect the other's differences and to value those, too.

Kate and Andrea succeeded in freeing themselves from secrets that divided them from their sisters. Feelings of shame and the fear of losing love are usually the motivations for secrecy within the family. However, there are some fortunate families that don't feel the need to hide matters of importance.

For example, Vera Johnson is the oldest of eight children who grew up in a black, Catholic family in Indiana. Both of her parents worked long hours so each of her siblings was assigned responsibility for one younger sibling. This duty was never resented or questioned. Most of Vera's friends also had a younger sibling they were responsible for—and they had to go home right after school to take care of that child. Despite her family's poverty and the racial discrimination they endured, Vera and most of her siblings went to college and have professional careers. Vera feels much closer to her sisters than her friends. When she has a problem, she'll call one of her sisters because she feels she has the most in common with them.

But one of Vera's sisters is the polar opposite of the others. Her youngest sister Edna has spent more years of her life locked up in prison than she's spent on the outside. Edna started her criminal career by snatching purses and worked up to being arrested for accompanying a male friend during an armed robbery of a convenience store. Vera is not ashamed of her sister. Although she doesn't share her values or lifestyle, she recognizes and admires Edna's ingenuity and resourcefulness in managing her life inside prison.

Edna also has never been treated as a secret in their family. Vera regards Edna as interesting, like all of her other sisters. When their father died, Edna's friends showed up at the funeral "dressed for the stroll," and the family appreciated their attendance at the service. When their mother died, Edna was in prison, and she could only get a two-hour leave for the funeral. So the Johnsons arranged the service to maximize the time Edna could be present.

Vera and her mother always wondered why Edna turned out so differently from the other siblings who all lead sedate and quiet lives that are centered on their families and their church. Interestingly, Vera and her mother speculated that Edna got into trouble because she didn't have a younger sibling to be responsible for.

Unlike many of the women I interviewed who considered it a burden to have primary responsibility for a younger sibling, Vera and her mother considered this a character-building experience. They thought Edna's problems stemmed from being the youngest child and not gaining the maturity that comes from sharing the work of the family. From what I observed in my research, refusing to harbor family secrets or to be silenced by shame is unusual. Many women I interviewed described major family secrets—usually in connection with illness, sex, or something that had to do with the body. In general, maintaining these secrets divided them from one another as it temporarily divided Kate from her sister Patty or threatened to divide Andrea from Shelly. Maintaining a secret tends to create considerable anxiety about its discovery, and secrets often inhibit intimacy or communication. In so many families I heard about, the most important things were never discussed or they were subjects that everyone danced around. In the O'Conner family, all the most important topics were taboo.

Mary O'Conner King, who is now sixty-seven, described how her mother became pregnant with her sister Joyce when Mary was ten and her mother was forty-six. Mary had no idea her mother was pregnant: "She was due in December, and I didn't know until September. She wore a big housedress."

Mary was very fond of her father. He was placid and easygoing, unlike her controlling mother. "He never hit us; he was nice to us." But he was an alcoholic, and when he smelled of drinking, her mother "would start in on him."

One day her father simply vanished when Mary was twenty and her sister was ten. Her father was gone, and he never came home. He'd cashed in two life insurance policies so it seemed he'd had a plan. The family was left without any money. Mary remembers that her father's disappearance could not be discussed at all. Her mother refused to speak about it, and Mary couldn't find out what happened. Her mother didn't want to find him; she thought he would just bring the family more trouble. Mary recalls this was also a topic you could not discuss with anyone outside the family. In fact, she remembered that even before her father disappeared, her mother never had any friends or social life because she didn't want anyone to know about her husband's alcoholism.

I asked Mary if she was hurt when her father disappeared. "Yes, but it was a relief. We didn't have to worry anymore. We didn't know if he'd be back, but gradually we realized he wasn't coming back." She tells me that years later her mother talked about wondering what happened to him, "but in those days you didn't even tell your priest you were having a problem."

Eventually, Mary and Joyce both married and became very close. Although Mary had felt partly like a mother to her sister when they were children, their relationship became equal after they were married, and the two couples did lots of things together. Mary's husband was considerably older than she was, and he died after suffering from a long and difficult illness. Then strange things began to happen concerning illness between Joyce and Mary.

> When I had breast cancer, Joyce was sympathetic, but she never asked me about it unless I told her something. She'd never bring it up on her own. During six weeks of radiation, she never asked, "How's it going? Are you tired? In pain? What does it look like?"

She told me she was mystified by her sister's reaction. The first and only thing her sister had said when Mary told her she had breast cancer was, "Oh, then I have greater risk of getting it." According to Mary, Joyce had always been very caring and sensitive, so her response was a mystery. Once, Mary was having dinner with Joyce and her brother-in-law, Bill. Mary mentioned that a mutual acquaintance had surgery and wasn't looking well. Her sister said, "It's best not to discuss this during dinner. It upsets Bill."

More recently, Mary called Joyce, and Bill answered the phone. "Joyce isn't here. She and a friend are out of town for three days looking at property." Mary called three days later and asked Joyce about the trip. Her sister told her she hadn't actually taken a trip. She'd been in the hospital having a hysterectomy. "I was so hurt she didn't tell me," Mary said. "Somehow she must have thought if she told me I'd insist on coming, and she'd have to manage my visit. She's very controlling, and I am, too."

Mary and her sister have done many things together without conflict. They shared the care of their mother when she was ill, and they have owned property together, all without any problems. "I'm at an age when so many friends are going through tragedies and surgeries. It's a normal part of being sixty-seven. Maybe she can't handle it. She's deathly afraid of it."

When we discussed the prohibition against discussing her father's disappearance, Mary raised a good point: Families used to
be more secretive about problems and illness when she was a
child. In fact, several of the older women I interviewed had told
me that when they were young, they weren't told until the very
end that a parent or sibling was ill or dying. But Joyce will not discuss illness with Mary even today. It's possible that Joyce doesn't
like to discuss threatening topics that make her feel she's not in
control. Her father's disappearance when she was a small child and
her mother's controlling behavior may have made Joyce averse to
discussing anything that makes her feel she's not in charge.

Not all secrets are about maintaining control. Most of the time,
keeping secrets in the family is about shame or trying to protect
someone. But when people fear shame or the loss of love, they
often try to exert control over who will be entrusted with the secret. And sometimes they wind up keeping those who care a great
deal at a distance.

CHAPTER 6

Becoming Friends
as Adults

THIS IS A STORY of sisters who weren't friends as children but became best friends when they were adults. It's also about sisters who occupied opposite roles in the family when they were young, but were able to overcome these early divisions.

When Anna and her sister, Leslie, were children, their parents viewed Anna as beautiful and perfect in every way, while Leslie was labeled the ugly daughter and considered a difficult child. Anna and Leslie's story illuminates not only how sisters are differentiated by appearance, but also by their parents' perceptions (or misperceptions) of how well they behave. Almost every woman I interviewed recalled that she and her sister responded in opposite ways to parental authority. It was a recurrent theme that one sister conformed to their parents' values, while the other sister rebelled.

This was true of Anna and Leslie, but as usual, the reality turned out to be more complex than the perception. Anna, the beautiful, older daughter, outwardly conformed to her parents' wishes, but secretly she always did what she pleased without feeling guilty or worried about violating their rules. Leslie always argued with her parents, but she didn't actually disobey them, because she was too frightened of getting caught and losing their love.

Why do so many families have a "good" daughter and a "difficult" daughter? In some cases, the parents give most of their attention to the most beautiful daughter because they see in her a reflection of their own aspirations (mirror, mirror on the wall). The less-attractive daughter needs to argue with them or question everything they say in order to get any attention at all. Leslie only argued, but she was still perceived as more rebellious. Most people assume a child's rebellious behavior is what provokes rejection (this is what's often remembered), but more often, it follows a prior rejection.

I met Anna first, and her beauty hasn't faded. She described her childhood in a well-to-do Chicago suburb. Her family lived in a nice house overlooking a lake, and she was the oldest of three children. Her brother, Dan, who is three years younger, has been estranged from the family for the past twenty years. Her sister, Leslie, was born when Anna was nine. As a child, Anna felt she was the obvious favorite of both her parents. I asked her how she knew.

There was nothing hidden about it. To my mother, I was the perfect child. I was considered very pretty. As a child, Leslie wasn't—she became pretty as an adult. Growing up, it was always, "Anna is perfect," "Anna don't do that, you'll ruin your nails!" Leslie was always in trouble, no matter what she did. I didn't trust my mother's compliments, because I felt she was complimenting herself and that I was a reflection of her. I didn't trust her sincerity, and I think that instead of making me a warmer person, more involved in other people's lives, my mother's comments about my looks made me build an ice wall in front of me.

Despite her beauty and popularity with boys, Anna didn't remember a happy childhood.

My parents fought incessantly, and they weren't happy at all. It was mainly because my father was a gambler. He had a good business, and we had a comfortable life, but when it came to my mother, he never had any money to give her. He placed bets on everything—football, baseball, basketball. He bet on every game. Their fighting made it very hard for me—I was terrified they'd divorce. I remember telling a friend, "What will I do if they divorce—who will I live with?" That's what I remember most.

My mother was the stern one, and everyone loved my father. He was a sport who'd take everyone out to have fun, and he'd always pick up the bill. He was sweet and easygoing, except with my mother. No one realized she had reason to be angry. But he never gave her anything. Every morning, she'd say, "Tommy, you have to leave me money for food. I need to buy food." He'd say, "Tomorrow, tomorrow." Eventually he'd leave her ten or fifteen dollars and she'd have to make it last. My mother made all our clothes, even our bathing suits. Outwardly, my family looked fine, but it was because my mother made a penny stretch.

Anna's father came from a fairly wealthy family and had taken over his father's company, which manufactured plumbing supplies. Her mother came from an impoverished family—she was modeling hats during the Depression when she met Anna's father—and thought she was marrying a rich man. He was a rich man, but from the time he got married, he had money for everyone but his wife and children.

Anna doesn't remember much about her sister as a young child; she didn't have a close relationship with her, because of the nine-year age difference. She recalls her sister didn't like to sleep alone and would go from room to room, trying to crawl under someone else's blanket. "She'd wet the bed, so I told her she had to stay at the foot of my bed."

Mostly Anna remembers her little sister being a pest, always hanging around when Anna's boyfriends were visiting, until they'd give her a quarter to get lost. Leslie was resourceful from the start.

Anna had wanted to go to a progressive college, but her father would only allow her to attend a Catholic junior college (even though they weren't Catholic) where he thought she'd be closely supervised and safe. "I do remember I hated it. I got an allowance of twenty-five dollars a month, and the day it would come, I'd go to town and a movie, and that was it. I hated every second of being at school, because I had no money."

Anna promised her parents she wouldn't drink or smoke or go away for fraternity weekends. She told them what they wanted to hear, and then she did exactly as she pleased. She's amused that years later, when she told them how she'd disobeyed, they would never believe her, because they thought she was so perfect.

Sophomore year, one of Anna's college friends invited her home for the weekend, planning to fix Anna up with one of her brother's friends. But the minute her friend's brother saw Anna, he wanted her for himself. They met in May and married in December, when Anna was nineteen. Leslie was the flower girl at the wedding. By the time Anna was twenty-three, she'd had two babies. She and her husband were living in a Chicago suburb about fifteen miles away from her parents' house. She knew her mother and father were fighting, but not how bad it was.

One day, Anna got a call. Her mother had left her father and gone off to Paris, leaving Leslie behind with their father. At the time, Leslie was in the ninth grade. "My sister came home from school one day and found a note. My mother was gone."

She remembers her sister came to live with her for a few months after their mother disappeared.

> My father called me one day and said, "I can't handle it anymore. I need to be on my own; you have to take her." We had two little babies, and Leslie lived with us and went to our local high school. My husband, Johnny, always adored her. While my mother was away, my father sold the house that my mother loved so much and rented an apartment. He was able to do that because the house was in his name. My brother, at that point, was already married or living on his own. My father sold the house because he needed money to gamble or pay his debts.

Anna believes her mother decided to go to Paris because she'd always wanted to travel and her father had always refused. She'd been saving money and she just went. She came back four and a half months later because she'd run out of money or maybe because she felt guilty about leaving Leslie. "She thought she'd return and walk in, and everything would be okay. But my father wouldn't take her back. That was a shock to her. I think she lived with us for a couple of months." It took a while for Anna to engineer some kind of reconciliation between her parents.

Anna's memories of this episode are a little vague because she'd already married to escape her family and the college she hated. She told me Leslie suffered a lot more over their parents' discord and felt doubly abandoned when her mother ran off and her father dumped her at her sister's house.

———

WHEN LESLIE TOLD ME the story herself, she couldn't stop herself from choking up and crying. Forty-three years later, the memory still provoked a visceral reaction.

> I was outgoing and vivacious; I never stopped talking. Anna was beautiful, quiet, and glamorous. When I was a child, I was called double ug—for double ugly... Another difference was that I viewed my mother as very loving and warm, though Anna didn't see her that way.
>
> My father preferred Anna because she was quiet, reserved, and beautiful. My father said I would never get married because I talked too much and I asked too many questions. He wasn't affectionate with me when I was a child, but by the time he died, I believe he adored me.
>
> In our family, only beauty mattered. You didn't need an education. I remember my sister had a blue velvet bathing suit. She was tall and had big boobs. When she walked down the beach, every boy would look at her. She had an aura of running her own life. I remember my sister dressing up, and wondering why I didn't have glamorous coats and gowns. She looked like Elizabeth Taylor, and I was a ragamuffin—chunky, double ug.
>
> Anna was aware that my parents had a bad marriage, but I didn't get it. At the table, my mother would say things like, "Have your father pass the salt." Even in high school, Anna sat at the head of the table, across from my father.
>
> I did adore my father, but he didn't give me the accolades I

wanted. I remember sitting on the porch and asking him, "Daddy, do you love me?" He said, "What a stupid question. I won't answer such a stupid question." So I forced myself on him, like a puppy dog.

After my sister got married, the shit hit the fan. My brother left for the army, and Dad moved into my brother's room. My mother confided in my sister—she being married—that she was miserable. But I was fourteen, and I didn't know what was going on. Then, there was a huge fight between my parents in the middle of one night. My father had found my mother's plane tickets to Paris. I pleaded with them not to fight. My mother said, "I'm leaving tomorrow." My father said, "Leslie, come with me right now, or I'll never come back." My mother told him she was leaving and he'd have to watch me. He went to hit my mother, and I said, "Don't hit Mommy." She was forcing the issue. She was packing up. I told her, "If I don't go with him, he'll never come back." She said, "Stay here tonight. He'll have to come back."

I was panicking, and sleeping in her bed with her. She said, "I have to go, but I'll be back soon. I would take you if I could, but I can't."

I didn't know what was going to happen to me. The housekeeper told me that Dad had spoken to Anna, and that I needed to go to Anna's. I was begging my mother not to leave, but the next day the taxi came at four P.M. to take her to the airport.

My father gambled a lot, and he put the house up for sale after my mother left. He'd come home every night, and I tried to cook. I was mortified to go to school. Everyone was talking about my family. This went on for a couple of weeks. One day there was a change. He put me in the car and said I had to go to Anna's. He said, "I never liked you. I never loved you. Just looking at you makes me sick to my stomach."

At this point in telling her story, Leslie was choking up, and trying hard not to sob. Years after the event, the impact of her father's cruelty was still fresh for her as she relived it through her retelling.

When I got to my sister's house, I was crying, and Anna said, "No one will ever hurt you again. You'll live with me." She told my father, "I need money for Leslie. I need to transfer her school. She needs clothes for school." It was the end of August. My father said, "No problem. I'll give you twenty dollars a week for her." And he left.

I stayed with her for a couple of weeks. Then she told me my father was coming back to get me, and that I had to go back with him. He told me he was sorry for what he said, and told me he loved me. He told me the house had been sold and we were moving into the upstairs apartment in a two-family house. Around this time, I was starting to get sick with Crohn's disease, though it hadn't been diagnosed.

My mother was writing to me, and my relatives were telling me how bad she was. I wrote to her and said, if she loved me, she'd come home. I asked her how she could do this to me. She stopped writing to me then, and later, she told me she stopped writing because I'd hurt her feelings.

I didn't want anyone at school to see where I lived. I was always sick and missing school. Anna arranged for me to take a trip to Florida, to visit some cousins. Then she called my mother and said, "You must come back. I think Leslie is becoming ill from this." But my mother didn't come back for four and a half months. I think my mother thought my father would follow her there and bring her back.

When my mother came back, she told me that Dad was leaving, and that I'd be better off with her. So I lived with her in that apartment. She convinced me the whole thing was my fault. My father went to live with his sister, who'd recently been widowed.

Anna remembers that after she managed to negotiate a reconciliation between her parents, her father was exposed in a financial scandal. Anna and her husband had to bail her father out of debt, even though she and Johnny were only about twenty-five years old and raising two little babies.

Her father's business partner had discovered that he'd been cooking their books to cover up money he was stealing to pay his gambling debts. Anna and her husband and brother had to come up with money to pay off the partner so her father wouldn't be sent to jail. Their mother had no money of her own, so now her mother went to work and slowly paid her children back every dime she had borrowed. From that point on, her mother ran the family finances and exercised more control. The financial scandal took its toll on Leslie, too.

"My sister went away to college for only one year," Anna explained, "because my father said he couldn't pay for it anymore. I didn't realize how devastating that was for her." She added that Leslie took several years to get her college degree while working to support herself.

After her children were born, Anna wanted to get a job, but her husband wouldn't allow it. It was the late fifties, and all his friends had stay-at-home wives. "I regret to this day that I don't have a career. It was the most major mistake I made. At one point I said, 'I have to go to work. I can have Mother come and take care of the children, and I can go to work.' But all his friends had money and their wives didn't work, and he didn't want me to."

When Leslie was nineteen she was diagnosed with Crohn's disease—an autoimmune disease that has caused her almost constant pain and required several operations to remove diseased portions of her GI tract. She'd been suffering from it all her life, but no one had known what was wrong. By the time she was twenty-one, Leslie had married. After that, she moved to downtown Chicago while she worked and finished her degree.

Anna recalls this was the time when she and her sister began to become friends. Their husbands get along well, and the two couples have spent a lot of time together ever since. The sisters also see each other separately more often, and they talk on the phone almost every day. "But even when we're not talking, I still feel close to her," Anna told me. "She's the other half of me—the other me. I've always felt very attached to her, from the time she was an adult. And yet we're quite different. She's always had to work all her life, due to finances, and that made our lives different."

By the time Leslie married, Anna's husband was financially successful, and they had a home in the city and a country home on a lake for weekends and summers. When Anna and Johnny spend time in their country house, Leslie and her husband often join them. "Leslie has made a good living—they haven't traveled as much, but we can go together to the same restaurants and theatre. But it's all due to her, because her husband hasn't made any money until recently." Anna worries about Leslie's health and the stress of her sister's career, but she's obviously proud of her sister's achievements.

Anna's daughter has serious medical and emotional problems and lives in Hawaii. Her son is distant and lives in Europe. But Anna said she's always felt very close to her sister's children, especially to Leslie's daughter, Julia.

When I'd asked Anna if financial differences ever caused problems between Leslie and herself, she said they didn't and offered an example. She told me that a few years ago, her sister and brother-in-law were short on cash. Leslie's work is stressful because it involves expensive projects that run on tight deadlines. Anna recalls her sister sneaking out of bed right after major abdominal surgery to visit a construction site when she was doubled over in pain. All the work and financial stress were making Leslie's precarious health even worse, and Anna wanted to do something to help.

> I didn't even want to discuss it. Stress is not good for her. It's not worth it for her to die. I told my niece, Julia, to go to Leslie's apartment when she wasn't there and find one of Leslie's checks. If I had the account numbers, I could just wire money into her account. While Julia was looking for a checkbook, my sister came home, and Julia told her why she was there. Leslie called me, hysterical. I told her that she could make it easy or hard for me, but I was giving her the money.
>
> It had to be done, and we never discussed it again. It was never mentioned. I wouldn't have cared if I never got it back, but I knew she would return it if and when she could. It was done and that was it. It's never changed our relationship. That was about five years ago. Three weeks ago, Leslie gave me a check for half the money.

I asked Anna if she'd discussed the issue with her husband before wiring the money.

> I didn't tell my husband. I didn't want to say to him, "Should I or shouldn't I?" There was no decision to make but my own. I also didn't want anyone to know, for her sake. It's nobody's business but my sister's.
>
> Whenever I get the rest back, when it's paid in full, I'll tell my

husband. I have my own bank account—money put aside for my retirement. Actually, I made money on that loan, because it would have gone into the stock market, and I would have been killed when the market dropped.

Not everyone has enough disposable income to extend a large loan without worrying about it, or to do it without consulting their spouse. But Anna didn't hide behind her husband as an excuse for not helping her sister, and she handled the loan to Leslie in a way that made sure it wouldn't affect the relationship between her sister and her husband, which has always been close and affectionate. "Johnny has always adored Leslie. She was just a baby when we met."

Hearing about Anna's sense of discretion, I thought about all the people I know who, in anger, confide their marital problems to their sisters, or vice versa, without thinking about the consequences. Or women who complain about their sisters to their children, without considering the impact on those relationships. Later on, they're upset when the people they love aren't wild about each other. But they don't see that they've had a hand in undermining those relationships.

Of course, it's only human to complain to others when you're upset and angry. But a woman might well get over her anger with her sister or husband because there are many other reasons she loves them. But the people she complains to don't have a context for measuring or evaluating the complaints, so hearing them can lead them to be unsympathetic.

I asked Anna whether her refusal to gossip about the loan or her marriage was a decision she'd made after thinking about it, or something that came naturally to her. She said she'd never thought about it. "I just knew instinctively you need to draw a fine line. In any relationship you're walking a fine line and you need to draw a line to keep everything working well. I'm a very private, close-mouthed person." She also attributed her sense that one should do the right thing as a lesson she learned from her mother, whom she considers a model of strength.

Anna had voiced some complaints about her mother's behavior when she was growing up. As an adult, she developed respect for her mother when she understood all the problems her mother had to face and deal with, including those created by her warm and charming father. "She's the strongest woman I know. She's ninety years old, and she still drives her car every day and runs her own finances. She looks wonderful... My mother taught me that you do what you need to do."

Her father never stopped gambling, even after Anna and her brother bailed him out so he wouldn't go to prison.

After my father died of a stroke [eighteen years ago] my mother discovered that he was in great debt, and she paid off every dime that he owed, even though the bookies weren't coming after her. She was shrewd about the stock market and paid off all his debts because she felt morally responsible. He'd left her nothing but debts. He had no life insurance. When she was going through his papers she also discovered that he'd been giving money to a woman who'd worked for him for thirty years— paying her rent and for things in her apartment and sending her children to summer camp. She didn't tell us about this other woman for a very long time after he died, but she was upset.

Was her father having an affair with this woman? I asked. The financial support made it look like he was, Anna admitted, but they didn't know for certain. "My mother was suspicious. She agreed it didn't make any sense, if she wasn't his mistress. But she had no proof, and to my knowledge, my mother never confronted the woman. My mother did like painting my father in a bad light, not that you had to use much paint on the brush."

I also asked Anna if her husband had minded paying her father's debts when they were first married. "He resented having to pay off his debts, but my father was a very loving man, and Johnny adored him. My brother also contributed at the time, but we had more money so we gave more."

Then Anna told me about her brother's break with the family, or as much as she knows:

> After we bailed my father out, my brother worked for my father for years. Something happened, and they had a terrible fight. My brother said my father owed him thousands of dollars, and it was so ugly he would take him to court. My father's brother was a lawyer and a judge in family court. My father and uncle discussed it. My uncle had never gotten along with my brother, and my uncle wanted my father to sue my brother.
>
> Leslie and I wanted my father to just give my brother the money, and we told my mother to call my uncle and tell him to drop his action against my brother. I said, "Give him the money"—it was probably ten or twenty thousand dollars—"Is it worth it to fight?" She agreed with us, but she told us it was too late. My uncle had already filed papers against my brother in family court.
>
> My brother left the business and he never spoke to any of us again. He felt that we sided with our father. He felt if we weren't 100 percent for him, we were against him. The last thing he said to us was that he knew things about our father that we didn't know, but he didn't want to get into it. He wouldn't tell us. I'm

dying to know what he meant, but he hasn't spoken to any of us for twenty years—he won't answer our calls or letters—and whatever he was talking about will go to his grave.

I found it interesting that in this family full of conflicts and permanent rifts that Anna and her sister didn't have any fights. Anna could recall just one source of tension with Leslie—her sister's relationship to their mother.

There was a period, about four years earlier, when Leslie stopped talking to their mother—in fact, they didn't speak for two years. Anna tried to stay out of the feud but felt they were both trying to drag her into their conflict. She couldn't even recall why they'd stopped speaking to each other. They had always bickered over trivial things, ever since Leslie was a child, because Leslie was a more open person who felt compelled to express her true feelings. Anna said she had learned to just agree with her mother and then ignore her and do what she wanted.

I'm not as emotional or as compassionate as my sister. She's very warm and she's affected by things, while I distance myself. She gets involved, and she becomes angry.

I do remember one thing they were fighting over. My sister was getting rid of some old sheets that were full of holes, and my mother wanted them. My mother saves everything. She wanted the sheets even though they were tattered and torn. Leslie said, "I'm not giving you these. If you need sheets, I'll buy you new sheets."

I said, "Leslie, just give her the sheets." I would just give Mother the sheets and say, "Who gives a shit if she wants to use old sheets even if they're old and torn, and you would use them to mop the floor." They had a major fight over this.

Anna thinks the pattern goes back to when Leslie was small.

> My sister was always more confrontational with my parents. If
> they said, "No, you can't do this," she'd argue, "Why can't I?" I
> would say to her, "Leslie, just say yes and do what you want." I
> must have told her this a thousand times. But she couldn't do it.

I suspect their mother had learned she couldn't cross certain
lines with her older daughter, but that her younger daughter had
more trouble establishing limits. Perhaps Leslie wouldn't give up
the sheets to her mother, not just because they weren't usable, but
because her sheets were personal items, and unlike Anna, she had
trouble protecting her boundaries.

When their father was hospitalized in a Chicago medical center
for six weeks after his stroke, their mother chose to stay with
Leslie, even though Anna had always felt she got along better with
their mother.

> It's funny she could stay with my sister, but she would have
> known not to ask to stay with me. We wouldn't have argued, but
> I would have been jumping out of my skin, and she knew that.
> My sister said, "Come and stay with me." If I had to have my
> mother, I would have rented an apartment for her, rather than
> have her live with me.
>
> I'm not as affected by what my mother says as my sister is. I
> became a colder person. She's warmer. She needs people more
> than I. I could live in my castle by myself and be happy. My sis-
> ter has a more people-personality.

After Leslie and her mother began speaking again, they both
complained about the other while Anna tried not to get involved.

My mother would bring [something] up and say, "But don't you think she was wrong? Oh, you'll just take Leslie's side."

My sister would complain that Mother never called her. I told her, "Leslie, if you wait for Mother to call you, she'll never call, because Mother is too tight to spend the money on a toll call." She never makes long-distance calls. She would never call us from Florida—that would be like calling from the moon. I told Leslie, "Look, you don't want to have a daily conversation with her. Just call her once a week."

Anna also attributes her sister's sensitivity to the shabby way she was treated as a child, especially when her parents just dumped her when they were fighting. "Mother doesn't understand how my sister felt about that. She feels my sister overplays that. She says, 'Oh, I wasn't gone that long.' I told her it was months."

Anna implies that Leslie has more anger with their mother than she's willing to recognize, and this can be frustrating. But other than that, Anna expresses nothing but love and admiration for her sister and says she couldn't imagine being without her. And they have a lot of fun together.

"We do our secret plastic surgery together. We do everything together. She picks me up, or I'll pick her up. We do things our husbands don't know about. I'm always the test case, because I'm nine years older, so I need it before she does."

When I asked Anna if they can really have plastic surgery without their husbands finding out, she laughed. "I'll pretend I'm black and blue because I bruise easily. There are things we get away with, and things we don't."

When they make their secret outings to the plastic surgeon, is it like being children and having mischievous fun together? I asked.

Absolutely! We weren't kids together because of our age difference, but sneaking off and having plastic surgery is like being
naughty again. I'll call her and say, "I'm going over, do you want
to meet me?" It's more fun to do it with her.

———

AFTER I MET WITH Anna, I then called Leslie to arrange her interview. For a moment, I was confused. The woman who answered
the phone sounded just like Anna. Then I realized Leslie and Anna
had nearly identical voices—something I've sometimes noticed
with sisters.

When I arrived at her apartment and the door opened—I was
surprised again. At first, I thought it was Anna. Then I realized this
wasn't quite Anna—the woman standing before me was shorter,
but otherwise, she bore a striking resemblance to her older sister.
This was the last thing I'd expected from sisters who'd been labeled
as beauty and the beast when they were children.

I looked again. They had the same eyes and similar hair, and
their facial contours were very similar. Later I thought of their
joint outings to the plastic surgeon. Either their surgeon was mold-
ing them both into a signature style, or Leslie had opted for the
Anna look. Or maybe they hadn't looked that different in the first
place. Like her sister, Leslie is very pretty and seemed twenty years
younger than her fifty-eight years.

The broad outlines of the childhood Leslie described were consistent with what I'd heard from Anna—but now I heard the story
from the perspective of the younger, less-favored daughter. In her
childhood, Leslie had observed her older sister a lot more than
Anna had noticed her. In some interesting respects, her view of
the family differed significantly from Anna's. For example, she
told me their father clearly preferred her sister, but she felt their

mother was closer to her. I have no way of knowing which is true, but it was obvious that Leslie had been much more concerned about winning her parents' love—perhaps because she'd had to work so much harder for their approval.

After telling me how beautiful her sister was, Leslie explained the niche she found for herself.

> Because I couldn't compete with her on that level, I had to be noticed by my accomplishments instead of my looks. I could draw and paint. I was creative and ambitious.
>
> My sister was always the most popular belle of the ball, she always had boyfriends. I thought she was a goody two-shoes, but she wasn't. I was truly the goody two-shoes but my parents always thought I was the bad one. I wasn't secretive. I'd fight with them. If they said the world was square I'd say it was round.

Given that her sister chose a different strategy—of doing what she wanted but hiding it from their parents—I asked Leslie why she always chose to fight with her parents. I've noticed that the child who is rejected often becomes more rebellious. And it usually follows the rejection, rather than preceding it.

> I thought I was smart. I was honest to a fault. Anna asked me, "Why do you tell them everything?" But I thought, How could I tell a lie? She thought they would never find out what she was doing, and I couldn't keep a secret.

I thought about these opposite responses of sisters to parental authority, and what they signify, because it was such a repetitive theme in my research. Almost every woman I interviewed identified one

sister who conformed to their parents' values—at least outwardly—
and one who constantly argued. In this case, the reality was more
complex because their outward postures didn't match their actual
behavior; Anna didn't fear the consequences of getting caught and
Leslie did. Because she couldn't win her father's approval as the
beautiful daughter, Leslie became a young entrepreneur. At age
seven, she gave art lessons to children who were three and four.
With the quarters she earned, she'd buy presents for her parents.
She shined her father's shoes. She always tried to please them while
Anna didn't even have to try.

In one way, Anna took the easy way out by avoiding a fight with
her parents and never feeling guilty about violating their rules
while letting them keep their idealized view of her. And at first
glance, it might seem that Leslie was just asking for punishment
when she insisted on telling her parents that the earth was round
when they said it was flat. Was she just accepting her disfavored
role, or doing something healthier—expressing her strength (she
was confident of her intelligence, if not her beauty) and the right
to assert herself?

I've gone back and forth on this. Leslie paid a price for arguing
with her parents—they considered her difficult and preferred
Anna's surface agreement. But Leslie also retained her ability to be
authentic and genuine, to express what she felt.

When Anna counseled Leslie to follow her example to avoid a
stupid argument, I have no doubt she was trying to help her.
Anna had been rewarded for letting her parents think what they
wanted to think and she hated to watch her sister become unhappy. I think she may have seen Leslie struggling to separate
from her parents, and she was trying to help her do it the same
way she had.

But the two sisters were so different that the same strategy wouldn't be effective for both. Leslie doesn't think or feel like Anna. And there was a downside for Anna, too. Hiding who you really are and what you really think in order to avoid conflict also has a price, even it's easier in the short run.

When she married, Anna didn't argue with her husband when he didn't want her to have a career, a concession she now regards as the biggest mistake of her life. It's true, as she says, that in the 1950s middle-class women were expected to stay home. But Anna was not any woman. As Leslie said, she had an aura of being in control. Anna has also said that she admires her sister's warmth and greater engagement with other people and feels the "wall of ice" she erected against her mother also turned her into a loner.

Anna received the rewards of royally succeeding in the conventional ways open to beautiful women of her era: admiration, love, and security. But she didn't get to display all the talents that lay beneath her obvious beauty. Leslie was criticized for being argumentative when that wasn't considered a desirable trait in a woman (her father told her no man would love her because she talked too much). Arguing may not have made her the favored child, but she learned to be confident in her intelligence. Each sister chose the path that was available, given her position in the family.

While I was in high school, I was always sick. I'd visit Anna, but I thought she was bossy. She was acting like a mother-guardian, not like my equal. Her husband, Johnny, always liked me; we connected. He'd always say, "Leslie, come with us" instead of trying to get rid of me. I don't think Anna was that thrilled to have me around. He was like a big brother. There was so much turmoil in my family. I had Crohn's disease, but it hadn't been diagnosed yet.

Leslie also remembered the terrible fights in her childhood about money, and how her father had money for himself and all his relatives but none for his own family.

My father came from a well-to-do family, and he was used to luxury. His secret life was giving himself the luxuries he was used to having. He wouldn't give my mother any money. Once I kept asking him if I could have Pappagallo shoes—all the girls in my school wore them. He told me he had no money, and that I should ask him again on Friday.

On Friday I asked him, and he told me he had no money. But he always had big wads of money in his pocket and he would say he didn't have it. And he came home with a cashmere suit and all these silk ties for himself. I remember he came home the next Monday and gave my mother fifteen dollars for the shoes I wanted, but instead of getting me Pappagallos, she bought me three pairs of five-dollar shoes from the cheap shoe store.

My father gave money to everyone else. If one of his relatives needed money, if his sisters or brothers had a problem, he would give them money.

I mentioned that Anna told me how her mother discovered he'd been secretly giving money to his longtime secretary and paying for her children to go to camp while he had no money for his own children's food or clothes or college. Did Leslie think he was having an affair?

No, I thought there was something going on with a different woman, but this woman he gave money to was his secretary for thirty years, and she was unattractive. He wouldn't have been having an affair with her. And anyway, my mother told me he was impotent then.

I thought it interesting that Leslie couldn't imagine her father sleeping with a woman whom she considered unattractive, while Anna and their mother thought he probably had. I wondered if Leslie couldn't imagine her father having an affair with an unattractive woman because he'd been so critical of her looks.

I was also struck by her mother's comment about her father's supposed impotence. I assume their parents did not have a good sex life. They slept in separate rooms, which didn't strike Leslie as odd, even when she was fourteen. I thought her mother's comment was insensitive: Do daughters really want to hear such things about their father?

Anything is possible. Perhaps their father wouldn't give their mother money because she didn't want to have sex with him. Perhaps their mother said their father was impotent to preserve her own self-esteem when she felt spurned.

Whatever happened, Leslie was more reluctant than Anna to criticize her mother, though she couldn't disguise how abandoned she felt, even after all these years.

It seemed to me in Leslie's comments and behavior there was still a residue of the devastated child; she was still trying to idealize her relationships with her parents. Since she was a child, she couldn't fully acknowledge how badly they'd treated her. By her own description, she couldn't see what was going on right before her eyes. To really see their weaknesses, at the time, would have made her feel even worse. So by accepting her role as the bad child and letting them blame her for everything, she was able to maintain a better image of them, and therefore an illusion of control. If she were the bad one, she could always act better and win their love.

The pattern continued: "I started college, and then Daddy pulled me out. He said he had no money to pay for my school. So I worked during the day and went to school at night. I did part-time modeling—for petite sizes. But I was going through agony and I was hospitalized for what they thought was appendicitis."

When Leslie was eighteen, she also had her first cosmetic surgery. In her quest to become beautiful like Anna, she underwent an operation to make her nose thinner. There were complications of hemorrhaging from the surgery, and everyone was horrified, including her father. She recalled that, at the time, her father remarked that changing her nose was not going to change her life—the implication being she still wasn't attractive to men. Later, he acknowledged how much he must have hurt her for Leslie to want to look like someone else.

The discomfort of her cosmetic surgery was nothing compared to her lifelong suffering from Crohn's and the many surgeries she needed as a result. According to Anna, Leslie never complained. And Leslie was grateful to her sister. "I was sick for two years before I was diagnosed with Crohn's. From the time I was sick, Anna was always there. She'd be rushing back and forth to the hospital, throwing out the mean nurses. She took over the role of mother, and I was taken care of."

Leslie married (she and Anna are still married to the men they chose when they were young) and by the time she was twenty-three, she'd had her daughter, Julia. When the couples were first married, they would meet for dinner, and Leslie would insist on redoing her makeup three times before leaving their apartment. Her husband thought she was out of her mind. Why was she so worried about how she would look to her sister and brother-in-law? She tells me Anna has always called her "pretty," not beautiful, and it made her feel self-conscious.

But after her first child was born, Leslie recalled getting angry when Anna introduced her as her "little sister." "I had a child and I told her, 'This is it. I'm not a baby. I'm your sister. I'm your equal.' After that, we became friends."

Anna had simply told me she wasn't close to her own children. But Leslie offered a fuller account, in the course of explaining her admiration for her sister. I decided to include it because it explained a great deal about how and why these sisters had grown much closer as adults. According to Leslie, Anna's daughter had sustained some neurological injuries that left her emotionally unfit as a mother. Anna, wanting to do what was best for her grandchildren, supported giving custody of the children to her former son-in-law when he and her daughter divorced. They agreed to an arrangement where Anna took her grandchildren every weekend from the time they were two years old.

Her former son-in-law had moved to Minnesota, so Anna would take a plane from Chicago to Minneapolis every single Friday to personally pick up the children, and she got on a plane every Sunday night to return them, making two round-trips a week so she could spend weekends with them. For eight years, she made these trips because she wouldn't put them on a plane alone.

In Leslie's view, Anna's "phenomenal" effort for her grandchildren made her a warmer and more emotionally open person: She was focused on helping others instead of making herself glamorous to please her husband.

Johnny wanted Anna to be movie-star glamorous. For the first twenty-five years of her marriage, she just had to be beautiful. Now she was coming out of her shell to give herself to others. Her heart opened up to the children, and as a result she has two grandchildren who adore her. I think she's amazing.

I'm alive today because of my sister. At one point I was down to eighty pounds because of Crohn's. I wasn't absorbing food and I was dying. My sister found a doctor who was able to help me, and she got me to fly to Florida with my daughter, who also has a touch of Crohn's. My sister found out about injections from Germany that allowed me to stop losing weight. She was with me and found every drug that could help.

It's always interesting to hear the differing perspectives of sisters. I don't feel that either Leslie or Anna was more honest, but they had different needs. Anna could make a more realistic appraisal of her parents, one that recognized both their strengths and limitations, because she grew up feeling that she had their admiration.

Leslie was treated badly as a child by both her parents. When she became older, she felt her parents were closer to her, partly because her children were closer to them. I suspect Anna was not competing for their parents' attention. She didn't need to, because she'd obviously won the competition when it mattered most— when they were children. Since their youth, she'd given Leslie advice about setting limits with them. But it's hard to give up the wish of being the favorite child, so Leslie continued to try to make a genuine connection with her parents and to win their love. She hasn't given up on her brother, either, although she hasn't seen him for twenty years. Even her daughter tells her she is idealizing her brother and is being unrealistically hopeful; but Leslie continues to hope for a reconciliation:

My brother had a rift with our father, and because of my mother, he separated from us. Soon after that, my father had a stroke and died. I think he's feeling guilty and can't deal with us. I haven't seen him for over twenty years. My daughter's getting married, and I asked her, "Should I send Dan an invitation?"

My daughter said, "You see him as you did when you were young—playing baseball, playing football. But as an adult, you didn't have a relationship. He won't answer."

LATER, I THOUGHT about Leslie's impulse to send the wedding invitation to her long-estranged brother. My first thought was that she should send it, as long as she didn't expect him to answer. She might have gotten a pleasant surprise. When people get older they often can't even remember why they were angry, or whatever made them angry starts to look very trivial compared to the wish to connect to people who were important in our lives.

Relationships can always change. Anna and Leslie started out as the top dog and the underdog, but the sisters became best friends who admire each other tremendously. Look at what happened to Leslie herself. She was able to change from being the "ugly" and disfavored daughter into a beautiful and talented woman who eventually felt loved and valued by her father and mother. She had the pleasure of having children her father adored. The fact that he doted on her children probably took some of the sting out of being rejected by him as a child.

But then, I had second thoughts about the invitation to her brother. This is her daughter's wedding day, and it would be unfortunate if Leslie focused too much on her brother. Leslie's daughter understood that her mother's behavior is often still driven by feelings of loss. It's wonderful to make a happier connection to the past, but the most important thing is to move beyond loss and to live in the present. Privately, I decided it would be fine for Leslie to send the invitation only if she could put it in the mail and forget all about it, like extending a loan only if you never expected to see the money again.

The sisterhood of Anna and Leslie offers an important lesson because their relationship had everything going against it. They started out on the most unequal terms, constructed as opposites—one beautiful, good, and desirable as a woman; one "ugly," bad, and unlovable. Anna not only had the advantage of being the preferred daughter but also of growing up before the family really blew apart. And she was healthy, unlike Leslie who developed a serious disease by the time she was a teenager. The nine years between them also separated them. They grew up in two different eras of their family.

What made all the difference is that Anna didn't buy into their parents' perspective on their relative value as daughters and young women. Instead, she stepped in to help her sister and let her parents know when they were acting like babies. She always saw much to love and admire in Leslie, and in Leslie's daughter—even when her own daughter brought her pain. She wouldn't take their mother's side when her mother complained about Leslie. She formed an alliance with her sister and, as a result, she wound up with a wonderful sister who is her dearest friend.

Leslie also didn't blame Anna for being the preferred one, and even though she wasn't originally the family beauty, she found a different avenue for asserting her value and worth. In the end, both sisters wound up with good lives, and their lives were much better for having each other.

PART TWO

The Imagined Sister

CHAPTER 7

Empathy, Listening, and Understanding

THE SISTERS IN part 1 had close relationships, and if they'd had problems, they had largely worked them out. In part 2, I focus on sisters who still face conflicts in their efforts to get along. Conflict doesn't imply a lack of attachment or love. When relationships are easy, we're not always aware of what makes them work. Looking at sisters who are currently more divided reveals more about what draws sisters together or pulls them apart.

In this chapter, I start with the problem of empathy, which is almost a prerequisite for being close. Why are some sisters able to listen and understand each other, while others just feel frustrated or angry every time they hang up the phone?

Women often complain their sisters don't empathize with them. But empathy requires more than projecting yourself and the way you think and feel onto another person. It requires fully seeing the other person and imagining how they think and feel in their situation, not what you would think or feel if you were in their place. Putting yourself into another person's shoes requires putting yourself into their mind, not just their situation. So, one of the obstacles to empathy is forgetting that your sister is different.

Another obstacle is that empathizing with a sibling might threaten a wish or illusion or make us feel guilty. If you were favored by a parent, it's hard to empathize with a sibling who was heavily criticized by that parent. Putting yourself imaginatively in her place would force you to reevaluate the parent you love.

Many women I interviewed felt enormously frustrated that their sister couldn't just listen to them, when they were upset, without immediately giving advice. This is a common complaint, and it's also a problem between friends. Some people are better than others at lending a sympathetic ear without imparting their opinion or wisdom, but I think most people can learn.

In an earlier story I related, Lizzie wanted her sister Charlotte to listen to her when she was in anguish over the terrible medical ordeal her husband was going through and her fear that she might lose him. Instead, Charlotte kept offering advice. But when Lizzie told her sister what she really needed, Charlotte got the message and started to respond appropriately. Before that, she was responding to what *she* needed; by giving advice she felt she could make things better, which had always been her role.

It's easier to be empathic when other people say exactly what they feel or need. So if they're saying, and you don't have a clue, you might ask. Maybe they can't tell you exactly what they need because they don't know themselves, or perhaps they're afraid to.

When it's your sister, it shouldn't be that hard to figure it out, as long as you keep reminding yourself to relate to the person she is, rather than responding to what you would need or how you think your sister should be. You do have a long history with her and you know a lot about the circumstances of her life. You need to think about her particular needs and fears as well as the immediate circumstance.

Lizzie knew about illness and how to deal with the medical world. When her husband spent a week in the intensive care unit, she didn't need to hear from her sister what was likely to come next and the steps she could take. She had the medical advice of cardiologists who knew more about her husband's condition than Charlotte could have known. What Lizzie really fears is losing the people she loves and being left alone. When Charlotte was able to listen to Lizzie express her anguish, Lizzie felt less alone. When Charlotte told Lizzie what to do to make herself feel better, Lizzie felt that her sister didn't want to hear about her pain, and she felt even more alone. When her sister offered advice instead of just listening to her, Lizzie felt she was being told her feelings of grief were not acceptable.

Lizzie's situation presents the hardest challenge for an empathetic listener because no one wants to imagine that kind of pain. Charlotte would rather not think about her sister's vulnerability to loss or how she would feel if her husband got sick. It's too threatening. This is when people often start to give unasked-for advice to ward off their own anxiety.

To use another example, we've all known mothers and daughters who are so closely identified with each other that they criticize traits that they see in each other that they don't wish to see in themselves. I think this process operates in sisters, too. It's probably also one reason why so many women feel criticized or controlled by their mothers, or why they are so much more aware of their mother's flaws than their father's. There's probably more mutual identification, and we don't like to look in the mirror and see something that bothers us.

Why is one woman able to listen and empathize with a sister who is in pain, while another seems not to have the capacity? I found some sisters who shed light on this question. Unlike Lizzie and Charlotte, something stopped them from getting the message.

The Depressed Sister and the Impatient One

Nancy Packer was born in Michigan in 1942; her sister, Patricia, was born five years later. They also have a younger brother who moved away from home as a teenager and rarely contacts the family. Their mother was determined that Nancy and Pat would marry physicians in order to have the financial security and social standing she had missed as a child. In this she succeeded, but nothing else went according to her plan.

Nancy married a physician, but their daughter, Susan, committed suicide when she was thirty, and their son suffered from such serious depression that he could never finish college.

Pat married a psychiatrist who lost his medical license after a public scandal revealed his sexual relations with a patient and his problems with substance abuse. And Pat's troubles with her son and daughter were eerily similar to those suffered by her sister. Like her nephew, Pat's son was thrown out of college a few weeks before graduation. He fell into a clinical depression and hid in his mother's attic for the next two years. Pat's daughter converted to Islam (she'd been raised a Catholic) and disappeared under a full veil, exposing only her eyes from that time on. Then she made an arranged marriage and moved to Saudi Arabia.

One would think that their common grief over their children might bring these sisters together. But there was often anger or disappointment between them, and they couldn't understand or help each other that well. Nancy was the sister I interviewed first.

Nancy told me her father was quiet and withdrawn and her mother was the efficient, active, outgoing one, the "hub of the wheel." Nancy feels her sister's personality follows their mother's pattern while she's more like her father: Pat is outgoing while she's an introvert. When they were growing up, their mother raised them to attract the right husbands with music lessons, skating lessons, a year abroad. But Pat was accepted into the Junior League after Nancy had been rejected.

Nancy's constant refrain was that she would not participate in empty social rituals and she didn't like being around lots of people, especially strangers. She began by saying her husband is a dermatologist, but she won't go with him to medical meetings:

> I'm not interested in people I don't know and who don't care about me. My sister would go, to fill the social void. I won't be an addendum to a male. Anyway, I think we are both controlling. We learned that from my mother, and it caused abnormalities in our families. My daughter suicided in 1995 at age thirty.

I was surprised by this matter-of-fact announcement of her daughter's suicide, without any lead-up. But maybe she needed to have the primary fact of her life placed squarely before me.

> I had a friend—a physician—who gave me a book about schizophrenia while my daughter was alive. I saw my daughter having the kind of thoughts described in the book. I attribute a lot of her suicide to my mother. There were so many things related to my control of my daughter; she didn't have a chance to develop her own persona, and neither did I. When my daughter was a

senior in high school, she was a beautiful blond who sang and
played the piano. I encouraged her to do this because my sister
and I had played the piano. I led her down the path I followed—what's good for me was good for her. She didn't know
who she was.

After quoting a line she attributed to Tennyson, about remembering who you really are, Nancy mused, "I was under my
mother's thumb until she died. I thought she had the answers and
acceded to her opinions—her opinions about people, about who
has value and who doesn't."

Turning from her own family, Nancy gave an account of her sister's family problems, which appeared as serious as her own. She
described Pat's troubled son and daughter and explained that
her sister's former husband, a psychiatrist, turned out to be "de-
praved" and was "ultimately delicensed"—a "drug, alcohol, and
patient abuser...It was in the papers...and the children read
about their father in the paper."

Although the sisters' father was ill and near death the week the
scandal about Nancy's brother-in-law appeared in the news, he
sent their mother to help her sister through her marital crisis.

After that her sister's daughter converted to Islam, and there'd
been a falling-out between Pat's second husband and her religious
daughter, because he wouldn't accept her daughter's extreme
modesty and insisted on walking around the house in his under-
wear. "My sister had to move her daughter out of the house. She
lived in an apartment, alienated from her mother, who'd sided
with her husband."

My sister's son started out as a genius like his father, but by high
school he was decompensated. He was expelled a month before

he graduated from college because of complaints others made to the administration. I don't know what happened—maybe he got thrown out for harassing someone. He was damaged by his father's self-destruction. After that, he hibernated for two or three years; he just slept and had no job and wouldn't take medication.

My sister's in a place where I am—she can't stand the Brain Pain. She just pulls back and we don't talk about it. She cut me off a lot of times.

At some point Nancy told me that her father's brother and an aunt had been in and out of mental institutions all their lives, so I asked her why she believed her daughter's mental illness was caused by intrusive mothering rather than inherited, biological factors. I told her I thought the theory of the schizophrenogenic mother had been abandoned thirty years ago, and wondered why she thought her mother's behavior, rather than unlucky genes, was the primary cause of their problems. She replied: "Yes, there may have been some predisposition, but that's not an excuse for the interactions."

[My daughter] started going downhill as soon as she got out of college. She was hospitalized several times. We didn't know what to do anymore.

She was dating a fellow and got engaged, and killed herself six weeks before the wedding. That was in 1995. From then until last summer I stopped working. I was decompensated. We went to a suicide grief center for three years.

She circled back to her theory of the origins of the problem in her childhood:

My sister was in the Junior League and I was envious of that. I had
asked to join and was turned down. I made my daughter become
a debutante because I wasn't accepted into the Junior League.

I was the older sister, and it was the same for my mother and
me as it was for me and my daughter. My mother didn't want a
baby when I was born, and I didn't want my daughter. It's possible my mother was more ready for my sister. My sister was
more adept at everything than I was. She's outgoing and opti-
mistic. My sister is a social person, and I'm rough-edged.

After she married, Nancy moved to Seattle and her parents
moved there also. Her mother wanted to be near her and to help
her. Nancy's mother proceeded to take over Nancy's motherly responsibilities, without relinquishing any of her own: When they
lived in Seattle she still picked out Nancy's clothes.

When Pat's marriage fell apart and she was afraid her husband
was a threat to her life, their mother left Nancy and went to help
her younger daughter.

My sister didn't get any alimony and she got only limited child
support. My mother spent her own money to help my sister put
a roof over her head.

Pat went through her divorce in 1985. When Mother moved
back to Michigan to help my sister, it flipped the scale for my
daughter. My daughter relied on my mother so much because I
let my mother be the mother of the family. As long as my
mother helped me, my husband didn't want to get involved.
He's milk-mild and didn't object.

Since my mother died [the year before Nancy's daughter
killed herself], I talk to my sister a lot. I feel there's a connection
that could grow only after Mother died. My mother wanted to

mediate all the communication between us. I'd say, "I'll call Pat" and she'd say "Oh, don't call her, she's so busy."

Nancy told me her husband was very much like her father.

A lot of the time, we marry our parents. My father would sit in the living room and make a fire and watch the fireplace. My mother would sit in the TV room and watch TV. They never slept in the same bed, and I've never slept in the same bed as my husband. I'm not into sex on an ongoing basis. It's been hard for me. I should have been a nun. I could have become a mother superior.

My sister lost her job recently and didn't talk about it. I didn't say much about it. I saw it coming. She was having interpersonal problems with people she had to work with. My friends call me on my daughter's death date and her birth date. But my sister avoids it. I'll tell my sister I don't want Susan's existence denied by not talking about it. Pat said she didn't want to make me feel bad. But she didn't want to feel bad.

I'm conjecturing. She doesn't want to deal with her pain or other's people pain. I've told her I need to talk about my daughter, but she avoids it . . . I'm almost like the younger sister looking up to an older sister, because she's stronger than I am. She's insightful and I use our talks as homework. It could be I did that even when we were younger. She's not controlling like my mother—she's a do-good control type. She wants a fix. I tell her to just listen, and I don't want or need a fix. It's hard for her to do that.

I WASN'T SURPRISED that Nancy's sister had a different view of the family. Nancy's depression and lack of energy got on Pat's nerves, and she found Nancy to be very controlling. When Nancy slumps into a sluggish depression, Pat thinks she should do a hundred push-ups to psych herself up.

"I take after my mom and my sister takes after Dad. Their union was dysfunctional because my dad was passive-aggressive and my mom was a control person." She tells me her father's brother snapped at twenty-three or twenty-four and was put in a county institution; his sister took over his guardianship. She learned from her mother when she was an adult that this uncle had been let out of the hospital for holidays, but Pat never met her uncle or even heard about him when she was a child.

Pat tells me she finally understood everyone after reading about the Hartman color-coded profile of four basic personality types.

I'm a Red—mostly business oriented, much less oriented toward emotions in relationships.

My sister is a Blue personality. She manipulates relationships, either openly or at times deviously. Blues are very wonderful in having committed, deep relationships. But Blues can be so overpoweringly dependent they destroy relationships.

My being a Red and my sister being Blue has posed real difficulties over the years. This will give you a clue. My son's birthday was yesterday. He's twenty-seven and had significant depression during the last ten years. Three times he wasn't functional for at least six months. When my sister and I were all young and having babies, we had wonderful times together. My mother brought our families together by planning and organizing the visits. My mother did all the engineering, making sure there was food there.

My sister is a very needy person. I've married two firstborn persons, and I find they are often inward and selfish. Normally my sister is good at remembering these things. But when she called yesterday, she didn't mention my son's birthday at all, and she didn't send him a card. Instead she just left a message saying how long I could expect this interview would take, so I'd be prepared.

What I've found in the last ten years is that my sister's attitude is "If I don't want to deal with it, I won't. If I don't want to clean the kitchen, or get groceries, I won't do it." Her constant refrain is, "I'm not gonna push myself." She keeps talking about how much she's done for everyone else, and now she'll do things for herself.

I'm also a control person, but not as controlling as my sister or mother. I'm the second child so I'm lighter and more clownish.

When Nancy's daughter was suicidal, I was working full-time at a stressful job, but I was on command for talking with her every day. There were hysterics. Nancy puts a burden on me when she tells me, "I don't make other friends. You and two other people are the only ones I can talk to." It's a compliment to say I can talk to you, but there's pressure to be there and give to her.

Control is a difficult thing in relationships. Poor Nancy's not physical. She probably didn't marry the right person, but she made the best of it. Our mother told us you don't get divorced. I got divorced because I picked a psychiatrist who lost his medical license having relationships with a patient who got her revenge when he wouldn't get rid of me and marry her. The situation got ugly and I couldn't stick around. I considered a women's shelter. I'm not sure my sister appreciated that. She is within herself and thinking of her needs. But I love her dearly and know she would care for me in destitution.

My niece, Susan, is not with us. Six weeks before her marriage, with her wedding dress lying on her bed, she killed herself. None of us were crazy about the bridegroom. I didn't think the wedding would happen. I didn't even buy a plane ticket.

My sister bought a sweater for me that was 100 percent wool. I told her I don't wear wool, it's itchy. She saw it in a catalog. I told her to return it, and she insisted I keep it. "This is what I'm giving you; this is what you'll like."

She was browbeaten by my mother. My mother would do the same thing. She'd buy something she'd like and say, "You'll love it." I was able to fend off my mother's control, but my sister took the brunt of it. My parents lived with my sister when her children were young. My parents had some financial problems and my mother would live near one of us. My mother knew my psychiatrist husband wouldn't put up with her. He'd had to do a big job to wean me from her when we were newly married. She saw the handwriting on the wall.

So my parents went to live with Nancy in 1969. Nancy needs help. She's always been helpless and my mother made her helpless and this was gratifying for Mom. My sister didn't have enough energy, and her husband wouldn't say, No, she can't live here.

Commenting on Susan's suicide, Pat thinks that Nancy was unrealistic and refused to see the true situation.

Here's a girl who wouldn't leave home. Her paranoia was so extreme she'd lost touch with reality. You would think her therapists might have said she isn't in any condition to get married. But they weren't on the right track. They were so desperate to find anything that would make her happy and functioning they were willing to go along with it. They were willing to grasp at anything.

She killed herself six weeks before the wedding. Did the suicide come from the pressure of getting married? Maybe she was
asking herself, "Oh my god, what did I get myself into?"

Pat also complained about her sister's wish to come across as an
intellectual.

She's very academic. She loves big words, but it comes across as
artificial. You need to use words correctly. Why not just use
simple English? She does it to impress. She was always a hard
worker and would study all night. She worked very hard because she was determined to get an A. I enjoyed life more—I
was more social. I still like to meet perfect strangers on the
street. She was always more of a loner.

My mother tried to treat us fairly, and give us the same op-
portunities. Money was a focal point; my mother was always
concerned about it. Her parents had divorced when she was
eight and that turned a child into a social outcast in those days.
Mom was also dealt the blow of having a lopsided physique.
She had huge balloon legs that were misshapen. Given her
background, and her financial worries, she raised us both to
marry doctors.

As for her own children's problems, Pat attributes them to their
father.

Both kids, due to their father's problems, chose situations or re-
actions where they ran for cover, either through depression or
choosing a life of complete structure. My daughter was attracted to the underdog of any kind, ever since kindergarten.
My daughter is a Muslim now, and we're all Catholic. She went

to Senegal as an exchange student. She made several other trips and when she came back, she was changed. When I picked her up at the airport, she was dressed so nothing was showing except her eyes. Even her hands were covered with gloves. It was so overwhelming. I fought it tooth and nail for a while. We went to a priest and nun, and tried to reverse it, but we couldn't. Sooner or later, I decided I was better off saying, I respect what you do, let's try to get along.

She was indentured and would only work with Muslims. When she was twenty-six, she said, "I know I'm supposed to be married." Her religious adviser knew only one man who was available to marry, an engineering student. They got married three weeks later. He's Saudi Arabian and now they live there. I try to stay in touch because I don't want to sever the ties. I call every week, but all the initiative is coming from my direction. It's such a different culture, and her husband isn't overly supportive of her ventures. They have a child who is twenty months old and I only saw his picture two weeks ago. They don't allow pictures. This was on e-mail; they won't let you have a picture you can freeze and frame.

My son is doing somewhat better. He's functioning in school. He won't take medication because his father did. Some things happened with my son that I haven't told my sister—not because she's not worthy—I think I don't tell her because I don't want it brought up at an inopportune time or to hear her discuss it academically. I'd just remarried six months before when my son came home a month before graduating college. He'd shot himself in the foot at the last minute and now instead of graduating he went on disability and went to sleep in our attic for fourteen months. I'd have to go up and see if he was still breathing. He inherited many problems from my first husband, who had bipolar illness.

Pat told me she knew from year two of her first marriage that her husband was crazy. She reported that when the children were teenagers, her husband made them clean the floor with a tooth-brush, to teach them a lesson. But she didn't explain why she stayed with him, other than learning from her mother that divorce was a mistake.

I asked why their common problems hadn't brought her closer to her sister. Pat tells me their problems have actually created the degree of empathy that's there.

Her son is like my son; it's scary—it's almost identical. My nephew was a high achiever and he also has a father who wasn't there for him, but not like my son's father. My children's father was out of his mind.

The day after my husband blew up, my mother came and helped me serve him with divorce papers. Dad was near death, but he said, "You go and be with Pat, she needs you more." My mother came and lived with us after my father died. She lived with us from the time Dad died until two years later, when the kids were ten and twelve. She was the mom, and I was gone every day at work. It was fabulous to have that support. Here I am forty years old, going out on dates, and she's up watching for me to come home.

She was in good shape—she went out to bars with me, be-fore she got married again, or she would have lived with me for-ever. The man she married had six kids and lived across the street. She was close enough to help with the kids after school. She was sixty-nine, young enough for me to rely on her.

Pat remarried five years ago. How did the children feel about her second marriage? I asked Pat.

Both of my kids were happy to see me get married at the time. Unfortunately, my husband made an error with my daughter, and he doesn't take responsibility. When we got married, she was already converted to Islam and had covered up her body. She'd offered to mow the lawn, and was sitting on the lawn mower. My husband leaned over and put his hand on her knee instead of putting it on the machine. She wanted an apology, and he wouldn't give it. That ended the relationship. He's a bigoted person, so I couldn't take him to visit her, where they might have had a truce.

Her sister's depression and withdrawal from the world are extremely irritating to Pat.

If someone calls you, for god's sake, you should psych yourself up. When I talk to her, she's so lethargic. She's depressed, and it comes across. It's hard for me. I think you should get up and do a hundred push-ups to get yourself in the right state of mind. I wish I could do more.

As our interview drew to a close, Pat may have felt guilty for complaining or felt that she left me with the wrong impression. She wanted to end by stressing her affection for her sister.

I honestly do feel my sister and I have a very close relationship. Our relationship's built solidly over time, even if it was due to Mother's initiation. The initiator's not there anymore, but we didn't fall apart. I love and value her dearly, and she's had a tough road. I don't want you to feel I'm only criticizing the poor dear.

I have no doubt that Pat was being sincere and not just append-ing these remarks out of guilt or discomfort. I suspect she was venting her anger in reaction to the phone message she'd just re-ceived from Nancy and her sister's failure to remember that it was her son's birthday, especially after Pat had spent years helping Nancy deal with her daughter's suicide.

Obviously, Pat was extremely annoyed, but if she hadn't been attached to Nancy, I doubt she would have been so upset. It was sad that these two highly intelligent and perceptive sisters had reached this impasse in their communications. They'd both suf-fered terribly over having such troubled children, despite all their efforts to help them. Because of Nancy's dependence on Pat, they reminded me a bit of Arlene and Claire from chapter 3, except Pat and Nancy were much angrier with each other. They'd also been dealt a great deal more sorrow. After an unhappy childhood, Ar-lene's life was good and her children were happy and well. Claire might have felt that she wasted her life because she didn't have children or a career, but she also didn't have to face the anguish of losing one child to suicide and seeing the other turn out to be clin-ically depressed.

Like several of the sisters I'll discuss in part 2, Pat and Nancy had conflicts that divided them. But I thought they each showed courage and honesty in describing their painful feelings, when many people would not even wish to acknowledge these feelings or share them with anyone else.

THE RELATIONSHIP BETWEEN SISTERS is always deeply affected by the relationship each has had with their parents, especially with their mother. So there is always something of a triangle in the bonds between sisters and their mother.

From both their accounts, it seems that the relationship between Pat and Nancy was largely mediated by their mother, the
"hub of the wheel." Pat felt they'd continue to have a relationship
after their mother died, and Nancy felt they could only have a relationship after she died. But any way I looked at it, it seemed their
mother was still the central figure of their sister bond, long after
she was gone.

For one thing, after their mother's death, Nancy apparently
shifted her emotional dependency to her sister, asking Pat to be
her listener when she'd withdrawn from the world. As much as
Nancy complained about her mother's control, she was very
dependent on her; she attributed her daughter's illness to her
mother's moving away and mentioned that her daughter killed
herself shortly after her mother died. After their mother's death
and her daughter's suicide, Pat seemed to assume the position her
mother had formerly held, becoming the dominant one and the
authority: Nancy said she drew lessons from their talks, while Pat
referred to Nancy as the "poor dear."

Both describe their mother as controlling, but they couldn't
have more opposite ideas about how their mother affected them.
Pat identifies with her mother, in being a high-energy, take-charge
person. She feels that her mother helped her enormously in raising her children. She also feels it was her mother who organized
the family holidays that initiated an adult relationship between
herself and her older sister.

Nancy, in contrast, describes herself as a destructive mother
who modeled her behavior on her own destructive mother. Her
mother left no room for her to develop an independent self, and
she did the same to her daughter. Her mother wasn't ready for her
birth, and Nancy wasn't ready for her daughter's birth. Rather

than helping, her mother ran her life. Even after Nancy married and had children, her mother moved in and became the mother of the family. She blames herself for her daughter's death, but sees her mother as the one who was pulling all the strings.

I was also intrigued by how differently the sisters viewed their roles in their children's troubled lives. Sisters often compare their children to their sisters' children to measure how well they have performed as mothers by using their sister's experience as a yardstick. I often heard more about the problems of my informants' nieces and nephews than about their own children's difficulties. I don't think competition was always the reason. I'm sure some just wanted to protect their children from exposure.

While Pat didn't minimize her children's problems, unlike her sister, she didn't dwell on her own role in these events (if there was one). She thought her children's problems mainly stemmed from their father's destructive behavior and his public humiliation.

Unlike Nancy who blamed herself and her mother, Pat didn't question her judgment for remaining in this marriage for fifteen years or for not removing her children from her husband's destructiveness. It's possible she lacked the power to keep him away from the children, but she didn't even raise the issue. His drinking, drug use, and abuse of his children and patients didn't happen all at once.

She said she knew from the start that there was something really wrong with him. Pat had a simple explanation for not leaving him earlier: Her mother told her it's not a good idea to divorce. She felt her second husband's bigotry and refusal to apologize to her daughter had alienated her child, but she didn't view herself as implicated in their conflict. However, when it came to her niece's suicide, she wondered if Susan might have been pushed over the edge by an engagement her parents should never have allowed.

I can't know what happened to Nancy's or Pat's children, but the current scientific thinking is that clinical depression and schizophrenia are primarily caused by biological factors, though some unknown environmental factors may contribute to schizophrenia. Depression may also be triggered by the loss of a loved one or the loss of self-esteem, but especially in the most severe cases, it's currently believed that there's usually a biological foundation that makes people vulnerable to other forms of stress.

Whatever the real causes, we learn a lot about people by how they account for problems, and these sisters couldn't be more different in their thinking or how they responded. As both sisters observed, many of the circumstances of their lives were eerily similar, but they responded to them in opposite ways. Nancy responded by acting depressed, self-blaming, and helpless, asking her sister for support. Pat became angry at what she sees as Nancy's passive behavior and chose to see herself as the strong, constructive one. In contrast to Nancy, Pat doesn't spend a lot of time examining her own behavior: She finds the answers she needs in the Hartman color-coded graph of human motivation. Nancy feels Pat is unwilling to listen to her and conjectures this is because Pat doesn't want to face her own pain. Pat feels she listens to her sister all the time, and that Nancy is oblivious to the pain that she's suffered, too.

One reason these sisters get so frustrated with each other is that although they accurately perceive their differences, they expect the other to think, feel, and act like themselves. They clearly see the person before them, but they don't relate to the person who's there.

Pat isn't offering Nancy the kind of empathy she wants. But why does Nancy look for empathy from Pat, when she can see that Pat doesn't operate this way? To act empathically, one must be willing to share the other person's particular experience of her situation, actions, and feelings. The ability to act empathically requires imagination and identification. People are different in their capacity for this activity in general, and furthermore, we all find it easier to empathize with some people and situations more than others.

Even though Pat has shared many of Nancy's outward experiences, her subjective experience is very different. She doesn't allow herself to get depressed, and she doesn't dwell on how she may have harmed others or on the losses she has suffered. She doesn't like to feel helpless or guilty.

Nancy is correct in saying that Pat doesn't want to go to these places. So why does she keep asking her to? The answer is that she's not relating to her Real Sister; she's relating to the one who is driven by her wishes. I strongly suspect Nancy wants her sister to give her something she didn't get from her mother, or something that she's missing from her mother. Nancy says that she's always regarded Pat as the "big" sister, even though Pat is younger.

Many of the women I interviewed are usually aware that their husbands or partners don't always think or feel the way they do. But they often forget to apply this insight to their sisters. They often assume their sisters should think or act as they do because they're both women and they grew up under the same roof.

Pat makes the same mistake as her sister. She thinks doing push-ups would alleviate Nancy's depression, because she finds that exercise useful. If you are a person who likes to take charge, it is very difficult to empathize with someone who is depressed—especially when that person seems determined to defeat any attempt to help her see things less negatively.

Pat understands things by categorizing them. In addition to the color scheme of motivation, she finds other categories useful: older/younger siblings; like mother/like father. She thinks she's more like her mother—a take-charge person, and that her sister is more like their dad, who was passive. We all tend to do this, but people can't be fit so easily into boxes. Although Pat is the apparently dominant one in their sister relationship, I find it interesting that Pat chose two husbands she couldn't control, while Nancy, who laments that she acceded to all her mother's wishes, chose a husband who was "milk-mild" like her father.

These women, like so many others, talked about the problem of "controlling" mothers and sisters. The word "controlling" came up so often in our discussions that I considered the use of the term and realized it covers many different situations. It's easy to feel controlled even by someone who doesn't mean to control you. If your sister is passive or depressed and conveys, like Nancy, that she can't do anything without your help, you may feel controlled by her dependence because you feel obliged to take care of her problems. She may or may not be intending to control you; it's partly your response to her helplessness that makes you feel controlled.

This is an example of why it's so important to recognize and distinguish the Real and Imagined Sisters that we and our sisters are relating to. It's possible that Nancy is asking Pat to "mother" her at the same time that she wishes to have an equal and reciprocal relationship with her sister. In Nancy's mind, an equal and reciprocal relationship means a mutually disclosing one—for example, sharing problems and grief concerning children. Many of us want our sisters to play both roles at different points over the years, although Nancy is probably less aware that she's asking for mothering in addition to asking for an equal relationship. She clearly sees that her Real Sister doesn't wish to dwell on or discuss the aspects of her children's lives that she has no power to control. Her Imagined Sister would not only be her mother, but would share her definition of how to be close and equal sisters. Pat has made it clear that she has a different way of addressing problems. Nancy sees her Real Sister, but she relates to her Imagined Sister.

Pat feels controlled by her sister because she likes to feel she can handle problems. It's understandable that Pat might not want to engage in the type of conversations that Nancy desires, but she feels controlled because at some level Pat feels obliged to take care of Nancy. Both sisters have said they identify Pat with their mother who took charge of things and managed her daughters' lives when they were in need. Perhaps Pat would feel less obliged and therefore less controlled by Nancy if she recognized that she and Nancy both have identified Pat with their mother. To some degree they both imagine she should do what her mother used to do, and that is one reason why Pat feels so controlled.

CHAPTER 8

Outsider Sisters

OUTSIDER SISTERS TAKE MANY different forms. The outsider might be rendered invisible and ignored, or else attacked and devalued. Either way, the outsider is made to feel excluded and not really part of the family. Usually, she's not the preferred child of one or both parents, and once her parents treat her as a misfit, their views are often accepted and echoed by her sisters. In this way, the outsider suffers a double rejection: first by her parents and then by her sisters.

Looking at outsider sisters gives us a good view into some of the dynamics of families that support or destroy sister bonds. In all families, there are unconscious projections and identifications. Parents usually see good and bad parts of themselves in their children, and children also identify themselves with their parents: "She gets that from her father" or "I'm more like my mother and my sister is more like my father" are familiar comments. Statements like these usually refer to the identifications that are conscious and recognized. But we're also deeply influenced by projections we're not aware of.

Children actually internalize aspects of both their parents, including their critical voices. When parents unconsciously project feelings or traits they hate in themselves or in another person who makes them angry (their parent, sibling, or mother-in-law) onto one of their children, it's destructive because a child has no way of defending herself against these imputations. Children almost always accept what their parents tell them, and there's also a tendency for these projections to be accepted by other family members.

If a mother identifies more with one daughter, that child often becomes the "good" one. The "good" child is sometimes nice to her less-favored sister, but more often she doesn't question her parents' judgment. She usually doesn't acknowledge that her sister is being scapegoated by their parents, because it's not in her interest to notice, and she doesn't want to think her parents are destructive. As a child, she usually ignores her sister's pain to avoid guilt, though later in life she might reevaluate her family's behavior. Being the "good" child makes her feel loved and valued. Who could resist the pleasure of being the favorite? But as adults, sisters do have the opportunity to reexamine the roles they were given and figure out how they came to be.

It's not just negative feelings or traits that get projected onto children. Parental wishes and hopes that haven't been fully realized (for beauty, brains, athletic talent) also get projected to children who are rewarded and idealized. They become the "good" ones, as long as they don't resist or disappoint the parent.

There is a small price to pay for being the "good" one. The favored child often becomes dependent on her parents' approval or has difficulty establishing her own independent feelings or views. But on the whole, this child enjoys a great advantage in life. It's wonderful to feel like the good one: If the projections aren't too limiting or controlling, the good child starts out with higher self-esteem that she can carry into life.

The "bad" child isn't so likely to have high self-esteem. But, on rare occasions, the role has a few potential advantages. As long as this child can find someone else who appreciates her and recognizes her (another relative, a teacher, a peer, a lover, or a partner) she can free herself from her parents' judgments. She may become more independent than the child who relies on parental approval or never needed to venture into the world for recognition. But the rejected child may also remain too attached, hoping to get the approval that was denied.

There are different reasons why parents choose one child or another for a positive or negative projection. The identification might be based on birth order—a parent often identifies with a child who occupies the birth position they held—or it might be based on physical attributes or talents if a child looks like them or a loved person or looks the way they wished they had looked. A parent might be critical of a child because she resembles their mother or mother-in-law in some way.

The Invisible Sister

Audrey Bliven grew up in a suburb of Houston. She has felt a bit like an outsider in her family, not so much criticized as unrecognized and invisible. Audrey was born in 1955 and has an older sister, Delia, who was born in 1943. "My mother's explanation for the twelve-year difference is that my sister was born when she wanted a baby, at age twenty-three, and that I was born, when she was thirty-five, because my father wanted another child. I could have been an accident."

Growing up, Audrey had little interaction with Delia, and no one encouraged any relationship between them. Her sister married at eighteen, when Audrey was six or seven. But Audrey admired her sister from afar.

Delia was my beautiful older sister, and I wanted to be like her. She was the second runner-up in our town's beauty pageant, the year before she left home. I remember she wore a white strapless gown with a sequined sash and had a bouquet of flowers. I thought she was the greatest. As the runner-up beauty queen she got to do all these neat things for public relations.

The local restaurant chain had a truck that was shaped like a hot dog in the back. She got to sit on top of that truck and drive past everyone in town. I was so impressed. She was tall and slender with olive skin and blue eyes and dark hair and high cheekbones. She looked like a lovely, mature woman. I was a chubby little girl and never thought I would get to look like that. She was really special. I looked up to her more than I looked up to my mother. She was what I regarded as beautiful.

I wonder if that wasn't a function of age. My mother was older when I was born. I remember the Clairol shampoo commercials with a beautiful young mother with her kids. My mother wasn't twenty-five when I was a child. She was in her early forties.

I thought I should look like my sister, but I didn't. I'm much shorter, and I was a chunky little round kid who was struggling to keep her weight down. She didn't have those problems. My parents didn't make me feel bad, but other relatives did. My sister met her husband at her senior prom—he was another girl's date—but my sister stole his heart. This is a story that was often told in my family.

But there was another story that wasn't often told. Her beauty queen sister became pregnant soon after her prom and the family had to put together a small and rushed marriage. Audrey's sister got married the January after she graduated from high school and became a full-time wife and mother of two children. "They've been married for over forty years. I don't think she's ever been deeply unhappy."

Audrey doesn't have many personal conversations with her sister, because she knows that whatever she tells Delia will be repeated to their mother. Delia and her mother have always been closer, and Audrey feels invisible to both of them.

I didn't marry until I was thirty-one, and I'm sure my parents had given up hope that I'd marry. So I had many years where my sister was married with two children growing up and she owned her own home. On every holiday, our family gets together, and there's been no room for variation. We always spend the entire day at my sister's home. Whenever I suggested something different, they wouldn't do it. I've always had to spend all of Christmas Day from early in the morning at my sister's house.

Before I married, when I lived in an apartment, I would have liked the family to gather at my home, once in a while. But it was an unspoken rule that we always had to go to her home because she had a house and her children—it made her the center of the family.

When I got married, I moved fifty miles away from where my parents and sister live. On the first Mother's Day after I married, I wanted everyone to come here, but they didn't want to make the long trip. I had to go there.

Audrey's husband would rather stay home for Christmas, but neither her parents nor her sister want to make the long drive, and now she would worry about her aging parents if they did. So nothing has changed; even though she's married, she still feels invisible to both her parents and her sister.

> When I was a kid, I was very shy and really clinging. I tried to stick close to my mom, but she'd take off. She was reserved and less demonstrative than I wanted. I remember we'd go shopping and I'd ask her opinion about something I was trying on, and she'd say, "What I think doesn't matter. Do you like it?"

Some women might think Audrey was fortunate, remembering how their mothers tried to control what they wore. But Audrey had a different problem: She couldn't get her mother to notice her or admire her. When she asked for her mother's opinion in the dressing room, she was probably hoping her mother would say she looked nice. When her mother refused to comment, it must have been painful for several reasons: because her mother was withholding herself and her approval, and because her mother didn't even notice what Audrey was asking for. It all made Audrey feel unseen.

It's often assumed that when one sister feels less attractive and less able to compete in the sexual marketplace than her sister, it's because their father preferred her sister. But that's not always true. In this case, Audrey felt her father was affectionate. It was her mother who designated Audrey's sister as the desirable woman. It's not clear why. Perhaps she felt closer to Delia: Some women make their oldest daughters their confidantes and Delia embraced her mother's lifestyle. Perhaps she admired Delia's beauty and chose to vicariously identify with something she felt she lacked.

Unlike Delia, who parlayed her beauty into an early marriage, Audrey went to college and eventually got a job she loved, working closely with high school students as a counselor. When an essay

she wrote was recently published in an educational newsletter she
sent copies to her family. None of them said anything about it.

> I felt this reaffirmed how little they understand what I do on a
> daily basis. My physical location living fifty miles away from
> them reflects the situation. I always go to them and help them
> with their lives, and they never come here, and they don't know
> anything about me.

When Audrey and her husband first married, they tried to have
children, and discovered they had fertility problems. Then they
considered adopting children, but Audrey's husband developed
significant health problems, including a major depression. For the
past six years, he hasn't been able to work, which makes Audrey
feel that adopting children is probably not an option.

She's frustrated that she can't discuss her feelings or the pressures
she feels about her husband's unemployment and depression with
her family, because they don't have any understanding of what depression is about. "When you have an illness that people can't see,
they think it doesn't exist. My parents and sister are clueless, even
though I've tried to explain. My sister doesn't key into John's depression—she thinks he should just get a job and he'll pop out of it."

Delia, like her mother, has done little work outside the home.
She raised her children and now that her children are grown and
have children of their own, Delia works fifteen hours a week. It
angers Audrey when her mother keeps saying how busy poor Delia
is, working fifteen hours a week and doing things for her grand-
daughter. "But I work forty hours a week and come home and my
husband needs attention. I've been vocal about it, but all I hear is
how my sister must be worn out, working fifteen hours a week.
Poor thing!"

From early on, Audrey's mother apparently identified with her first daughter, who became the beauty queen just when she was becoming middle-aged. She seemed to pass the tiara to this daughter, so it's not surprising the family gathered at Delia's home; Delia and her young children had become the domestic center of the family. For years, Audrey was made to feel like the single sister who was only an "appendage" to her family and her married sister's family.

In some families, the underdog in the competition for most beautiful and desirable is acknowledged, at least, for her brains and academic achievements. This form of success was usually considered the runner-up prize for women in Audrey's generation. In some families, intelligence is more valued, but Audrey's achievements aren't even noticed. Of course, beauty is easier to buy than intelligence, and perceptions of beauty vary widely once you get outside one family. But the confidence that one will be a good wife and mother often comes from comparisons with a sister and messages sent by parents.

Although Audrey feels unrecognized, she's also relating to her Imagined Sister instead of the Real one. She still describes her sister as the beauty queen and can't imagine that her sister has ever been unhappy. This indicates she's not seeing her Real Sister; instead she's relating to her own childhood projection. Her real sister was knocked off her throne early, by an unplanned pregnancy, right after her high school graduation.

Trying to get to know her sister better, Audrey recently asked Delia why she chose her husband. Her sister answered that she couldn't remember—it was so long ago. "Maybe it was his powder-blue convertible," Delia said.

Delia's answer floored Audrey. She told me she couldn't imagine how a woman wouldn't remember the qualities that had attracted her to her husband; she certainly does. But Audrey was thirty-one when she married, mature enough to think about these questions. Her sister was eighteen and pregnant when she hastily married. Even not knowing her, I could understand Delia's reply. Perhaps she was thinking of the naïveté of her teenage years, and how quickly one could go from riding in convertibles and beauty queen floats to pushing baby carriages.

When Audrey said she couldn't imagine that her sister had ever been unhappy, it struck me that she wasn't seeing her Real Sister. There aren't many people who get through life without ever feeling unhappy. Audrey told me that when Delia was a small child, her father was away at war, between her first and third birthdays. It's likely her mother was anxious during those years, and maybe that's why her mother was so close to Delia; she was left alone with the child. Given her less-than-ideal start in life and shotgun marriage, I doubt Delia never had an unhappy day.

Audrey was made to feel invisible in her family, and her sister has done little or nothing to recognize her, in childhood or now. But Audrey is also relating to the Imagined Sister of her childhood. Although she is asking her sister questions in order to get to know her, she may not be able to hear all the answers.

The Bad Sister
of the Saintly One Who Died

In 1935, when Amy Robb was seven years old, her aunt Louise showed up at her school one day, telling Amy she'd be staying at her aunt's house for a while. Amy was delighted. She liked her aunt Louise and her cousin Martha.

After a couple of weeks, her aunt brought her home and all their relatives were gathered there, looking very somber. There was food on the table. Amy was told that her older sister, Lucy, had gone to be with Grandma and that her soul had gone to heaven.

I was confused. We lived in Wisconsin, and my grandmother lived in Minnesota. I thought of souls as part of the feet. I wondered, Did they cut off my sister's feet?

Every Saturday, for several months, my mother would take me to a mausoleum and cry, and then we'd go home. I thought maybe my sister's soles were being kept there. I didn't understand what death was.

Eventually, my mother stopped taking me to the mausoleum because her sister Louise told her it wasn't right to bring a child there. But my mother never recovered from my sister's death. She'd always been restrictive, but she got much worse. She told me I couldn't skate anymore because I'd hurt myself. She became very compulsive about cleanliness, and she'd get hysterical if I didn't stay clean. She constantly wrote secret letters to my dead sister, telling her how much she loved her.

My sister, who was seven years older, had died at home. She'd had a cold, and suddenly strangled on mucus, in my mother's arms. She probably died of polio.

I'd always been more rebellious, and my sister was more compliant—my mother never had to discipline her. After she died, she became Saint Lucy. Everyone always said that Lucy was too perfect to live.

I wonder if Amy decided that she had to be bad to avoid her good sister's fate. Or maybe her mother's anxious and controlling behavior or the contrasts to her lost, perfect sister were enough to make her rebellious. But Amy started to identify with being the bad sister. She fought with her mother constantly. Her father was more sympathetic, but he wouldn't intervene on her behalf in her fights with her mother. She recalls her mother would bake angel food cake, probably because it reminded her of her dead child.

Amy's mother was also very negative about sex. Amy remembers that when her mother turned forty, she had a hysterectomy and her parents got twin beds. Sex was never discussed in their home, but her mother made Amy feel guilty about sex and frightened her about becoming pregnant.

Her aunt Louise was the only adult she could relate to. She'd complain to her aunt that she wished her mother would try to understand her, and Louise would reply that her mother probably couldn't, because she'd never had an original idea in all her life.

To escape home, Amy fell in love and married very young. Her first husband was getting a Ph.D. in biology and they moved to Ann Arbor. By the time Amy was twenty she'd given birth to twins, a boy and a girl. While her husband was at work, and her twins were asleep, Amy was having sex with the next-door neighbor. She and her husband both had affairs, but the one she described that caught my attention was Amy's affair with her dear aunt Louise's son-in-law: the husband of the cousin she liked and used to play with.

Did she ever feel guilty during the affair with her cousin's husband, I asked her? She told me she hadn't. She assumed her cousin wouldn't have sex anyway, because on her honeymoon she'd had a skin problem that had turned out to be a cancer, and she'd needed to have a leg amputated. Mainly, she had worried about alienating her favorite aunt if Louise found out she was sleeping with her daughter's husband. And she felt she was bad, and that her badness was connected to sex.

Amy is psychologically sophisticated, so I asked her if she thought that sleeping with her cousin's husband, betraying the sick daughter of the aunt she would have preferred as a mother, might have had anything to do with her envy of her sick and virginal sister. Amy laughed and said she'd never thought about it that way, but agreed it was certainly possible.

Her identification with bad children continued for most of Amy's life. She taught troubled teenagers who were under the supervision of the youth authority. Of her own children, she felt most identified with the younger, "bad" daughter. Her oldest daughter seemed to be the saintly reincarnation of Amy's sister: a good and compliant girl who achieved great success in school. Her fraternal twin became an engineer. Amy's next daughter was rebellious in dress and behavior. Amy felt her second daughter had problems because she could never live up to the achievements of her older sister—something Amy could certainly identify with. The oldest pair and the younger daughter may have had different temperaments, but Amy's reaction also illustrates how children's birth order elicits different parental identifications and projections.

The Disinherited Sister

Ruth Berak, who is eighty, grew up in Philadelphia with her parents and her sister, Marion, who is now eighty-four and lives in Arizona. They've both become widows in the last few years; Ruth is still professionally active, as a fund-raiser for a nonprofit organization.

Ruth always assumed that she and her sister had the same mother and father; she learned only in her early twenties that

Marion was actually her half sister. The subject was so upsetting to Marion that although the sisters are otherwise close, they've discussed it only briefly and once, sixty years ago. It remains a taboo topic even though Marion was denied her rightful share of family inheritances. For different reasons, they both went along with not mentioning the family secret.

Ruth explained:

My half sister was born to my father and his first wife. Her mother died in childbirth, and my sister was named for her mother, Marion. My father married my mother three years later and I was born after nine months—so there's a four-year age difference between us. These facts were a well-kept secret.

I didn't find out that my father had another wife or that my sister had a different mother until I was twenty, after my father had died. I was dating the man who became my husband, and he was distantly related to someone related to my father. He knew about my father's first wife, and just assumed I knew, and one day he mentioned something about it. I told him, "You're mistaken—you're wrong. How can you say things like that? It's not true." But I asked my mother and learned what they'd never told me.

It wasn't until the next summer that my sister and I talked about it. She got very upset. She told me she first learned about her birth and early childhood when she was seventeen years old. She'd just gotten her driver's license and my father said, "We'll let you drive" to visit his sister. En route, he told her the truth about her birth, and she was so upset she almost smashed the car. She made my parents promise not to tell me. She was afraid I wouldn't love her anymore or care for her if I found out she was only my half sister.

My sister claims she has no memory of anything before I was born. I've learned that after her mother died my father put her into some kind of foster home for three years, and she came back only after he remarried. I only know that she was boarded out—he didn't disclaim her. I don't know if he visited her during those years. I have no idea if she lived with a relative or a friend. She claims her memory starts with my birth. I'm in a crib and she brought her friends in to see me and she was trying to pull me out between the slats until my mother came in and rescued me. That's when her memory starts. That's when she first had a mother for the first time, a family that was hers.

Ruth remembers a happy childhood, surrounded by people she loved. She and Marion shared a room, and they were close. She wasn't that wild about her father, who was a hypochondriac and always had to lie down because he wasn't feeling well. Ruth thought her mother catered too much to her father's illness complaints and his insistence on having his shirts ironed a certain way. Ruth really adored her maternal grandfather and grandmother, who lived down the street. They were very affectionate, lots of fun, and she and her sister spent a lot of time with them. The sisters spent the summers with their cousins at their grandparents' summer home on a lake.

Her grandfather owned a factory that made office supplies, and his three sons were in the business with him. They earned a lot more than her father did, and Ruth now suspects that her mother was disappointed and unhappy in her marriage.

Ruth doesn't have any memory of her sister being treated any differently from herself. They didn't look alike, and they have different interests now. But they each got to go to the college they chose (which was unusual for women during the Depression and World War II).

Their father died at age fifty-six, when Ruth was eighteen. A few years later, Marion married a man who became a successful businessman. Neither Ruth nor her mother was that wild about the man Marion chose to marry. But though she initially considered him abrasive, Ruth came to feel that her brother-in-law (who died a year ago) was a good husband to her sister. Ruth also made a happy marriage in her early twenties, to the man who first told her about her sister's childhood.

In their work lives, the sisters went in different directions. Ruth organized museum exhibitions and Marion worked in her husband's accounting business. As a parent, Ruth was far more fortunate. Ruth and her husband (who died five years ago) had children and grandchildren who are devoted to her and whose high achievements fill her with pride. Marion adopted one son who did not have children, and Ruth isn't wild about her nephew. Her sister and brother-in-law wound up losing most of their savings trying to set up their son in businesses that never worked out. Ruth tells me she has no idea why her sister didn't have biological children. "We never discussed it—my sister is very secretive."

It seems that Marion had all the bad luck and Ruth always had the good luck. But this never divided them. The two crises in their relationship came when Marion was surprisingly disinherited by their mother and years later, she was disinherited by her maternal uncle.

Her mother died suddenly when Ruth and her sister were in their thirties. Marion and her husband had moved to Arizona, so Ruth saw her mother more often. She learned just before her mother died that her mother was angry with Marion and planned to leave her entire estate to Ruth by not making out any will at all. Her mother dropped dead in her garden soon after, without any will, having told both Ruth and a lawyer about her intentions. Because Ruth was her mother's only legal heir (her mother had never legally adopted Marion), her sister had no legal claim to any part of the estate, which included whatever their father had left when he died ten years before.

Marion was hysterical. I'm not exaggerating. She kept saying, "Mother didn't like me." I was left with this dilemma. Knowing what Mother wanted, and that my sister was heartbroken, I decided I couldn't live with myself if I didn't help her. I said to my husband, "What should I do?" He said, "I can't tell you what to do." I told him I had to live with myself and do what was right. I didn't want to look back and say I should have done something else.

I divided all the liquid assets absolutely equally, and there was quite a bit of money for 1955. But I kept the shares in the family business that my mother had inherited. For a year, I was furious with my poor dead mother for doing this to me. I told my sister that I was sure our mother meant to leave her the money and just didn't get around to making a will. The business was sold many years later, and I didn't feel guilty about keeping that. The business meant the most to my mother. By holding that, I was honoring my mother's wishes, and by sharing the money with my sister I tried to do something for her. Her husband resented it—he once made a remark that I could have done more.

The same thing happened when Ruth's uncle died. Their mother's younger brother had no wife or children, and he divided his estate among the biological children of his two sisters, but left almost nothing to Marion.

Years later, my uncle died. I was like his daughter because my mother wasn't around. He'd discussed his will with me and told me he wasn't leaving anything to my sister. I pleaded with him not to do that. He left a token amount to Marion and divided the rest among my cousins and me. I was the executor and my sister was very upset and hurt and she had every right to be. She and my uncle were very close. It was a terrible thing to do.

I guess my family lived a lie. If my uncle cared about my sister he wouldn't have done that. All that time he was alive he didn't treat her any differently. I guess he didn't count my sister as a member of the family.

I asked Ruth if she has any idea why her mother didn't want to leave anything to Marion. "I can only speculate," Ruth replied. "I guess my mother resented her because she regretted her marriage to this man with this child. That's what I've come to think. My sister was nice to her—she was a dutiful daughter. I lived a little closer. My mother died when my daughter was a year old and my sister didn't have a child. No one will know why she did what she did."

At this point, Ruth did confess to some pleasure she took in being the one who was loved the most.

This happened recently. A cousin had a cousins party and there were ten of us there. We're all very close because we all adored my grandfather. Biologically, I'm the oldest. My sister was in Arizona and she wasn't there. Someone said, "Ruth, you're the matriarch of the family." I said, "No, Marion is" and it hit me. I wanted to say, "But I am. I'm the oldest." I didn't. For the first time, I wanted to be acknowledged as my grandfather's oldest. I was eighty years old. I knew I was his favorite. I was his first and favorite.

I admire Ruth's honesty and insightfulness; this wasn't an easy thing to admit, even to herself, but who can blame someone for wanting to be the favorite? I also felt her concern for her sister was deep and sincere. She was torn between wanting her sister to feel equally loved and admitting she enjoyed her position as the favorite grandchild. Not dividing the shares in her grandfather's business that she inherited from her mother probably had a lot to do with her attachment to her grandfather. It was easier to share her parents' money.

I considered, briefly, if it might have made any difference to Marion if Ruth had shared everything with her—her entire inheritance from her mother and her inheritance from her uncle. But Ruth was unusually generous and magnanimous and it wouldn't have changed the fact that Marion's worst fears were based on reality; she wasn't really loved or truly counted as one of the children by her mother or uncle.

When I asked Ruth about her brother-in-law's resentment over Ruth's not sharing their mother's entire inheritance, she recalled that when she gave Marion half the liquid assets, her sister had said to her husband, "I told you my sister would do something for me" and her brother-in-law had said, "It could have been more." I asked how she felt about that remark. "I said to myself, screw you. That's the way he is. I didn't let it bother me. I thought I had done the right thing."

I suspect few sisters would have been as generous as Ruth, and that many would have kept all the money. In other cases I've heard about, when preferred children inherited all or most of the money, they simply decided they must have deserved it.

Ruth's speculation about her mother's motives strikes me as reasonable. There was nothing in Ruth's description of her sister to indicate any reason why Marion deserved to be disinherited.

Recently, Marion paid a visit to Ruth, and Ruth was determined to get her sister to talk about the taboo subject—the fact that she had a different biological mother. They hadn't discussed it for sixty years. But Ruth was so afraid to upset her sister, she let the opportunity pass. "We'll both die not having talked about it. I felt there needs to be closure about this. We both know this. Why can't we talk about it? It seems silly. I feel it's hanging there." But she put her sister's feelings first.

As much as Ruth truly doesn't like deception, she inevitably got caught up in a family custom of not seeing or hearing or knowing. There are so many things she doesn't know, that she never asked because she was part of a family that kept secrets and had unspoken rules about what you could talk about and what you couldn't. Even in families without major secrets, the most meaningful subjects are often avoided.

I imagine Marion must have always sensed that she wasn't loved like Ruth, and that her position in the family was precarious. She'd been left in foster care during the first three years of her life. After learning the truth at age seventeen, she may have felt responsible for her mother's death because her mother had died in childbirth, and then she'd been "boarded out"—to use Ruth's language—just like a dog. She probably knew that her family wasn't so fond of her husband. She might have hoped she'd be rejected less if she kept up the pretense that she was a full member of the family. Ruth didn't notice any difference in the way they were treated. The preferred child rarely does. But that also suggests Ruth didn't want to see what might have been obvious. If her mother and uncle didn't include Marion in their will, it's likely they were treating her as an outsider all along.

Ruth says her feelings about her sister didn't change when she learned about the circumstances of her birth. I'm sure she didn't love her any less. Just before her sister visited, Ruth happened to mention to one of her oldest friends, who'd known them for fifty years, that her sister was actually a half sister. Her friend was shocked that Ruth had never mentioned this before. "My friend said, 'You're kidding. Who was her mother? Who was she?' I said, 'I don't know—she was this woman my father married.'" Her friend asked her why she'd never spoken of it, and Ruth told her that it never mattered to her. If what Ruth meant was that she didn't love her sister less, I would believe that, but it's hard to understand how it wouldn't have mattered.

I would have guessed that family secrets are hard to keep. Almost always, someone, inside or outside, knows the secret and reveals it, as Ruth's husband innocently did. But in listening to sisters' stories, I've often been surprised at how long major secrets are preserved, even when several family members know the truth.

I suspect that in many cases there are hints or clues that a member could pursue if they really wanted to know something. But usually a family taboo around knowing encourages members to look away. For example, the identical twins in chapter 1 were a little suspicious when their mother wouldn't discuss their birth, but they let it go.

Ruth recalled seeing something that might have aroused her suspicion. "Once I found a picture of my mother in a newspaper clipping—it was the announcement of her engagement. I started to read it, and she snatched it out of my hands. I thought that was odd. Later on, I realized she didn't want me to see the date of her marriage, because my sister was born before they married." I wonder why Ruth's mother kept the wedding announcement where it might have been found.

Ruth valued her sister's feelings more than she valued money, and she showed a concern for the disfavored child that isn't all that common. And to Marion's credit, she didn't blame Ruth for being the favored child. She appreciated her sister's generosity, unlike her husband who complained that Ruth could have shared even more. Marion also took pride in Ruth's grandchildren (bragging about them as if they were her own), although she never had children of her own.

Ruth and Marion's mutual generosity protected their bond, in spite of others who might have ruined it.

Toward the end of our conversation, Ruth's thoughts turned to her grandparents and all the loved people she had spoken of; now, only her sister is left. "Here I am, eighty years old. Once I stood in the middle of a circle surrounded by love and affection, and one by one they've all dropped out of the circle, and I'm almost alone." But she and Marion still have each other.

CHAPTER 9

Sisters Who Leave and Sisters Who Stay

SOME SISTERS LEAVE THE WORLD of their family by choice, not because they have been rejected. It's their greater talent, ambition, or independence that pulls them away. Educationally, culturally, geographically, financially—they distance themselves from others in the family. But unlike the disfavored daughters who separate because they were unappreciated, these daughters often remain the favorite child, even though they're not around on a day-to-day basis.

But the successful sister who leaves is often not that well liked by her sisters who remain closer to the world they came from. They may resent her because she's favored even though they were the "loyal" children. I also discovered that in families with three sisters, there's almost always an alliance of two sisters against the third, especially if the odd one out was the most successful or moved into a different social world.

One important lesson I've learned from interviewing sisters is not to impose my expectations of which one would be the envied sister. What happened in the Lewis family really opened my eyes.

The Unmarried Sister

The oldest of the Lewis sisters, Nadine, now forty-five, was a high academic achiever and is now the director of a nonprofit organization. Of the three, she is the only one to have gone to college and to have a professional career, which is odd because their parents had both gone to college. She's also the only of the three sisters who didn't marry and have children. Nadine spent her senior year in high school abroad and then left for college (a highly selective one) and never moved back, because she needed some distance. Her parents and two younger sisters live in Ohio. Nadine lives in upstate New York. She told me she thought she represented something of a separate and different authority figure to her sisters when they were younger—not one related to their parents.

But that was not how her younger sisters spoke about Nadine. I'd expected to hear about Nadine's academic and professional achievements from her younger sisters. Their marriages, according to Nadine, had moved them into a working-class milieu. But Norma, the middle sister, made no reference at all to Nadine's achievements or to looking up to Nadine when they were young. Norma just recalled Nadine as a "bookworm" who stayed in her room and "read a book a day." She spoke of the adult Nadine not as a successful professional, but as a single woman without children who had not done what she should have to find a man for herself. Mindy, the youngest sister, thought it might have been her parents who first labeled Nadine the "bookworm" and "loner."

There was always more tension between Nadine and Norma (the oldest and middle sisters), while Mindy got along with both. But if either sister felt any envy about Nadine's middle-class life and professional success, they didn't show it. They just described Nadine in terms of what she hadn't gotten in life, and they had—children and a husband. Interestingly, both younger sisters described Nadine's unhappiness on their wedding days some twenty years before. They assumed Nadine was upset when they married because she was the oldest and single.

Despite their conflicts, I sensed this family was close and concerned about one another's lives. The sisters all get together about six times a year with their parents, and Norma and Mindy talk to each other more frequently. Nadine and Norma were less than two years apart, and they fought a lot as children. Both of them remembered that Nadine had the verbal ability to make cutting remarks, and that Norma would just punch her in the nose. Mindy was the buffer: "When we took car trips, I was squashed in the middle seat between them, because my parents didn't want them fighting."

All the sisters described their mother as very kind and well-meaning but a little difficult to deal with; they described their father as being around less of the time, when they were growing up. They felt their parents had not shown any favoritism, and had been accepting of each daughter. But their parents did not get along, never acted as a unit, and they disliked their parents' arguments. Nadine said she was especially uncomfortable when her mother tried to use her as friend and confidante during her teenage years, frequently complaining about Nadine's father. Her mother told Nadine that she would not have married her father if she hadn't become pregnant with Nadine. I asked Nadine if hearing this upset her, and she said that it hadn't. Her parents were still together, after decades of fighting, so they had obviously chosen their shared if contentious life.

But since Nadine had said she'd resented being used as a confidante, I still wondered if her mother's remarks hadn't been troubling. When mothers use their children as confidantes this way, it suggests they are trying to reverse roles. In making that remark, Mrs. Lewis was acting out of her own needs, not Nadine's. This usually happens when a mother hasn't had her own dependency needs met by her mother. Unconsciously, she tries to get one of her daughters to mother her by listening to her troubles and giving her support and advice. If the oldest daughter begins to resist (and Nadine did leave home early), the mother tends to move on to the next daughter.

Norma, the middle sister, described herself as the "black sheep" of the family—into drugs and alcohol when she was young. Nadine recalls that Norma would "spoil" Christmas celebrations, because she was drunk and wouldn't show up. Norma resents what she sees as exaggerated descriptions: "I was in a horrible depression and drank one Christmas Day."

Nadine had told me she was concerned about Norma's mood swings—she'd been diagnosed as manic-depressive, an illness their mother's mother also suffered from—and Nadine was worried that her sister's medications weren't working properly.

When I spoke to Norma, she immediately told me about her bipolar illness and that she was either very silent or had a "motor-mouth." I talked to her on a day when she spoke rapidly and non-stop, without pausing for a breath. As all the sisters had told me, Norma doesn't mince words and she freely expressed her annoyances. "As a young adult, when Nadine came back from working abroad, she said nasty things to me. I'd say, 'I'm with someone and I'm raising children,' and she'd make snide remarks, like 'Aren't you perfect.'"

Norma also told me how her brother-in-law, Mindy's husband, had described the three sisters and their flaws: "Bitchy, Bossy, and Bessie. Nadine is Bitchy, and I'm Bossy, and Mindy is Bessie." Norma added, "All three of us talk in a jokey way. He's not mean to his wife. We all laughed when he said it, it fit in a way. We can laugh at ourselves."

Despite the complaints, this family remains in close contact, and seems to strive for mutual tolerance. They all belong to different churches and have very different feelings about such issues as abortion and politics, but they don't argue about those things. Of the three sisters, I felt Norma openly expressed the most anger, directed toward Nadine and her mother. She still remembers that Nadine looked unhappy at her wedding, twenty years before:

Nadine felt excluded because we didn't consult her on the bridesmaid dresses, but she wasn't living close by. And clothes aren't important to her. We didn't intentionally exclude her, but we hurt her feelings. We're couples or mothers, and she's a single female and the oldest. I don't think she'll ever be married. She's never tried hard enough. She hasn't dated for years. Now she's forty-five and she set herself apart and she has her bitchy side. Mom's been praying for her. But you have to try and she doesn't. Anyone who's hurt or lonely at her age should join a gym or go somewhere or put an ad in the paper to meet someone. She could join a singles' group. You can't just wait for an accident to happen—and she hasn't tried. But she should know she could trust us to take care of her.

Nadine had admitted to me that she felt lonely and would like to be married; she still hopes she will find the right man. When she was younger, she had been drawn to men who weren't right for her—gay men or alcoholics. She broke off one relationship with a man because of his drinking problem. Last year, she took a "leap of faith" and became the foster mother of two teenaged girls, sisters from a troubled family. Nadine explained that being a foster mother to two teenagers had been easier than she had expected: "The best thing I've ever done. I've had roommates who were harder to live with." Nadine's father was initially concerned about her decision to become a foster mother, but now her family is supportive and tells the girls they are part of the family.

Being the only one who hadn't settled into a domestic life, Nadine felt that, ironically, she was treated like the "youngest child even though I was the oldest sister." I thought it might have been the way they patronized her for not being married, but she didn't say it.

> I used to think I would have kids on my own if I didn't get married in five years, but I kept extending the deadline from thirty to thirty-five to forty. Having my own kids seemed less and less likely to happen. I wasn't sure I could handle it with my job. I saw an article in a church council newsletter about becoming a foster parent for hard-to-place adolescents, and I thought I'd check it out.
>
> I love babies, but I'm approaching my forty-sixth birthday, and how much energy do I have? I love my nieces and nephews and my friends' kids. I hope I'll get to play with the children my girls have someday.

After talking to Norma, I got the feeling that Nadine's decision not to adopt a young child was influenced by her family. Norma recalls:

> She wanted to adopt a baby, and we advised her against it. She's had bad allergies, and pulmonary bronchitis. You can't handle an infant as an older single parent. It's not realistic. She wouldn't get any sleep. And all the illnesses they get. I think it was a

wonderful idea for her to adopt the two teenage girls—it's wonderful for the whole family.

While Norma had ignored Nadine's many interests and professional accomplishments by reducing her to a "bookworm" who
just stayed in her room, her appreciation for Nadine's becoming a
foster mother was genuine. Perhaps because Norma's life is focused on her family, she doesn't recognize the valuable aspects of
Nadine's life that aren't family oriented. She seems to feel closer to
her younger sister, Mindy. In fact, she's disappointed that Mindy
doesn't have more time to spend with her. She'd always hoped she
and Mindy would raise their children together, and babysit for one
another, but they lead separate lives.

Norma does admit that her daughter, Laurie, is very fond of her
aunt Nadine, and they get along well, but Norma was offended by
a casual remark Nadine recently made:

> My younger sister, Mindy, is more happy-go-lucky, not as nega-
> tive as Nadine. My daughter goes to a Christian school, and
> someone asked if Laurie would stay in a private school. We felt
> like she needed a tight rein and discipline. So I said Laurie gets
> so much out of learning the Bible and wants to be a minister.
> Nadine goes, "Laurie? Hah! Oh, you've got to be kidding." Like
> a put-down. How could you say if she could or couldn't. She's
> seven. How can she say what she'll be like.

I wasn't there to hear the tone, but I can imagine words like that
being said with affection rather than judgment. I wondered if
Norma is still reacting to Nadine's cutting remarks when they were
young. Norma thinks her parents treated all the girls fairly, and
that her mother means well. But she feels her mother is denying

the fact that Norma has bipolar illness, when her mother's mother had it, too. In fact, Norma feels that she was the only one who could get along with her grandmother, because they understood each other this way. "I realized she became manic first, and then she'd get drunk. Not the other way around." I suspect this was a way for Norma to explain her own problems with alcohol, too. But my mother isn't afraid to accuse me of having her mother's negative traits. I said to her, 'Look, I'm not your mother, I'm me.'"

When Norma was a teenager she was enlisted to take care of their very difficult grandmother, because her grandmother had been cruel to their mother and their mother couldn't deal with her. At one family gathering, Norma pointedly announced, right in front of their mother, that when their mother got old, Mindy would have to take care of her because she and Nadine had already put in their time taking care of their grandmother. Not a diplomatic remark, but Norma justifiably felt she had already assumed one of her mother's responsibilities.

Mindy had the fewest complaints, and she also told me she doesn't like conflict. She did mention that when she was young, Nadine was off doing exciting things—things she could never imagine doing herself. This was the first time I'd heard any praise for Nadine's independence or her interest in the wider world. Mindy felt closer to Norma as a child, and it was Norma she admired and tried to imitate. "My parents said she was so artistic, so I tried to be artistic."

Mindy sees herself as a follower, because she was a younger sister. Like Norma, she focused on Nadine's single status:

She watched her two younger sisters getting married, one year after the other, and she wasn't happy. She was depressed because she'd broken up with her boyfriend. She wasn't happy at my wedding. She thought the bridesmaid's dress I picked out for her was ugly. She sat around and sighed and was lost in her memories. She was near tears. We understand it—but don't burst in tears now.

Overall, for the past ten years our relationship has been pretty good. I can feel when she's down. I know she wanted to be married but she didn't find the right guy. She's a wonderful aunt. She always has goodies for the kids, so that's neat. She's good at being an aunt.

Mindy also worries a little bit about Nadine's expectations of her foster children. "It's really neat to see her mother side, and she genuinely loves the girls and they are great kids. But one of them made other plans on Thanksgiving to be with her boyfriend, and she was crying, 'I just got the kids and they're breaking free.' The other girl is more attached to her."

Mindy also recalls that Norma had to be the go-between for their mother and grandmother.

She's used up her tolerance of older people and she doesn't want to deal with my mother's aging process. Norma had to deal with my grandmother. My mother felt too sensitive and too hurt by things her mother said. She's still like that. I don't like conflict among family members, so I stayed away. I'm a peacemaker. I tried to avoid my grandmother because she wasn't nice to my mother and I feel close to my mother, and she hurt her.

Nadine also intervened to help my mother and put my grandmother in a treatment center. That made her into an enemy in my grandmother's view. I tried to stay innocent and kept out of it. When my grandmother died, my two sisters and my mother were more broken up about it than I was. She was a pain in the ass.

Mindy appreciates Norma's directness, but she thinks Norma can be too confrontational and insensitive. "When my parents were visiting her, my dad is a yeller and my mother knows how to push his buttons. Norma said flat out, 'You can't argue in our house. You should consider taking Prozac.' She's direct, and my grandmother was like that, too. She said what she was thinking."

As for her parents, "They are proof anyone can stay married. They've been annoying each other for forty-five years. We've learned to have a commitment to love each other. Even if you're mad, you don't quit speaking. We're always celebrating holidays together, and birthdays. We always make an attempt to be close, to make up, and consider the other person's point of view. We enjoy each other's company 98 percent of the time."

I did get the feeling, talking to all three sisters, that for all their complaints, there is a genuine family loyalty. It surprised me that Nadine's interesting work life and travels hardly came up in anyone's discussion, except her own. I understood that Norma and Mindy might not share all of Nadine's interests, but they didn't show much interest in recognizing the full person Nadine is. Both Mindy and Norma said that Nadine was involved with their children, but I didn't see a reciprocal attempt to appreciate the good things in Nadine's life, other than her recently acquired foster children. I think this may be a common experience for outsider sisters: What counts most is what the family values most. In this family, what counts most is whether you have a family. Nadine has given a great deal to others through her work, but she and her sisters focus on what she doesn't have—a husband and children of her own.

The Star

Another woman I interviewed who was the most educated and successful of her sisters and the only one to move far from home, also became the outsider, like Nadine. But Lila also had the most enviable marriage, so she wasn't vulnerable to her family's judgments of her life.

Lila Robb is a striking-looking computer software developer who lives in Miami with her husband, David, a businessman. The second oldest of four sisters and the first in her family to be born in the United States, Lila grew up in a Guyanese Indian family near Washington, D.C. She told me that a large segment of Guyana's population is made up of Indians who emigrated from India or England, and they adhere strictly to their traditional culture. Her mother had been raised by Indian parents who moved to Guyana from England, but when her grandfather died, her grandmother arranged for Lila's fourteen-year-old mother to marry a much older man, a twenty-four-year-old Guyanese Indian.

Lila's oldest sister, Christie, who is twenty-nine, was born in Guyana when her mother was not quite fifteen. Soon after her birth, Lila's parents moved to Maryland, and Christie was left behind to live with her grandparents. Lila was born the next year, when her mother was sixteen. And two more sisters followed her—one is now twenty-three and one is sixteen. Her parents didn't bring Christie to Washington until they'd established some financial stability. By that time Lila was three and Christie was five.

Her father's many brothers soon followed him to Maryland, so Lila grew up in a Guyanese Indian community with her father's extended family, including cousins she liked, and uncles she didn't. She hated how the men ruled their wives and treated them like slaves or housekeepers. Until she went to college, Lila and her sisters led a restricted life. "We couldn't hang out. I had to study. We weren't allowed to get phone calls. I helped my mother with her chores."

Now, Lila's older sister doesn't speak to her parents or to anyone in the family except, rarely, to Lila's twenty-three-year-old sister. Lila tells me that Christie defied her father, first by hanging out with the wrong crowd at school, smoking and trying to be cool, and then she broke away from the family by moving in with a black man her father didn't approve of. Their father wanted his daughters to marry either Indians or white men, but not African Americans. Lila has heard rumors that Christie's husband is a drug addict and an ex-felon, and that he doesn't go to work, so Christie supports her family with low-paying work.

According to Lila, Christie has held a grudge against their parents for leaving her behind in Guyana for five years—a grudge that Lila considers to be selfish and stupid. She thinks her sister should understand that their parents were struggling and trying to make a better life for the family. At the same time, Lila deeply resents the way her father has treated her mother:

> My mother was never in love with my dad. He's traditional, old-fashioned, and he's not social. He would hit her, and they'd never go out to a restaurant or to a movie. She had to cook and clean all day. Right before I entered college, she left him for a while and took me with her, and we moved to her mother's apartment for a few weeks. My older sister was left at home with my dad and two young kids, and she left them to live with her boyfriend.
>
> My mother got a job as a caretaker for old women, making sure they eat and go to the bathroom. My father owns a convenience store with his brothers. My mother always told me and my sisters that we should go to college and get a job so we wouldn't be dependent on a man.

When my mother moved back with my father, she was afraid to go alone, so she took her mother with her. The house was a gross mess and she cleaned it up. My father used to hit my mother when I was a girl, and I hated it. We told him off. We've called the police and she's gotten restraining orders. He knows if he hits her now, she'll call 911 and press charges.

Lila lived at home or with her father's relatives while she commuted to college and a wider world opened up to her. "I was shy growing up, very reserved. But I started to go out to happy hours, and dancing. I had a surge of self-confidence. It took a lot of time for me to gain the social skills other people had, but now I feel confident. I started coming home at six A.M. and my father wouldn't say anything to me. I had fun because he couldn't control me anymore."

She was also amazed at how many wealthy Indians she met in college whose families arranged marriages for them if they hadn't found someone on their own—wives would be imported from India; husbands located in the matrimonial pages of Indian American newspapers.

"My girlfriend's parents were getting her pictures of marriageable men from Dallas and Chicago. This is about marriage, not dating. Before, the girls didn't have a say, but now they can reject someone they don't want. My girlfriend met a few of these men and turned them down."

After she graduated, Lila got a job in a mutual fund corporation. She dated Indian men from wealthy backgrounds in the United States or India. They were very different from the men in her father's family, who believed girls should never go to bars, should be virgins when they marry, and become domestic slaves to their husbands and their husbands' families. "My cousins were dating Guyanese men, and there was such a difference. Those men were so possessive, and my cousins couldn't have any friends. I thought, Fuck it. I knew I wouldn't marry a Guyanese Indian."

Lila's twenty-three-year-old sister did, and Lila feels sorry for her. "He has a job, but he's lazy. She works harder and takes care of their kids. Her husband watches TV and doesn't help out. Those men expect service. And if you marry them, forget about your family. The man's family is the only one that counts. So my sister doesn't get to see my mother unless he's not home."

While Lila was breaking away from the life that was expected of her, she knew her cousins and uncles were gossiping about her. "They thought of me as a slut or a ho [whore] because I'd go to bars with friends." Women in her Guyanese Indian family were given limited options. "They mold you to get married and cook and worry that your mother-in-law won't like the way you wash the pots." Of all the female cousins she used to play with when she was a child, Lila is the only one with a college education. The boys, on the other hand, went to college.

Perhaps with her mother's and sister's experiences in mind, Lila took her time choosing a partner. "I waited until I was twenty-five and fell in love with a white guy, and we're very happy. My husband got a great job offer in Miami, so we moved here." Lila now has a good job and is considering graduate business programs.

Although she doesn't live close by, Lila remains close to her mother. Even though she's still paying off her college loans, she sends her mother money every month, and a few years ago, Lila helped her parents buy a house in the suburbs, to get them away from the influence of her father's family. Her husband, David, helps her parents with their mortgage payments.

My dad's family breeds this stuff—that you should hit your wife. Mom went to his family's house and his youngest brother, who is forty years old, said jokingly, "Why don't you slap her around?" My mother should have said something, because now she talks back. My father knows if she walks out, I'll take care of her.

My husband is so good and supportive of her. He doesn't mind sending money to her—he sees how she waits hand and foot on my father, and he feels sorry for Mom.

Lila hates what has happened to her oldest sister. As children, she and Christie used to play games together and take walks in the park. "I don't understand what happened. Why she won't talk with us. If she talked to me, I'd be open to her." One of her father's brothers recently died, and her oldest sister showed up at the funeral but would speak only to Lila's younger sister. "Maybe if I'd gone to the funeral, I might have said, 'Snap out of your ego trip and talk to your parents.'"

In a way, she's reproduced my mother's situation. She's suffering with a guy who doesn't work. She has three kids and she has to take care of everything.

My twenty-three-year-old sister and her family were living in a small apartment, and my brother-in-law's parents gave them money to get a house. They wanted to be near my mother, so my mother could take of her kids while my sister goes to work.

Lila feels closest to her sixteen-year-old sister; she's the only one left she might influence. "She just took her PSATs. She needed help and she'll ask me about colleges and school projects. But she won't discuss personal things with me because she's afraid I'll tell Mom, because I'm close to Mom."

It seemed to me Lila is like many oldest daughters in closely identifying with her mother. In effect, she occupied the position of oldest daughter, even though she was born second, since Christie spent her earliest years away from her mother and didn't join the family until she was five. It's fairly common for parents, and especially mothers, to be more intensely involved with their first child; it's their first experience with being a mother so they're more anxious and also more entranced. Their later children represent a less novel experience, and their attentions are also more divided with each additional child.

Of course, each child elicits different feelings from his or her parents, so later on, there are many different bases for positive or negative identifications. Mothers often shift their focus to their second daughter, if the first pulls away. But the intensity, anxiety, novelty, and exclusiveness of the first relationship and the absence of siblings as alternative figures for the child to engage with may explain why the bond between first daughters and mothers is often closer, or why first daughters are frequently more identified with their mothers and more anxious to please them.

I asked Lila why she thought she was close to her mother, while her older sister isn't speaking to her. As frequently happens with a favored child, she wasn't that tuned into the experience of the disfavored child. Lila felt her sister's resentment about being left behind in Guyana for her first five years was selfish.

Mom reached out to all her daughters. But I cared more. It bothered me to see her crying or not having money. She gave up her life to help us. I feel it's selfish not to care for her. I wish I had closer relationships with my sisters. I go on vacations with my friends, and I wish I could do it with my sisters.

I can't relate to them that way. I don't know what they think of me.

But Lila fears they just think of her as someone who's rich and should support them. She recalls going out for a meal with their mother and her two younger sisters. When it came time to pay, her twenty-three-year-old sister told the other one, "Don't leave money; wait for Lila. She always picks up the check."

"Does the money make them jealous?" Lila wonders.

They'll see I buy shoes that cost $150 and they'll ask me how much I spent on them. But I put myself through college, and I'm saving. I never put them down. I have to be careful around my dad's family when they ask me questions. They keep asking me how much I make. I'm not gonna tell them. I leased a new Passat—big deal, it's not a Porsche. My mom heard my father's relatives saying, "She thinks she's better than us."

I don't know what they say. Maybe they hate me. I don't know. They didn't ask for me this week, at my uncle's funeral.

I've worked so hard to be where I am. I don't know why my oldest sister is the way she is. My parents were strict with both of us, for our own good. My sister did hang out with the wrong crowd. She was so into this guy. My friends are totally different. They're more like me. They're independent; they like to travel and go out. They come from solid families. My husband's family is very good, and very accepting of me, but they don't know about my sisters. They just see my parents, and David doesn't tell them anything and they don't ask.

I asked Lila if her sisters' remarks hurt her feelings. She answered that they just make her want to succeed more.

The Betrayed Sister

Tonia Frette is an acting teacher in her early forties. She lives in Los Angeles with her partner, Roger, who's an architect. She was raised in New Hampshire, the oldest of three daughters. Her two younger sisters still live within ten miles of their childhood home. As a teenager, Tonia was forced to take care of her two younger siblings, which she resented.

Her sisters have a very different lifestyle than Tonia. One married a born-again Christian and adopted all his views. She's very judgmental about anyone who doesn't share their beliefs. Both of her sisters have made remarks that express their view of Tonia as the "weird" sister who lives with her boyfriend in California and didn't get married or have children.

Recently, both of their parents died (within a year of each other), and from Tonia's point of view, the most precious thing her mother left behind was their summer cottage in Maine. It was designed and built by their mother's grandfather, and Tonia's happiest childhood memories were of summers spent there. Her mother had owned only a third interest in the cottage; she'd been an equal partner with one of her sisters who had no children and a brother who had died and whose share had gone to his son, Tonia's cousin Fred. Tonia and Roger loved this cottage and its beautiful setting and her great-grandfather's craftsmanship, so Tonia had mentioned many times to her sisters that she wanted to make sure they all kept access to the house. Tonia also felt that she was the only one of her generation who appreciated its original beauty, and she believed that her mother had assumed she would protect it.

She learned too late that her sisters had secretly colluded to buy their aunt's share, without telling Tonia. That meant her sisters had a majority and controlling share, their cousin Fred owned a third, and Tonia's interest was reduced to 11 percent. She was shocked when she learned what they'd pulled off behind her back. When she asked them how they could betray her this way, they denied any responsibility and blamed it on their cousin Fred, saying he thought they should "downsize" the number of owners and centralize control of the house into fewer hands.

Tonia was devastated. For one thing, she and Roger loved the house as it was, and she could see that her sisters and their husbands were planning to "gloss it up" and transform it into a suburban-looking second home. Even worse, she felt stabbed in the back by her sisters, who didn't even have the decency to be honest about it, passing off the blame to their cousin.

She recalled feeling horrified as a child when her mother kept having babies that she had to care for. She'd been pushed out from the epicenter of her mother's love and saddled with responsibilities that weren't fair. Now she was being pushed out of the house that was her most cherished tie to her mother and her childhood.

Several older sisters I interviewed were, like Tonia, given the responsibility of raising their younger siblings. Sometimes these sisters became close with their siblings in adulthood, and often they didn't. There are several problems here: one is giving excessive responsibility to a child, a second is that children who are getting very little of their parents' attention are likely to take out their anger on one another.

I didn't get the feeling that Tonia was at all interested in controlling her younger sisters, but I encountered other cases where a sister who had to sacrifice her childhood by mothering younger siblings developed a controlling attitude toward them, and was hurt and angry when they asserted their independence. From a child's immature perspective, making a big sacrifice should at least earn adoration and obedience. A child can't understand that her charges don't want to be controlled.

Once, when looking through a trunk in her parents' attic, Tonia found an old photograph of herself going to her senior prom, all dressed up in her gown. Scrawled across the photograph, in red ink, were the words, "My fatso sister!"

There is something absurd about this defacement of Tonia's prom night photograph. Even now, in her forties, Tonia has the graceful, lithe body of a dancer—which she's always had. That her sister took the photo of her and secretly mutilated it with her angry red pen must have been a measure of her resentment and envy.

The way that sisters deal with the division or disposal of their parents' belongings and the way they treat each other at the time of a parent's death are very good indicators of their entire relationship. Even as adults, Tonia's sisters couldn't accept or appreciate her life, which had moved away from theirs. In childhood, she had power over them because they were left in her care. It was not a role she wanted, but her sisters probably made her the target—much like a stepmother—for their anger over not being cared for by their real mother. As adults they formed an alliance, finding safety in numbers, to take back her power and her mother's blessing.

Disputes over Dying Parents

Of all the punishments felt by the sister who leaves, the most painful is when she's excluded at her parent's deathbed. Typically, because she's been home the least, she's probably less ready to let go of her parents. Sisters who have a good relationship are usually sensitive to each other when their parents are dying. The death can bring them even closer. But I've noticed that angry sisters can not only be oblivious to each other's pain but remarkably cruel at this emotionally wrenching time. They are all feeling loss, and the worst may come out among sisters who haven't worked out their problems before.

The sister who's been far away often feels guilty about her absence. She may also find reasons to criticize the decisions of the one who was left in charge. The sister who's been around the dying parent resents any suggestion that what she has done might be less than perfect. In her view, the sister who left relinquished any right to determine what should happen in the end. It can end up in a permanent rift or in lasting regrets.

Maria Acosta grew up in a middle-class Colombian family; all five of her siblings were sent to the United States for college. While in school, Maria met and married an American man and eventually settled in the United States. Separated from her family in Colombia, Maria found that she mainly missed her mother. Maria had always felt that she was really her mother's confidante and favorite daughter.

Maria's sister Alicia is eleven years older; Maria dubbed her "the General" because she felt that Alicia was very controlling.

As their parents grew older, it was The General who was most involved in their care because she'd returned to Colombia and lived near them. But Maria still felt her mother was closer to her. "Alicia resented me because she didn't have a good relationship with my mother. She was rebellious as a teenager and they didn't get along well."

Every year, Maria made at least one trip to Bogota, and spent a couple of weeks there, visiting her mother. When her parents celebrated their fiftieth anniversary, Maria returned to Bogota for the celebration. As she was leaving, she got an uneasy feeling.

I had said good-bye to my mother at the airport many times. But that September she whispered in my ear, "I will never see you again."

She had leukemia and she was very tired, but she didn't say anything about it because they were celebrating their fiftieth anniversary, and she didn't want to spoil the occasion. When she said, I'll never see you again, it hit me so hard. It left me very worried, and I told my husband, because she'd never said anything like that before. Maybe I was afraid to say, "What's going on?"

That was in September. My mother died in November. They called me on Tuesday to say my mother was very sick, and I'd better come. I arrived the next day, on Wednesday, and she died on Saturday. It was very hard for me because my mother was in the ICU by the time I arrived. They wouldn't let me get close to her. She had septicemia, and they were afraid I might give her something worse.

I told my mother I was there. She knew. But I had to say hello from a distance, without embracing her. I was furious with the doctor and my sister. She had taken over, and she wouldn't let me near my mother.

I should have told my sister to jump in the lake, because I wanted to embrace my mother. They didn't let me near her. She was already in a coma when they let me get close. I didn't get to say how much I loved her.

My sister said to me, "I told you to visit more often." She was very resentful of me because she'd never had a good relationship with my mother, and when my parents got sick she had to deal with it. But there was nothing I could do because I lived here, in the United States.

Maria suffered a long time about the way she lost her mother. But in time, she ultimately forgave Alicia. "She was dominating and strong-willed, and I am, too...Now that she's in her sixties, she's mellower, and I'm fifty-four and I see life differently. I accept things and overlook things more than I used to. Her opinions aren't worth arguing about and she did have the burden of caring for our parents."

Sister Alliances

The alliance against the sister who leaves isn't inevitable. And alliances against the sister who is preferred aren't inevitable, either. The favorite daughter can make the choice to ally herself with her sisters, and then her favored status might not be so resented. I end with a story about three sisters where there was clearly a favorite and they didn't let their mother divide them. In this case, none of them moved far from their parents.

Susan was the oldest of three daughters born to a mother from Japan. Their mother had been brought to the United States when she married; severed from her family and culture, she never adapted to the move, and she remained depressed and angry for the rest of her life. She felt that her oldest daughter should be her constant companion—a role she considered to be traditional, and her due. But Susan felt her mother leaned on her because she'd never made friends here or worked outside her home, or learned to speak very much English.

Their mother made it very obvious that her oldest daughter was the preferred child; Susan was the sole executor of her will. Susan didn't accept this role without protest. "I teased her that she'd better appoint all my sisters as coexecutors, because she was going to drive me into the grave and would probably outlast me." In a way, Susan's mother had reversed roles, expecting Susan to make up for the mother she had lost. All her demands of Susan were rationalized as a way of fulfilling her obligations as a mother to instruct her oldest daughter in the proper way to live: "It's my duty as your mother to tell you..." was the preface to nearly everything she said. Susan felt her mother was jealous of Susan's own family. Her mother rarely asks about Susan's husband and took little interest in her grandchildren. It appeared that she wanted Susan all to herself.

All the sisters found their mother to be trying, though her excesses also gave them something to laugh and gossip about. Since their mother would try to divide them by telling each one the unpleasant things their other sisters had supposedly said about them (usually twisting and embellishing their words beyond recognition), the three sisters had made a pact to tell each other every critical remark their mother had attributed to any of them so they could clarify their real remarks and prevent her from driving them apart.

Now that their children are adults, every summer the three sisters take a two-week vacation together, without their husbands, because they really enjoy each other's company and have the most fun when they're alone and unencumbered by other ties. When their mother complained to Susan that she wanted to be invited in the holidays, Susan was firm about protecting her sisters' time together. If their mother came, it would spoil their vacation. Using her mother's words on duty and obligation, Susan explained they would miss her terribly, but they felt they had to sacrifice her company because they had a duty to put their father's needs first, and their father could never survive for two weeks without their mother.

Nadine and her sisters felt their parents treated them equally even though the sisters wound up with very different lives because of their varying talents and interests. That equal treatment from their parents has probably helped them maintain caring contacts even though Nadine's sisters don't relate to anything she's done except having chilren. Lila thinks her sister Christine is unreasonably resentful over being left behind in Guyana for five years when their parents first moved to the United States; in Lila's estimation, their mother treated them equally, and her greater success is due to her hard work. Tonia and Maria had interests and talents that moved them away from their birthplaces, so they weren't around when decisions that deeply concerned them were being made by others.

It's just a fact of life that whether or not parents love and treat their children equally, the circumstances of life will always create some inequalities among siblings. They have different talents and interests, they are born into their family at different times, and they wind up close or far from their birthplace because of other choices they make. But even if they're unavoidable, differences and inequalities don't need to divide sisters as long as they recognize each other's different needs and perceptions.

I have frequently noticed that, among families with three sisters, two are close and one is left out. On the other hand, I've also noticed that sisters pair up with a "closest" sister when there are four or more sisters. So alliances might grow around common interests rather than a primary wish to exclude someone. But even in families with three sisters and a mother who clearly favored one of them, divisions aren't inevitable. Susan's family is a good illustration. Susan and her sisters didn't let their mother divide them. They recognized that she tried to do this because she viewed anything that didn't revolve around her as a threat. They didn't blame Susan for being preferred, and she didn't view her mother's favoritism as evidence that she was more worthy. Most of all, they took practical steps to protect their sisterhood. They knew that relationships take work, and they made the efforts to secure what they valued.

CHAPTER 10

The Wishful Sister

THIS IS A STORY ABOUT NORA, a sister who kept giving and giving to her older sister and couldn't bear to see that her sister was incapable of returning her love. Why do people keep giving so much to a relationship or have high expectations for it when the other has never given much back? The inevitable comparison is to obsessive romantic attachments, where each rejection or disappointment only spurs the unrequited lover to make ever greater sacrifices, she's so desperate not to lose the object of her affections.

Thinking about Nora, I realized that sisters can also have a kind of unrequited love. Like romantic sufferings, these relationships are fueled by illusions. The wishful sister can't see her sister as she truly is because she thinks she needs her sister to give her what she never got from her mother. She may be desperately seeking someone she can depend on.

At fifty-two, Nora is a warm and attractive woman with dark hair and deep green eyes. She lives in Manhattan with her husband and her youngest daughter. Until she asked me to sit so that the light from the window would come from behind her, I didn't realize that she's legally blind.

Nora's sister, Fran, is fifty-four, and lives in Virginia. They haven't spoken in six months. Until recently, Nora thought they had a close and loving relationship; it took a dramatic event for "the scales to fall from [her] eyes" and for her to realize she'd always been blind to how one-sided that love really was.

I grew up on the Maryland shore, in a summer beach town that also had year-round residents. My sister Fran was born first. She lived with my mother and biological father until I was born two years later. When I was born, my parents separated and they never lived together again.

My mother had two little babies to support, so we moved into her mother's apartment and my grandmother raised us while my mother went to work. My grandmother lived in an apartment building right across the street from the ocean. We lived there until I was eight—a tiny little female group. My father was a serious drinker, and once in a while he and his mother would show up to take us out. I was about thirteen the last time I saw him.

My sister and I felt like we were a burden to my mother; for six years, until she remarried, she had to take care of us and her old mother.

I was born with a serious vision impairment—I'm legally blind. Early on, everyone knew I wouldn't see very well. Maryland has services for the blind, but there wasn't much service in the town where I lived. When I was six, someone came from the Commission for the Blind—I don't know how they found us; I went to a Catholic school—but after that, I got to go to a summer camp for blind children. For ten years I went to that camp for two weeks every summer, and then I worked there as a counselor for four years, so I was quite involved. Those two weeks every summer were my only contact with visually impaired kids.

I work at a vision research institute now, and we do all these things to help blind children and their families. But when I was a child, we had one visit a year. They'd say, How are you?—I'd say, I'm fine. Do you need anything? I'd say no. And then they would leave. But they were good people. They paid for me to go to college and graduate school, and I loved going to that camp. But this affected my sister. She thought that I was privileged and lucky to go to the camp. No one ever paid for her to go to camp.

My sister was supposed to walk me to school; I had no idea where the school was in relation to our apartment. I needed concrete landmarks, but the way we went there and back was always through alleys and labyrinths—small spaces in the back of apartment buildings and houses.

I was very, very dependent on Fran. I couldn't orient myself without landmarks, and it never occurred to my mother or anybody else to think it might be good for me to know how to get to school by myself, in case I lost my sister.

I know she didn't like taking me to school, because a cousin who was her age would walk with us, and—this is one of my strongest childhood memories—they'd say, "Poor Nora. Too bad she has the chicken pox; too bad she can't be with us today."

I'd be chasing after them, and I was mad, but I had to stay close. I knew they didn't want me to walk with them, but I had no option. I had to stick with them. We'd enter the school through the back way, and I was very disoriented. I had no way to learn the lay of the land.

I didn't tell my mother or grandmother my sister and cousin were mean to me, because I had no friends of my own. My sister was my total playmate until I was in the third grade and we moved. My grandmother was very strict, but she wasn't well, and she didn't keep track of where we went. We had 100 percent freedom, and we could go anywhere. My grandmother never asked where we were going.

My sister always took me across the street to the rock jetties on the beach. It was like a seawall made of rocks. I was very timid—I was always afraid I'd slip off. She'd walk all the way down, on the rocks, and I tried to stay as close to her as I could without going on the rocks. This petrified me. I didn't know if she would fall, or if I'd fall if I got too close to her. I have no depth perception at all. I need to hold someone's hand.

Privately, Fran and I were friends when we were young. We played cowgirls and with dolls, but only when we were home. In public, we were virtual strangers. Even in high school, she was having a difficult time fitting in, and I was a tremendous liability in her quest for social status. So she wouldn't talk to me in public. If I passed her in the school hall, she wouldn't say hi. She didn't want to be associated with me.

After the third grade, Nora started to have an easier time than Fran. Being a bright and engaging person, she eventually made friends and she did well in school, unlike her sister, and even though she couldn't even see the chalkboard. By the time she was nine, she also got bifocals that allowed her to read standard-size text.

My mother married when I was six and we moved when I was eight. My stepfather had visited us, and we called him Uncle Ed. Suddenly, he was Daddy. I had no idea they were going to get married, but you accept whatever you're told when you're a child. When I was eight, we moved to a bigger house, and my grandmother moved with us.

When we moved, a whole new world opened up for me. I could see down long streets. I knew how to get to school. I had friends. I felt like I was born. Before that, I'd been so isolated, it felt like I wasn't awake.

Coincidentally, her new daddy was physically handicapped. He'd lost his lower legs in World War II, at the age of nineteen, when he was struck by a grenade. Her stepfather had a good pension because he was considered 100 percent disabled, and he also ran a candy concession near the beach during the summers. Nora remembers him as a hard worker, but neither she nor Fran ever developed daughterly feelings toward him. Although he was disabled, he never spoke about it with Nora and did nothing to help her adjust to her near-blindness.

I tried out for the basketball team and cheerleading team; I thought I could do everything then. No one said I was getting rejected because I was nearly blind. I did feel I was incapable because I wasn't landing on too many things I could do. They told me I could be the equipment manager for the basketball team. I thought that was fine.

Fran's struggles at school affected Nora.

Everything was difficult for her. When Fran had to take chemistry, it was a catastrophe for the whole family. No one could play the radio at home because she had to write up her lab report. When I took the dreaded chemistry class, two years later, it was so easy—even though I couldn't see the periodic table. I'd expected chemistry would be like death, based on her experience. For the first time, I realized that life didn't have to be so disastrous as it was for her. Everything was so hard for her—even learning to drive. I think she was very anxious from an early age.

Nora did feel out of the running when it came to boys or being friends with the most admired girls:

My sister and I both had the "second"-team friends, not the most popular kids, but a nice group of people. With my girlfriends in high school, I felt secure—it was great. I wasn't going to parties—I felt I looked weird—but we never discussed my vision impairment in my family, so I had no vehicle to deal with it. I felt very rejected, socially, by boys. But I thought that's just how it will be, and I had my girlfriends.

My mother was paying minimal attention; she didn't know how to understand my sister, or how to help her. My parents made her contribute some of her babysitting money to the family. It was their work ethic. By then they didn't need her babysitting money. She didn't get along with my stepfather; they didn't like each other. She was making bids for attention, so she fought with him over everything.

I asked Nora whether her sister was competing with her stepfather for her mother's attention.

My mother was devoted to him. She stopped working and spent all day driving my stepfather around. And there's not a lot of my mother to go around.

I shared a room with my sister, and one of my happiest memories was talking each other to sleep. We took turns—whoever's turn it was had to keep talking until the other fell asleep. We'd ask, "Are you awake?" These were moments of intimacy we shared before sleeping.

Fran was trying to go out into the world, and she had very nice taste. When she was young, she decided she would have a beautiful house and nice things when she grew up. In her effort to acquire social status, my sister bought expensive clothes from her own babysitting money, and it became a source of conflict. I didn't care about clothes and could ally myself with my mother. My mother was very practical and my sister was extravagant. My mother didn't like it that she wanted to spend money on things like that.

In high school, neither one of us dated. Fran felt terrible that she didn't go to her prom. I was in the same boat, but we never talked about it.

To compound the dating problem, Nora's counselor convinced her to go to an all-female junior college, and Nora followed this bad advice. But her sister had greater ambitions, as Nora recalls, and was always in search of a glamorous life. Fran made a friend in college who was dating a student at Princeton. Fran met Steve, her friend's boyfriend's roommate, and her social life took off.

I was at this Catholic junior college and regressing socially. Fran invited me to go on a blind date at Princeton—a date I agreed to with great trepidation. I had absolutely no experience with boys, and this was trial by fire. This was a date for a whole weekend.

Fran's boyfriend was named Steve, and they'd fixed me up with a friend of Steve's named Ross. Sometimes, I'm looking very hard at someone to follow what they're saying, and I don't see anything. Fran and Ross liked each other a lot. Steve was her boyfriend, and Ross was supposed to be my date, but she ditched Steve and started taking to Ross. She wound up marrying Ross—he became my brother-in-law.

In retrospect, Nora sees this event as a classic Fran.

She didn't think twice about screwing you. She should have told me she liked Ross, because I had no investment in him, but she didn't. I couldn't see what was happening until I saw them blatantly flirting. She screws you, and then she makes you feel sorry for her.

I think that was the first time I realized what she would do to me. Knowing how vulnerable I felt there—it was like I was walking around naked. I couldn't have felt more vulnerable than I did with so many guys there, walking around, and I was having trouble keeping up with the conversation. Ross was a difficult date: He was so smart, making quips—one right after the other—and I couldn't figure out what they meant. I don't like that kind of humor.

Prior to this weekend at Princeton, the sisters had been getting closer, and when Fran married Ross, Nora was her maid of honor. But Fran's social triumph soon turned into unending tragedies.

They married in 1969, in the middle of the Vietnam War, two days before my stepfather died. Ross did go to Vietnam, and while he was away, my sister gave birth to her first son, John. During this time, I finished college and earned a master's degree in special education for the visually impaired. I moved to New York in 1975 when I got my first job here—they hired me on the phone when I was twenty-three—and I met my husband a year later. After John was born, my sister gave birth to Billy and David.

When Billy was seven years old, he got leukemia. I was pregnant with my second son then. Ironically, we both had three children. They were some years apart since I started eight years later. Everyone rallied to help my sister and Billy while he went through chemo. At that time, they were just starting to have cures for childhood leukemia, and they didn't know what would happen to him.

When Billy was twelve, the leukemia came back, and that's really bad. This time he had a bone marrow transplant, and my mother and Pete—he's the man who'd been my mother's companion since my stepfather died—took care of my sister's other children while Billy was being treated. Initially, Ross was not compassionate, but he became a better person after they went through this. Billy recovered from the bone marrow transplant, but the doctors said they had no idea what all the radiation had done to him or what would happen. The kid stayed at home for a couple of years after the bone marrow transplant, having homeschooling.

Then Ross died suddenly of a heart attack, at age forty. It was so sad to see his life end like that. He was very intelligent and handsome.

Fran was a wreck. She'd been a stay-at-home mom, and her whole social life was with Ross. They'd moved around so much, and she didn't have many friends, and none in Virginia, where they'd lived since Billy was sick.

Billy started college and didn't do so well. He flunked out because he spent all his time skiing and doing things that were fun. I think he knew he'd better have some good times.

The next year, when he was nineteen, he came to live with us, because he hoped to go to New York University. My youngest son was eight, the age Billy got sick, and my oldest son was twelve. I think Billy had lost all those years being sick since he was eight, and he could reexperience those years living with my kids. It was very poignant. He had a wonderful year, but my sister hated it that he was here and that he wanted to live with me.

Billy was getting terrible headaches and it made me very worried. He acted as if they were nothing, because he didn't want to be sick. In June, Billy went home, and got a clean bill of health when he was examined. But just a month later, he was diagnosed with brain cancer. Now he had a death sentence, and he'd spent his last good year here.

You'd have to know Billy was dying, but my family, especially Fran, lives in a culture of denial. At Christmas he came here, and at Easter we went on a hiking trip. I think he knew he'd get more attention from us, because we adored him. Billy and I had a strong identification from being disabled. He'd been bald for years, from all the chemo, and he'd never fit back into high school after being sick. He'd had too many adult experiences. And my children loved him, because he played with them.

To do a bone marrow transplant in 1984, you had to do total body irradiation, including radiation to the brain. That's probably what did it. Plus, for a while they'd lived in a town where there was a pocket of childhood cancer...He died at home in 1993. Fran's other two kids are just waiting to die. Four years ago, Fran's youngest son, David, moved to New York and stayed with us for ten months. He lives nearby, and we're very close.

Fran's oldest son, John, also needed to run away from his mother. At one point, he got a new address and phone number and refused to give them to his mother for a couple of years:

He'd visit or call his mother occasionally, but he wanted their contact to be on his terms and to be the one who initiated the contact. I think that was a bold, brave thing for him to do. Fran thought he was troubled. Maybe it wasn't John who was troubled. She wanted those kids to take care of her after the two deaths.

When Billy spent his last good year with us, my sister wasn't even grateful that we were putting ourselves out for him, financially and emotionally. She acted like we were trying to keep him here. She'd call on Christmas and just ask to talk with him, like we were the enemy.

I've made a lot of mistakes, but I've devoted my entire life to kids, while Fran has devoted her life to her spouse—so this was a place for her kids to go.

Why would Nora keep opening her heart to draining experiences, when her sister was so unappreciative? I'm sure part of it was that she had an independent affection for her nephew and wanted to do whatever she could to give him some happiness, no matter how badly her sister acted. But there's more to it. Nora was still willing to accept mean behavior from her sister because for some reason she felt dependent on her, and felt she had to sustain the relationship at any cost.

She went on to tell me about Fran's romantic involvements after she became a young widow:

When things were bad, she would always go for these boyfriends because she needed attention and help. Whenever she was dating, she'd always be telling me all the personal details of her sex life that I didn't want to know. I tried not to let her go into it, but she didn't have any close friends . . . I also felt so bad for her. She had such a raw deal in her life, and she was always so lonely and unhappy. It got to the point where it was out of control. I couldn't take it when she started to complain about my mother.

I had the role as the listener; I'm the one everyone talks to because I don't offer an opinion they don't want to hear. I'm supportive, even though I often don't agree. I don't like unnecessary conflict, so I don't say things.

I thought we were very close, despite our little ups and downs until two years ago, this July. Her son John had just married, and she realized the man she was dating at the time was not going to marry her. Then, the very next week, she met Clark on a sailboat. At fifty-two, Fran was taking a sailing course. She's youthful that way.

I'm hearing all about Clark—okay, I'm used to her boyfriends. Then I hear that Clark had been married for thirty-eight years and his wife had been dead for only one month when this romance began. So in my listening role, I heard all about Clark, and it was worrisome to Mother and me.

She told me, "Clark says he'll be married by next July, no matter who it is." I told her that doesn't sound good, and she didn't want to hear it.

Clark is very controlling. My sister had a good job that paid for her social security and she was earning as much I do—even with all my degrees. Clark wanted her to quit, because he's older and retired, and he has more money. She didn't quit, but she went part-time. She also had a darling house, and Clark wanted her to sell her house, and move into his house, which she did.

He's such a baby and he's so selfish. Although he has more money than she does, they split everything fifty-fifty in their relationship. She went to a lawyer to review the prenuptial agreement Clark wanted, and the lawyer told her it was terrible and not to sign it. When she's feeling desperate, she confides in me. But she did what he wanted to keep him. She must have told Clark that Mother and I were worried about his making her give up her job and her house, because ever since then, he's wanted to have nothing to do with us.

As Fran got more involved with Clark, she needed Nora less, and cut her off progressively. Nora was supposed to bow out gracefully, just as she used to do when they passed each other in the hallway in grade school.

One day she told me, "Clark said he's not sure about our relationship anymore because he doesn't want all the excess baggage."

I said, "Are you, by any chance, referring to me as excess baggage?"

She didn't say no.

And that was where our relationship broke down. That was February. My mother's companion of twenty-nine years, Pete, died in May, and my sister got married in July.

First, she refused to come to Pete's funeral, even though Pete and his family had been so nice to my sister. Instead of coming to the funeral, she and Clark went on a holiday. They had to drive practically right by my mother's house on their way, but they didn't stop. I was astounded. My mom and Pete could not have done more for Fran while Billy and Ross were dying. Pete had cancer that had metastasized to his lungs. Fran said that she couldn't be around more sick people. She said, "I can't go to any more funerals in my life." It was phenomenally selfish.

She got married in July, and no one in the family was invited. Sometime later, my sister had the audacity to tell us they'd invited their friends for drinks at their wedding. I had actually gone to Maryland to visit my mother when my sister was getting married. I went there thinking that if I was there she'd invite me. She got married in the dead of summer when we always get together. My aunt—my mother's sister—also thought she would call. My aunt and my mother and I all got together and broke out the champagne. I was hopeful she would call.

Nora was devastated when there was no invitation from Fran. She felt like she was in mourning for the rest of the summer.

I'm trying to recover and ignore her, if possible. I did write her a long letter, because Mom's health started to deteriorate after Pete's death and because she was so upset that Fran wasn't at the funeral. It was just colossally embarrassing for her. Everyone kept asking, "Where's Fran?" Everyone in the family had helped her through her tragedies, sending her money and food.

In my letter, I told her she died for me the same day that Pete died. That the person I knew no longer exists. I told her, "If Mother dies, I'll hold you responsible. Don't you remember how we came to your aid when Billy and Ross died?"

She never responded to my letter, and I didn't call her after the wedding. I felt so hurt. I had shared, fairly willingly, in a lot of tragedy in her life. I had made many trips, prior to their dying, to help. That she had a happy event that she didn't invite us to was more than I could deal with. Maybe it was because Clark is tight with money, I don't know. I can't say. What scared me is how she has changed. I feel he has lots of control over her, or maybe she really didn't change, and I just saw it, and that's probably it.

Then it was tragic to me. Everything—going all the way back—came into a different focus. Like her taking Ross, when he was supposed to be my date. The year of her being mean to us when we were good to Billy, the last year of his life. A month ago, I was feeling I missed her, so we had a few polite phone calls, semi-caring phone calls.

Nora went on to say that no one in her birth family—mother, sister—really knows her anymore. She has been traveling around the world giving papers about international issues concerning the blind. No one in her family seems to notice or congratulate her.

It seems Nora's family has never appreciated her considerable strengths and achievement or her passion for helping people with vision problems. To be legally blind and travel around the world presenting papers at international conferences is a remarkable achievement.

Fran did apologize to my mother for not going to the funeral, and she's visited her. Now they are close. There's always been a triangle between my mother, my sister, and me. Always two of us talking about the third one. I was usually the one both were talking to because I was far away, and they live near each other. There's always a dyad, and one of us is always the outsider, and now it's me. I'd rather be out than have my mother be the one who is out, because she's breaking down.

I asked Nora why she craves this contact with Fran when her sister has never been caring or kind to her. She told me she really enjoyed Fran's visits and doing things with her and going shopping for clothes. She can't see well enough to know what is flattering to her, and Fran has exquisite taste. But Nora has close friends and surely one of them could go shopping with her, if her husband can't. I was thinking she might actually be better off regarding her closest friend as her "sister." Nora's answer to my question really explains the craving for Fran—it's a special kind of emotional dependence.

> I think I needed her. I didn't really have a mother. I didn't have a father. I needed her. I feel it's a tragedy because I don't have her. It can never go back to what it was before. I have a tremendous sense of loss. I just can't accept the truth that she wouldn't be there if I needed her. I can't understand how she didn't go to Pete's funeral. I saw it when she didn't defend me to Clark. She sacrificed me for Clark. How could she forget us, after fifty-two years?
>
> I guess I have a fantasy of a family that didn't exist from day one. My grandmother died when I was just turning fourteen. I missed her quite a bit. She didn't really talk to us, but she had a presence and provided care. My sister and mother are all I have—there are no other relatives. So I keep going back, like a magnet.

I think Nora hits the nail on the head when she says she is drawn back like a magnet because of the original loss. These escalating sacrifices to someone who won't give back do have the quality of an addiction. The wishful sister just can't stop herself from trying to get a fix of something she feels she can't live without.

When you're younger you have fantasies that things will improve. The greatest tragedy is to lose hope. I have hope that my sister and I will know each other. It won't be what I wanted... It is hopefulness that fuels not seeing the truth. Or, I feel I could get depressed without hope.

I'm certain the sadness Nora would feel at giving up her sister bond is fueled by the original loss of growing up without a father and barely having very much a mother. Her sister wasn't much, but Fran was all she had. Now, whenever Nora has any feeling of loss or disappointment in the family she made—even a conflict with her husband or son—it may generate the old anxiety and make her yearn to feel connected and supported by the original family she never had, and her sister was the main connection.

Younger sisters who look to their big sisters for caring that should have come from a mother or a father in childhood often feel a double abandonment: first, by their parents and later by their sister, because their view of her is driven by their wishes rather than a realistic appraisal of what she's likely to give. Sometimes, that wish persists for a lifetime, despite countless disappointments. For some, wishful and unrealistic expectations of their sister just surge when a life event (a loss, a crisis, or even a happy event like having a baby) reawakens their needs or wishes for a mother to help them.

In a situation where there hasn't been much parental love or nurturing, it's not just the younger sister who unconsciously looks for mothering from her sister. The younger one is usually more aware of her dependency because it was so obvious when she was a child. But an older sister often extracts mothering from the younger one, too, by expecting her sister to be a constant audience for her life and her concerns. When Fran expected Nora to be always available to hear her woes, she was looking for a kind of mothering, and she didn't give it back. Parents are supposed to watch over children, not the reverse. Having missed that attention originally, Fran wants everyone (her children as well as her sister) to give it to her. And Nora has always accommodated Fran because her sister was originally all she had.

Maybe this transference of expectations from mother to sister occurs because, growing up, we share our mother with our sisters, so the boundaries become indistinct. Some sisters are able to give each other this kind of care when it's needed, and being able to count on each other is a priceless gift. It's the sisters who act out of blind hope, not heeding the warning signs, who really get into trouble.

PART THREE

Making Amends

CHAPTER 11

From Imagined Sisters
to Real Sisters

I'VE MOVED FROM SISTERS who are close to sisters who are divided. But these aren't fixed categories, impermeable to change. I want to end with sisters who found each other later in life and came into an unexpected pleasure. There are many women who don't have close sisters, or sisters at all. They say their friends are their true sisters.

It is often easier to be closer to your friends than your relatives; your friends often have a lot more in common with the adult you've become. I don't discount what friends have to offer that sisters might not provide. But there is still something powerful about family and biological connections that's just different.

I learned this from someone who grew up without biological relatives. Nina Silver was always looking for her birth mother, but she found something even better—her sisters. She also taught me that sisters aren't just about sharing a childhood. The biological connection is powerful and profound.

Discovered Sisters

Nina Silver didn't meet her two half sisters until she was fifty-three, but all her life she had fantasies they might be out there. Occasionally she'd hear about someone who looked just like her, and she'd wonder if that person was a relative.

Nina was adopted in Ossining, New York, when she was ten weeks old. Her adoptive mother told her about it when she was four or five. She didn't really wonder about her birth family until her pre-teen years, when she started to think a lot about her physical appearance and how she didn't look like anyone in her family. Her parents had also adopted two sons five and six years before they adopted Nina, but they were so much older Nina felt almost like an only child. She had friends who had sisters, and she always imagined what it would be like to have one: In her fantasy, a sister would be a friend for life and give her unconditional love and acceptance.

Nina's mother let her see her adoption papers when she became a teenager. In the late 1940s, when Nina was born, the adoption agencies didn't give out a lot of information. But a secretary had made a mistake, and her birth mother's name, Laura Mathis, had been left on the papers. For years, whenever Nina would travel to a different place in New York, she'd search the phone listings for that last name, and call up, asking if Laura was there.

I became more curious after I had children of my own. I thought I was mainly interested in learning about inherited health characteristics. But once I had given birth to a child, I thought a lot about what my birth mother must have been thinking and feeling. I just wanted to know about the circumstances of my birth and about health things. If anyone I called had said, "That's me," I probably would have hung up! I would just call and ask if they were related to Laura Mathis, and they would say no.

I had a friend who was also adopted and she'd heard of an organization that helped people find their biological relatives. We went to a meeting together and they told me that since I had a name, I could look for it in a statewide registry of marriages. I started looking at the year after I was born and found my mother's name in the registry. I sent away for a copy of her marriage license—it was public information. When I got it, it listed her husband's name, her parents' names, and where she was born—Queens, New York.

My mother's phone number wasn't listed, but I called her mother—my maternal grandmother. I was thirty-five then. When she answered the phone, I asked if Laura was there, and told her I was an old friend of her daughter's and wanted to find her. She just gave me my mother's number in Long Island and told me it wasn't listed.

I called my birth mother right away. When she answered, I asked, Is this Laura Mathis, and is this a good time to talk? I asked her if my birth date meant anything to her. She said no, but why was I asking? I told her I was looking for my birth mother, and I said I guess I had the wrong number. I don't know why I didn't push it. Maybe I didn't want to be rejected, or I thought maybe she couldn't speak then.

She said, "Wait, wait. You do have the right person." I could hear she was hyperventilating. She told me no one knew about this, and she would try to call me another time. That was twenty years ago. We had a relationship on the phone for eighteen years before we ever met.

She actually called me a day later and told me she'd never told anyone about this pregnancy except for her mother and a family friend who was a doctor in Westchester, where she went to stay until she had the baby. After I was born, she and her mother never spoke about it again. She was told she should just move on and put it all behind her. They went home a few days after I was born. She told me she would die if anyone found out about this, but she maintained a secret correspondence with me and we'd talk on the phone a few times a year.

She told me she has a very vague memory of my birth father. She'd become infatuated with an older military officer—he was about twenty-eight [when she was eighteen] in 1947. He had been in the war and was still in the service. She saw him only a few times, and he never knew she was pregnant. This is what she told me. I've wondered if she's covering up something—if maybe he was married. I've wondered if she knows more about him. I've also thought maybe she doesn't know who my father is; maybe she was having sex with more than one man and doesn't want to admit it.

She'd call, or I would call. We always had to be careful, to make sure her husband wouldn't hear anything. In the 1940s it was considered immoral to have sex if you weren't married. She swears if her husband had known about her pregnancy, he wouldn't have married her. Or if he found out later, it would have damaged their marriage. My feeling is he might have felt betrayed she kept this secret for thirty-five years, and that it wouldn't have been good.

I did tell my mother I'd found my birth mother. She'd encouraged me to look for her, after I had children. My mother was very brave about it, but I think it was threatening to her. I asked my mother if she had anything she wanted me to say to Laura, and she said, "Yes, thank her for me." I told Laura this, and she seemed very touched. She said, "Tell your mother I said thank you, too." I didn't tell my adoptive mother that I was continuing to have conversations with Laura. I didn't want her to feel threatened, or to think I felt there was something lacking in my life with her. There's a curiosity that has nothing to do with feeling any lack. But adoptive parents always seem to think you feel that way.

About ten years ago, my adoptive mother passed away. Then Laura's mother passed away and her husband passed away—all within two years, around '94 or '95. She went into a deep depression for a couple of years and then she moved to be closer to her older daughter. I didn't know her address, but after a while, Laura told me I had siblings, but not their names. I didn't ask any questions about them; I didn't want to threaten her and make her feel I'd show up with a suitcase. She told me she had two daughters and a son, and eventually she told me their first names. She didn't want them to know anything about me—she was afraid they'd think badly of her.

Nina had always deeply missed having relatives she was biologically connected to. Before she found her birth mother, her only biological connection was to her children. Her adoptive mother and father had divorced when she was two, and her father had moved away. She'd gotten to know him only briefly; when she was an adult he returned to the Hudson River Valley to be near his family when he was terminally ill. Nina had relatives (grandparents and aunts and uncles) from his side of the family, but they never really accepted her as "blood." They never visited her on holidays or sent her birthday gifts. They treated her differently from the other children because she wasn't biologically connected—something that always hurt her deeply. So mainly, Nina had grown up alone with her adoptive mother and felt slightly suffocated because she felt her mother was controlling and wouldn't let her be her own person.

Nina is a striking-looking woman: very tall and slim, with a great sense of style. She always looks perfectly put together. She could have been a model, and ironically, both her mother and birth mothers were models when they were young. But despite her lovely appearance she always felt like an "ugly duckling" because she looked different from everyone else in her family. She also felt she never developed self-confidence as a child because her mother was controlling and didn't accept or approve of her choices and interests.

It seemed likely to me that losing her father at age two in addition to being ignored by his family must have added to that insecurity. But Nina dismissed this idea. She felt her adoptive father had not played any role in her life, and that he hadn't affected her. She attributed her problems to her mother's controlling nature. I think it's easier to recognize the impact of someone you've struggled with than the impact of a void.

I also wondered why Nina hadn't been as curious about her birth father. If her interest had really been to learn about her health background and the circumstances of her birth, finding her birth father would have been just as relevant. Her birth mother told Nina his name or what she thought was his name, but when Nina didn't turn up anything in a casual search, she stopped pursuing it. Perhaps she feared jeopardizing her relationship with her birth mother if she pursued her birth father or actually found him, since it was very obvious that Laura didn't want to discuss this part of her life. Nina told me she always felt a deeper connection to her birth mother because her mother had carried her for nine months, and being a mother herself, she knows what that feels like.

I wondered if the early departure of Nina's adoptive father led her to think of parents primarily in terms of mothers. To separate herself from her adoptive mother, Nina had gotten involved with a "bad boy" when she was fifteen, married him at seventeen, and wound up having two children right away, instead of going to college first, as her mother had always planned. That marriage ended after six years, but she later married a loving and supportive man who has been her husband for the last twenty-five years. Together, they've raised her children from her first marriage as well as his children from his first marriage. So she's seen an example of a good father.

After Laura's mother and husband died, she really had no good excuse for keeping Nina at arm's length or not wanting to meet her. It disappointed Nina that Laura still insisted that she must remain a deep, dark secret. The idea that Laura's children would think badly of her for having had premarital sex and getting pregnant when abortions were not available seemed absurd in the current context.

Actually, Laura's oldest daughter, Linda, discovered the secret by accident when she was helping her mother close up her grandmother's house in 1995. They were going through a trunk in the attic, when Linda discovered a little pencil drawing of a baby on a yellowed scrap of paper, and, showing it to her mother, asked what it was. Laura was overwhelmed when she saw the picture. She had drawn it the day she had given up her baby, so she wouldn't forget what her baby looked like. But her mother had taken the sketch away and told her she must put the baby out of her mind. Laura had always assumed her mother had destroyed the drawing almost fifty years before, and she became agitated when she saw it. So she blurted out the story to Linda and admitted that she'd been corresponding with Nina for the past fourteen years. She also made Linda swear she would not tell a soul about it—not even her sister or brother or husband. So now Linda was in on the secret, which she dutifully kept for three years.

Nina felt hurt that her birth mother wasn't that thrilled about her reappearance, and that she remained so guarded with her. So she didn't push for a meeting. At one point, she had to go to a conference on Long Island near where Laura and her daughter Linda lived, and Laura finally said, "Well, let's do it. Let's meet when you come." This was seventeen years into their phone relationship.

I told her I'd call at a certain time, after my conference was over. But when I called, there wasn't any answer. I didn't try again. When I got home, my husband said, "Guess who called?" My birth mother had been calling my house frantically, claiming she didn't hear the phone ring when I called. My husband told me he'd had a long conversation with Laura, for the first time.

A few months later, I was having dinner with a friend and she said, "You know she's getting older. She's in her seventies. Are you ever going to do it?" Some months later, my birth mother called and said, "Let's do it." The next day, I drove back to Long Island.

Linda had helped to prepare food and bought flowers for my arrival. She wanted to meet me, but she thought my first meeting with my mother should be one-to-one, so she'd left before I arrived. The second time, they both came up to Westchester together, and they spent several days at my house. I had a relationship with Laura, because we'd been speaking on the phone for nearly twenty years, but I'd only heard about my sister during the last few years.

When I first saw Linda, I was disappointed she didn't look like me. But she has a great personality. She's very bright and funny and entertaining. She makes you laugh. We like doing a lot of the same things, and I really enjoy hanging out with her. She has a daughter in college and a son from a previous marriage. My other sister, Kim, lives in Florida, and she comes to New York only once a year. She and my brother were finally told about me after my first visit with Laura. My brother is quite young—he's sixteen years younger than I am. He's forty, and Kim is forty-six or forty-seven, and Linda just turned fifty. They were all happy to find out they had another sister—and they couldn't understand why their mother had burdened herself with this secret all her life.

Kim is very different from Linda. She's very earthy and spiritual. She's into healing, and I think she always wants to heal me. But they're both very loving and receptive and welcoming. They say we are sisters, and we're starting from here. We'll make our own memories and blaze our own trail. Linda told me she wants to make up to me for what their mother did—depriving me of knowing my family. But I said that wasn't her responsibility.

Nina imagines she would have been a more self-confident person if she'd grown up with Laura as her mother.

I think my birth mother allowed Linda to do her own thing, because her mother had been so controlling. My birth mother raised her children to feel independent; they're very confident so they're different than I am, in that way. I also think they are way prettier than I am. I look like my birth mother. Linda looks like her dad, and Kim looks like a combination of my birth mother and her dad.

I never found out anything more about my birth father. I get the feeling Laura doesn't want to get into it. Linda is actually more interested in this. I think my mother is resistant because either she doesn't really know who the father is or maybe she's protecting someone like a married man. Or maybe the officer from the air force was married. I can tell she doesn't want to go there.

She just told me she met this guy at a dance. He was a paratrooper lieutenant, and she fell head over heels in love with him, and ended up in trouble. She didn't tell her mother until she was four or five months pregnant. She didn't go back to tell him. She barely said his name to me. Is she trying to protect someone? She told me she used a neighbor's name on the adoption papers. She's given a name to me, but it's not the right spelling because I checked military records and it's not there.

Maybe she's not sure who the father is, and as a mother she doesn't want her daughters to know she was promiscuous. Parents think they need to be moral puritans to set an example. I don't think she'll tell me. If I had a name, I'd want to find out about him. What do I have to lose? I often look at my kids and wonder, where is this coming from? She told me he was very tall, and I'm tall and my son is six feet four.

Having a relationship with my sisters and my mother gives me a connection I didn't have before—to something real. I'm not in touch with the adopted cousins I grew up with, but there isn't a week that goes by when I don't hear from both of my sisters—a letter, a picture, or a phone call. And they stay in touch with each other. Once a year, Linda goes to Florida, and Kim comes to New York.

They are saying I'm an equal part. When Kim comes to New York this year, they're all meeting at my house. I'm wondering if they feel responsible because of their mother . . . the sins of the mother. They are sweet and responsible. Do they really want to do this, or do they just think they should do this? I hope they're not just doing this because they are wonderful people.

I don't trust other people very easily—that they mean what they say. I've heard it's related to not bonding. My first husband used to say, "Do I have to crawl across the freeway to convince you I love you?" I felt that really young. I wanted unconditional love, but my mother was controlling and domineering. Her feelings and what she wanted were most important. She knew what was best for me. How to dress and how to wear my hair. I let her control me. It's why I got married so young—to get out. I met my first husband when I was seventeen, and married someone she didn't like. He was kind of naughty and irresponsible. I found him fascinating because he was so different from me. We were together for six years, and I was on my own for five. Then I met my second husband when I was twenty-seven. He's the only person I really trust. He's so responsible, more like the father I would have wanted—family-oriented, consistent, true to his word, independent, and smart. He doesn't criticize me. After I left home, my adoptive mother and I became good friends. She was wonderful to my kids; she was a wonderful grandmother.

I feel like my sisters are very good friends. They've known each other all their lives. They were there for each other's weddings and kids and birthdays. They are very loyal to each other, and never put each other down. Will I ever have that connection, because of the time and years we didn't have? They'll be in my life—I don't know how much, to be realistic. It takes time to have a relationship.

I know this is silly, but I've noticed a difference in how my birth mother acts toward them and toward me. She wasn't my mother. She has mothering things that happen with them and not with me. She told me, "We don't do gifts in the family" but she does gifts with them. She did mother them, and she didn't mother me, so I think it would be bizarre if there wasn't a difference, and it's okay. But I still notice it.

My sisters are trying harder than my mother to be like a family. They are all-accepting. They said, You'll jump on and we'll go on from here. There was one incident. Linda's daughter had her high school graduation and all the other family members were there. All the old aunties (from their father's side). I couldn't go, because my mother doesn't want them to find out about me.

I always wanted a sister, but that wasn't my goal in finding my mother. I wanted to find out what happened, and she made it possible.

Linda

I spoke to Linda a few days after talking with Nina. I was certainly curious to hear how they'd integrated these revelations into their view of their mother. Nina remembers her childhood as dull and constrained. Linda's recollections of childhood were the opposite. She began by telling me her father met her mother on a bet. The story they told about the meeting was that her mother was a gorgeous twenty-year-old redhead sitting in a Manhattan nightclub, and her father, who looked like Cary Grant, bet his friend a hundred dollars he'd be able to talk her into having a drink.

Making bets was her father's life. He was a professional gambler, a wiseguy and bookie who arranged bets on everything from horses to football. He also opened gambling casinos in Las Vegas and the Caribbean. He would come and go, like their fortunes. One day the family wouldn't own a car, and the next they'd have a Lincoln Continental convertible. One of Linda's fondest memories is when her mother (who could be overprotective) was diagnosed with tuberculosis and had to spend six months in isolation in a sanatorium. So her father took her with him everywhere on his usual rounds to pool halls and bars or wherever he was collecting money. When she was still in diapers, she remembers sitting in the back of his convertible with the top down and thinking this was the life.

Their father was the mystery man in the neighborhood. All her friends would ask, What does he do? She told them he dug for gold, because she thought that sounded exciting. But their unusual life all seemed very normal to her. She remembers that people were just drawn to him; he was so brilliant and funny and handsome. "He wasn't fun, but you wanted him to pay attention to you. He had power. We all wanted his approval. If you'd ask him, 'Don't I look pretty?' he'd say, 'I'd tell you if you looked terrible.'"

Linda couldn't quite figure out the relationship between her parents, because they weren't openly affectionate. Sometimes they'd have a drink and put on a Stan Getz album and dance around the living room. Her little sister, Kim, wanted conventional parents and would cry when they danced because she didn't think it was proper.

Linda remembers her mother being gorgeous when she was young. In retrospect, she thinks her mother was a wild and beautiful creature until she got her wings clipped by becoming pregnant and being forced by her mother to give away Nina. After that, Linda thinks her mother just went back into her cage, a passive object that her mother, and later her husband, could just move around.

As a child, Linda couldn't stand Kim, who was three years younger. She remembers her as being whiny and clinging.

She snooped in my stuff and would read my diary out loud. She snooped in my parents' room. One day she found the *Joy of Sex* in their closet. Nothing went by my sister. She was Inspector Clouseau. Why did she look for trouble, if she wanted everything to be perfect?

She'd cling to your leg, and she just wanted to be with her big sister. My mother didn't force her on me. She said, "Be nice to her," but I ditched her. She'd pretend to have asthma attacks if I was mean to her. I'd just push her down the stairs. We didn't become close until I became pregnant when I was seventeen, and my boyfriend was sent to prison on drug charges. After my baby was born she helped me, and we became very close.

When her parents first discovered Linda was pregnant, her mother became hysterical while her father was reassuring and made her feel safe and loved. He told her she could keep the baby and the family would help her.

Linda married her boyfriend, and he proved to be an abusive husband when he was released from prison. As I later heard from Kim, Linda's younger sister, he also began to molest Linda's younger sister when Kim came over to babysit. But Kim was too terrified to tell anyone what he'd done. Instead, she just stopped going to her sister's apartment.

One night, Linda's husband crawled through Kim's bedroom window only to find his mother-in-law there! Kim had gone out of town for the weekend with friends, and Mrs. Mathis was sleeping in her daughter's room to get a break from her husband's snoring. When Mr. and Mrs. Mathis demanded to know why he'd crawled into Kim's window, he claimed he was there to deliver drugs, but now Kim reported that he'd been molesting her, and nobody doubted that she was telling the truth. Linda immediately asked for a divorce, but her husband was frightening her. Linda recalled that her wiseguy father arranged to have her husband beat up to send him the message that he was never to come near Linda or Kim again.

Linda thinks she has always been totally unlike her younger sister. "Kim married a devout Christian and became religious herself, because it made her feel secure. She lives in a world she thinks is controlled by God and gives everything up to that. While I'll make something happen, she'll go with the flow of life. She's like my mother—very passive."

But Linda admired her sister's attitude when their father was dying of terminal heart failure in the hospital. At one point, he had a cardiac arrest, and Linda told me that if she had been in the room, she would have called a code blue and had everyone pounding on her father's chest. But Kim was there and calmly held him and told him he could let go. Linda feels he died in a beautiful way, because he was with Kim, and that she wouldn't have been able to handle it. She knew her mother would fall apart once her father died. With his death, she really lost both of her parents.

After their grandmother and father died within six months of each other, their mother became severely depressed, and never recovered. According to Linda, Laura sank into a chair and never got up. She was so completely helpless that Linda had to sell her mother's house and move her mother close to where she lives. She told me her mother is so anxious, she's driving her crazy. Linda and Kim are very close, but Linda feels a little resentful about carrying the burden of their mother while Kim is off in Florida, enjoying nature and living a peaceful life. "When I go on vacation, I need to put a girlfriend on call in case Mother needs something. What can I do? Kim is in Florida, and my mother is afraid to fly, so she won't go there. Nina can't do it, after not getting any of the benefits all her life."

Linda adores Nina; she says Nina's arrival in her life turned out to be the best thing that's happened to her.

From the moment I met her, I loved her. We were on the phone for three hours last night. When I met Nina, I felt I knew her all my life. I can't explain it. You don't need to know someone your whole life to feel she's your older sister. I think it's genetic. I love her like I love my sister Kim.

I feel I've always known her. She's like my mother. She looks and moves like my mother. Nina's not comfortable. She feels like the ugly duckling—the odd man out. She's insecure and puts herself down. She said she didn't expect to have a relation-ship with my mother, but they had a relationship on the phone, and in a way, she has a closer relationship with our mother than my sister and I do. Mother still reminds me to wash my hands and to call her the moment I get home. But Nina can talk to her, and they can relate like two women. It's because Nina is the way she is, so natural and normal.

Linda can't understand why her mother refused to meet Nina after her husband died. But after her mother blurted the truth to her, her mother made her swear she would never tell.

She told me she would rather die than have anyone find out, and she wished she hadn't told me. She told me she would kill herself if I told anyone. So I kept the secret, even from my hus-band and my sister, for over four years. I don't think my mother feels Nina's hurt, holding her off for all that time. Sometimes I want to smack her for being mean to Nina.

I want Nina to have fun and feel part of the family. Maybe I feel responsible because I didn't push the issue more. I probably could have made my mother see Nina. I should have pushed her, but she's so delicate and depressed. I have a lack of respect for the way my mother handled it, especially after my father and grandmother died. Because then it was only about her. She was afraid of what people would think. I see her now as more than just my mother. [I see her] as a woman who has weaknesses and failings I don't admire and more qualities I admire. I'm sorry Nina didn't get to know her when she was younger and less depressed.

I lost respect for my mother, but I'm not in her shoes. I don't have her anxiety or depression, so I really can't judge her. I'm frustrated, but she also could have refused to speak to Nina altogether. She did hang in there and had a relationship with her. She just couldn't visualize how it could be positive; she had no idea it could turn out well. Here's a child who reaches out to you. How could you keep her at arm's length?

It took courage for Nina to stay with it. I'd give up if someone wanted me to stay a secret in a corner. I can tell Nina is needy. Mom didn't send her a birthday card the first year we had contact, and Nina felt bad. It was an oversight. I said to my mother, "You didn't send her a card?" She asked me, "Is that something I should do?" It's still strange to her. She doesn't know what to do.

Nina's a gift. She's a lot of fun. If I'd met her and she wasn't my sister, she'd be my dear friend. There's no strangeness for me. I look at her, and she reminds me of Mom. The voice, the movements, the way she looks. Seeing my mother in her makes it easier to have a comfort level with her. She really is my sister.

I told Nina that even though I had my real mom and dad, I got a lot of stuff with it that wasn't so great. She did miss out on the fun we had. She'll openly ask all the questions—things she wants to know. What did we do on Halloween? What was Christmas like? She's so wise and brilliant, I don't want her to feel like the ugly duckling. I don't think of her as a half sister. I think of her as my sister.

Kim

Kim's memory of her shared life with Linda was very different, in major respects. In contrast to Linda, who adored her father and thought he saved her from her mother's overinvolvement, Kim experienced their father as distant and remote. She remembers him as rarely being at home. Kim felt nurtured by her mother's warmth and attention. Also, Kim believes Linda was jealous and threatened when their mother shifted her attention to her two younger children.

Kim agreed with Linda's description that she was an anxious baby and she remembers following her sister around. But, interestingly, she doesn't remember Linda being mean to her or pushing her away. Instead, she remembers that she was led by Linda into jointly tormenting their younger brother—waking him up in the middle of the night and "scaring the shit out of him" with frightening masks, or forcing him to swallow pill bugs, which they said were pills. She thinks Linda wanted to do this because Linda felt their mother preferred him. I was intrigued that Kim remembered being mean to her younger brother, but not her older sister being mean to her.

Kim admitted that she wanted parents like Ozzie and Harriet, and she didn't like it when they'd have a drink and would dance to

Stan Getz. "My parents would go out to nightclubs at 9:30 P.M. while all my friends had parents who went out at 5 P.M. for early bird dinners." She also confessed she was always snooping in their drawers, where she would find things that frightened her, so she didn't tell anyone. Once she found a deck of cards in their bureau that depicted couples in the act of intercourse—each card showed a different pose. Recently she told her mother about this childhood discovery and her mother said, "I can't believe you saw that." She remembers, at age seven, covering her nude body with her mother's silk scarves and lifting them off, pretending it was Elvis Presley who was pulling them off her body. She laughed when she told me that Linda interpreted her behavior as meaning that she was actually a sex maniac.

Kim told me it was the influence of the Catholic schools she went to that made her so nervous and fearful when she thought of her parents drinking or having sex. But I wonder if the fact that her father was a wiseguy and that his life revolved around criminal activities might have added to her anxiety. She explained that "I looked to religion for my security."

In high school, she met her first love. She remembers when they first embraced. They were at a party, and he'd taken his Pendleton sweater off, and Kim sneaked into a bedroom to try it on and he discovered her wearing his sweater. They were a couple for a year and a half, until she heard he'd kissed another girl. Kim said she looked into the future and worried he would break her heart and that she'd never recover because she loved him so much. "At that time, I was married to him in my mind. I thought, What if we're married with kids, and he hurts me and I can't recover. I loved him too much. I couldn't marry him."

So instead, Kim chose a man who would never hurt her: a devout Christian who'd been adopted and had never felt he had a family. She knew her husband was a good man and would never leave her. She met him when she was working in a dental office, and he came in with an impacted wisdom tooth. "I put film in his mouth, and I was impressed it was so clean. You'd think I was buying a horse."

A few years ago Kim felt she had to move her family far away, to Florida. She wanted to leave New York and be in a place where she and her family could live a more spiritual life and find their own identity. She misses the daily contact with Linda because they'd become very close once they both had children, but now she can focus on their spiritual life and living close to nature. She talks to Linda frequently and has long visits with her at least twice a year.

Kim feels that the problems she's had, including her frequent thoughts about her first love and a long struggle with bulimia, are somehow connected to her father's elusiveness. She doesn't idealize her father, as Linda does, but, like Linda, she wishes Nina could have known her mother when she was young and beautiful. "The pride of Mother's beauty—I enjoyed the fact that when Mom and Dad walked into a room, it turned heads. But there was a lot of poopy stuff."

Kim feels a little guilty that Linda has the daily responsibility of caring for their mother, but she doesn't agree that her mother is difficult. She thinks the main problem is that Linda needs to mellow out.

When she first learned about Nina, she was delighted to find out she had another sister. "I feel Mom in her. I feel this oneness. She looks like my mother. Now that she's in the picture, I feel less pressure about taking care of Mom. Nina can support Linda. Mom is not a burden, but Linda's so taxed emotionally, so Mom seems like a problem."

She told me how she learned about Nina on a visit to her mother:

Two summers ago, the day before I was leaving to go home, my mother said, "Come over, I have something to tell you." I thought she had cancer. I went over and sat on the couch, and she looked at me and said, "When I was eighteen years old I saw the most beautiful guy in a sweater. We were together for one night and I had a child and her name is Nina. She is fifty-four years old and I've been talking to her for several years. I want you to meet her."

I thought it was an interesting slip that Kim said her mother fell in love with a man in a sweater. It was Kim's first love who wore the sweater, and her mother's story was of falling in love with a man in a military uniform. One reason Kim moved to Florida was to get far away from her high school boyfriend, who is too much on her mind. But there is something eerily similar about most of the women in this family and their first loves. Nina, Linda, Laura, and even Laura's mother and Nina's mother all initially became mothers with "bad boys" or unconventional ones, and none of them lasted as partners or fathers. Like a Shakespearean drama, it seems the plots of one generation are revisited on the next, no matter how people try to escape their destiny.

———

WHEN I COMPARE Nina's two mothers, I think she grew up with the more solid one. Nina romanticizes what she missed, although Kim and Linda are the first to say their childhoods were far from perfect.

For Nina, finding her birth mother and sisters has filled a need that no one could fill before. She wanted to know what everyone wants to know about themselves: "Where did I come from?" "Who am I?" Although Nina knows, intellectually, that she's attractive, she's always felt like the ugly duckling because she was searching for her biological family.

The sisters aren't totally free of illusions. Kim doesn't recognize how difficult it is for Linda to take care of their depressed and anxious mother. Linda's memories of her father strike me as a little romanticized. Nina idealizes the life of the family she missed: She thinks mainly of how interesting the family was and doesn't see its dysfunctions. But, on the whole, I see all three women moving from imagined relationships to real ones.

Nina has a realistic view of her sisters: She's really enjoying them and thinks they are caring and welcoming and lots of fun. The hurt she feels when her biological mother doesn't treat her the same way she treats Linda and Kim reveals that Nina is sometimes relating to an imagined mother. She says she understands why Laura treats her differently than the daughters she raised, but the fact that Nina is still hurt at not being treated as a full daughter reveals she still nurtures a wish that her mother would be different from the woman who put off meeting her, even after there were no good excuses for doing so.

I also wondered why Linda and Kim kept remarking that Nina looked like their mother. Was it just a shock to see someone with her physical features, or were they seeing a resurrected, younger mother in her—the beautiful woman their mother was before she became depressed?

Or maybe, the moral of this story is that being a sister isn't just about sharing a childhood, which is what I have always thought. Maybe that sense of a biological connection with each other and one's mother, as Nina argued, is a really huge component of feeling a deep connection. Their relationship with Nina is untarnished by childhood rivalries. Unlike most adult sisters, they could relate to Nina as adults instead of as children.

The Sister Who Grew Up

The story of Diane and Sylvie taught me something about the workings of memory. Sylvie resented taking care of her younger sister, but Diane didn't notice it at all. Diane only remembered the good parts—that she got to be with her beloved older sister. This story is a lesson that we sometimes have no way of knowing when something we did meant so much to another person. Sometimes we remember the bad things we did, but they remember the good things instead.

When Sylvie was eight and a half, and her older brother Jack was ten, her forty-one-year-old mother gave birth to twins: Dan and Diane. It was the 1950s, in rural Michigan, and eight-year-old Sylvie was made responsible for caring for the babies, even after her mother recovered from postdelivery complications. Sylvie was the twins' primary caretaker, and she resented it.

The arrival of the twins also coincided with the family's descent into poverty. When the twins were two, their father was laid off, and his brother talked him into taking a new job selling insurance, which was a disaster, because he didn't have a salesman's personality. Sylvie remembers living in poverty from the time she was ten until she married at twenty. They were on welfare, and her cousin would bring over food.

When the twins were about eight, Sylvie's mother became sick with cancer (probably breast cancer) that had metastasized to her hip. Now Sylvie also had to help her mother move up and down the steps. Sylvie remembers her mother as high-strung, hysterical, and vain, though in retrospect she realizes her mother must have been anxious and depressed by her illness, which was never, ever, spoken of. After graduating from high school, Sylvie started working. When she was twenty, her mother died, and Sylvie married her boyfriend and moved to Illinois to get away from the entire family. Her older brother got married and left at the same time.

Their father was devastated by their mother's death. According to Sylvie, he'd been madly in love with their mother since he knew her in the seventh grade, but it seemed she'd never loved him the same way. Now he was left alone with the twelve-year-old twins, and he started to drink heavily.

He'd always been an alcoholic, but my mother had kept him under control. Now he drank all day, and he was obnoxious and abusive. Diane and Dan had a much more difficult life after Jack and I left. It affected Diane's life for many years. She was quiet and shy, and she thought she had killed my mom, because my parents never communicated anything about her illness.

Diane turned thirteen right after my mother died. I'm not sure I was at her confirmation—I'd already moved away. She went to high school, and my father became mean and nasty and awful and drunk. Diane later told me she had only one friend all through high school. She started drinking and smoking pot, and my father would go into a rage and badly abused her.

I brought her to Illinois and asked my husband if we could keep her with us. My husband said, "No. This is not our child." So she lived in poverty with my father and developed many problems which could have been avoided. Dan did well. He started to work his way through college, like Jack. But no one encouraged the girls in our family.

Diane became involved with an awful guy and got pregnant, then married and she got pregnant again. Her husband was out all night when she gave birth to her second child. So at twenty-four, she wound up divorced and with two kids on welfare and no child support.

She'd asked my father for help, but he wouldn't give it. Then, when she was twenty-six, my dad had a major stroke and no nursing home would take him. He was blind; he couldn't talk or write; he could barely walk and couldn't control his bowels. Diane and her two babies moved in with him, and she took care of him for seven years, until he died.

There were big financial issues that caused problems. My father had money coming in, and he paid his share of their rent. My older brother controlled the purse strings, while Diane was doing all the work. Some money was set aside for her, but she had to ask my brother for it because she wasn't that responsible with money.

When Dad got sick, I told Diane, "I took care of Mom and the whole family when she was dying. Now it's your turn to take care of Dad." I didn't feel guilty. I was pretty fed up with Dad then.

She worked at night in a restaurant at a minimum-wage job and dropped the kids off with a babysitter. A few years later, she met another guy who was a drug-using loser at that time, and she got pregnant again and married him. Eventually, he stopped using drugs and became a good father and Diane started college, part-time, while she was working.

When Diane was forty-one she developed breast cancer, which had spread to two nodes. She'd volunteered to be in a medical study and got a massive dose of chemotherapy that made her hemorrhage. I got a call that she'd lost 25 percent of her blood and might not live. She survived and had radiation treatments and went right back to work and school. She never complains or pities herself.

She rose from the bottom job, making sandwiches, and seventeen years later she's in the top management of the company—a chain of thirty restaurants. There are the owners, the vice presidents, and then Diane. She's opened several stores for them, and they love her. This spring she is graduating from college. I'm tremendously proud of her. I've had adversity, but not as much as she. She's earning a decent living and her husband, whom I've grown to love, also has a good job.

Growing up, I was like her mother, not just her sister. I was burdened as a child. Taking care of the twins kept me from having a social life. My family could have become divided because Dad treated Diane so badly, but we stayed close.

My husband left me after sixteen years of marriage. I thought we were working on things together, and I had no idea he was already involved with his young secretary. He was an alcoholic and irresponsible.

I don't feel guilty for not taking my sister to live with us when she was a teenager, but it would have saved her from so many problems. It wouldn't have been easy. She was a lost soul. When she came to visit us, when she was a teenager, she didn't want to go back to live with Dad. There was nothing there. No caring or attention or confidence building. So she rebelled against it. I don't take responsibility for the hard road she's had. She had a knack for making poor decisions and she's making good ones now.

I'm very proud of her, and I offer her support in anything she does. Our relationship is getting to be more of equals. I'm not a parent; maybe I'm a mentor. But I'm learning from her. She tells me what's happening in her business. When she has to fire someone or she doesn't agree with the other managers, we'll talk about it and I learn from her about how businesses work. I ask her about what she's learning in school. She has done things I haven't had to do, and I admire her courage and selflessness.

Several times, Sylvie said that she didn't feel guilty for turning Diane away when she was teenager: I wondered if she protested too much, or was trying to persuade herself. Of course, her husband was right. Diane wasn't their child. But being the caring sister she is, it must be hard for Sylvie to think about having left Diane when she'd been the only real parent her sister ever had.

Diane

Sylvie had described how much she resented the burden of caring for her younger siblings when she was an adolescent. But speaking to Diane, one would never have guessed it was obvious. She told me she had a happy childhood, until her mother died when she was twelve. Then Sylvie and her brother Jack married and left when she was thirteen. This was hard because she always felt much closer to Sylvie than to her mother.

Sylvie was the one who would come in and read stories. I can remember my sister interacting with me, but not my mom. I remember Sylvie laughing with me and giving us baths when we were younger. Taking us shopping. I remember she made us tuna casserole. I still make it—my kids hate it, but it brings back memories of my sister and brother and me together. She also made boxed pizzas, with Chef Boyardee. That was the coolest thing. Sylvie would do fun things.

Sometimes Sylvie let me sleep in her room when it was cold—that was so special. She'd be asleep when I came in. But just getting under her covers, I felt secure and safe. That total comfort, it's hard to describe. When I was a teenager and visited her, she taught me how to bake. She's a fantastic cook. I'd watch my mom, but she never taught me.

The only image I have of Mom is working in the kitchen or doing the ironing, and the last year of her life, when she was confined to the house, lying in a hospital bed.

I didn't know she had cancer and that she wasn't getting better until the day before she died. I learned later on that my mother knew she would die, and the doctors had told Dad and Sylvie and my older brother. But for whatever reason, no one told me or my twin brother, Dan. I'm sure they had good intentions. My mother couldn't get out of bed on her own, so I spent most of my time taking care of her.

I'd come home from school and sit and watch the soaps with her, but she didn't talk to me about life. I feel a lot of emptiness that I don't know her; I don't know who or what she was. I don't remember her personally.

When we were teenagers, my twin brother and I were left alone with Dad. Dan and I were close then, but once we were adults he went through a divorce and never talked about it. Sylvie is the one that all my siblings are closest to. She's the nucleus of the family. She's the one everyone will call and talk to. That's Sylvie. She's always said she's the mother.

But apparently, Sylvie was at least ambivalent about this role, and Diane had to accept the reality.

Even through my teenage years, Sylvie would tell me, "I'm not your mother," though I wanted her to be, because I needed a mother. She was struggling to establish her identity. She'd gotten married and moved away when everything was a mess.

At some point, when I was a teenager, I wrote her a letter and asked her to take me in. She wrote me a letter trying to motivate me but she said, "I'm not your mother. I can't take the place of your mother. You have to do this for yourself." She had to say that for me to understand. Maybe I realized I had to stop using her as a crutch.

I did a lot of soul-searching later in life and realized I needed to become my own parent. My life was out of control and going nowhere. It wasn't until I was in my thirties that I said, Where are you going here?

I shouldn't have married my first husband. I didn't love him. When I got pregnant, I was afraid of telling my dad, because I was brought up in the church. So I got married. Sylvie helped me find an apartment, but she knew it wouldn't last. I remember my sister during the wedding, just looking at me. She has a habit of studying people; you know she's deep in thought and contemplating, running out the scenarios. She could see my ex-husband for what he was. She knew right away, from meeting his family. I didn't. I was just trying to get out of the house. So I got pregnant and got out. That marriage didn't last five years but I got two beautiful kids out of it.

I was on welfare with two small kids, as low as you can go, spending time at Dad's house, because I had no money and nowhere to go. He'd cook me dinner. I asked him if I could come home until I got on my feet but he wouldn't allow it. He said, "You made your bed, now lie in it."

Then, Dad had a stroke. Everyone else had moved away, and I was the only one left. He couldn't live by himself, but they said he wasn't bad enough to be taken into a nursing home. I said, without thinking, "I'll take him in." I wasn't even thinking what it meant.

Diane told me how she resented being told by her brother and sister-in-law that her hundred-dollar-a-month payment for taking care of her father would be put in a savings account for her, but she couldn't touch the money.

They were telling me I wasn't responsible enough to have money, but I was responsible enough to take care of Dad. He lived with me for seven years. I couldn't go on a vacation or away for a weekend all that time. I heard my brothers were taking trips, but I couldn't do anything. I had Dad with me, and the kids. I tried to say, "Why don't you fly him out and let him stay with you for a month, so I can have a break?" They all said, "We don't have the facilities, and you said you would do this."

After two years, I got an entry-level job. But now I was putting money in the bank and I could buy the kids bikes and clothes. I still work for the same restaurant chain. I worked my way up to senior supervisor in charge of thirty stores. It wouldn't have been the career I'd have chosen, but things happen.

My relationship with Sylvie changed about four years ago, when I was halfway through college. I realized I was forty-something years old, and I wasn't a kid anymore. I didn't have to tell every problem to her. She's always known when I needed something, anyway.

One winter I was feeling down about something and a package arrived. It was a Christmas sweater set she saw on QVC. It came right before a party I had at work, where everyone would be wearing holiday sweaters, and I couldn't afford to buy one. I asked her how she knew I needed this, when I'd never had a sweater like it. She told me she figured it out from something I said. She has this way of really listening. She's always been that way.

Hearing about Sylvie's ability to choose the right sweater for her sister, I couldn't help but remember Pat and Nancy. Pat was furious that Nancy had sent her an "itchy wool" sweater and insisted she keep it even though Pat said she couldn't wear wool. Unlike Pat and Nancy, Sylvie and Diane know how to give and receive.

I have always idolized her—I still do. I thought she had no problems because no one in my family discusses problems. I have gotten to the point where I think we are equals and she tells me when her kids have the same struggles.

Five years ago I almost died. She was so supportive when I was sick, just hearing her voice on the phone. Sometimes I was too sick to talk. She understood that. I'd just be crying and she'd sit there in silence and let me do that. I couldn't get that from my husband and children—that level of understanding.

About eight or nine years ago, I went on a self-journey. I realized I had to become my own parent. I did a mental exercise where I see myself as a child. I saw how my mother handled it, and then I allowed myself as a child to be treated differently.

One time, it was the Fourth of July and I had on a pretty dress. We didn't get new dresses often, because we had no money. This was a special occasion. Someone told me not to go on the front porch because Dad had painted it. I went on the porch and I was terrified to see I had leaned on something and the paint was all over me. I hid in the yard. When my mother found me, she went ballistic. "How could you do that? I told you not to." She ripped the dress off me.

I remember going into this place. I am this little girl running into the yard, and instead of Mom coming out screaming and crying, she says, "I'm so sorry that dress is ruined. Let's take it off and see if we can fix it." She's sympathetic. I learned to become my own mom. Every time I remember something like that, I can do that.

I asked Diane how she learned this technique.

Out of accident. One night I was lying in bed and thinking, How could that have been if it was handled differently? I played it through my mind. I realized there is something here. After I did that, I cried. I realized I wanted Mom to do that. When I had my kids, I talked to them all the time. I joked with them and made a conscious decision to be the mom I never had.

When Sylvie moved after my mother died, I was very hurt. It was like Mom dying all over again. We'd shared a room in the apartment we moved to just before she married. When her wedding dress was hanging in our room, I would look at that dress and cry and cry and cry. I put up walls because of that hurt. I think it occurred to her, but she was trying to take care of herself.

Sylvie is a special person. She's so intuitive. She knows what someone wants. My twin brother will call and not have a real conversation. It's like talking to a stranger. Sisters have a special kind of bond, a level of understanding. It's almost like talking with yourself at some point.

I'VE NOTICED THE CHILDHOOD LOSSES that often drive sisters apart can also provide the motivation for keeping them together. I think these sisters were able to have an enduring and loving relationship because they didn't blame each other for what they didn't get from their parents and they were able to accept and forgive each other's limitations.

Sylvie said she was angry about having to sacrifice her childhood to take care of her younger siblings, but she didn't blame them. I've wondered why Diane didn't perceive or feel Sylvie's resentment when they were young. Is it possible that Sylvie showed nothing of her anger when she was forced to be a mother surrogate? Perhaps she just accepted her responsibility and didn't realize how much she resented it until later. Maybe Diane chose not to see what would have been too threatening, since Sylvie was all she had. People who are given little love in childhood often romanticize or idealize the meager offerings. When your mother seems like a stranger, the joys of discovering Chef Boyardee or getting to sleep in your sister's bed don't really add up to a "happy" childhood. But maybe Diane is recognizing and appreciating that she did have an extraordinary sister, even if her sister could not be her mother.

I wondered what kept Diane locked into seven miserable years of caring for her invalid father, especially after his cruelty to her. Was it the pattern of an abused child who clings to her parents? Or was she swayed by Sylvie's message—that this was her turn—and was she fearful that she'd lose her siblings if she didn't do what they wanted her to do?

In the end, as adults, Sylvie and Diane didn't blame each other for what their parents did and did not do, and it seems they never did. And they see their Real Sister and find much to admire.

CHAPTER 12

Conclusion
The Time to Make Amends

MOST PARENTS WANT their children to be good friends because they worry about what will happen to their children after they're gone. If their children are close, they feel reassured that none of them will ever be left alone or without anyone to help or love them.

Many of the women I interviewed had mothers or fathers who conveyed this wish, asking them to always look out for their sister or emphasizing the value of sister loyalty as a way to survive life's other losses.

There is wisdom here, in addition to love and concern. The sisters I met who are close feel they have something special that isn't found in other relationships. A few told me no one could make them laugh the way their sister could. One put it this way: When she's with her sister, they only need to look at a dog that's doing something odd and they'll burst into laughter, while no one else around them can understand what's so funny. Some sisters, like Anna and Leslie, enjoy doing something "naughty" together, like sneaking off to have plastic surgery. Ellie would rather be with her twin sister than with her grandchildren in her old age. Chasing after children can make you feel very old, while being with someone who understands you and makes you laugh can make you feel very young.

Other sisters found tremendous joy in bringing up their children—especially their daughters—together. Sharing their daughters' experiences was a way of reliving their youth together, as well as sharing the children they loved. For the Ryan sisters, gathering their children every summer and hanging out around their parents' swimming pool gave them a precious feeling of continuity over the generations, a seamless connection between their present lives and their happy memories of childhood.

For others, the special joy was being part of a large, extended family. And Nina's late-found sisters were overjoyed to discover they had a fun-loving sister they hadn't even known existed. Nina's sister Linda compared the joy of discovering Nina to being like a child at Christmas: You open up a big box, hoping it's the doll you asked for, and instead, it turns out to be a live puppy—a gift that exceeds anything you imagined. More than one woman told me that when she first got married and baked her first pie from scratch, her older sister stayed on the phone with her for two hours, guiding her through the entire process. Who else but a sister would do that? For Lizzie and Charlotte, the uniqueness of their relationship was the fact that together they had filled the void of their missing mother, and they knew they could always depend on each other to be there in any moment of need.

Other sisters who initially didn't get along so well made an important discovery when they honored their parents' wishes for them to stick together. Their relationship turned out to be something very special, especially after they lost their parents. Being close to each other was not only a way to pay tribute, but it allowed them to feel their parents' presence. They acted in a caring way toward their sister—even when it wasn't easy—to repay the care their parents showed to them, or they acted as their parents would have or would have wished for them to act. In doing this, they felt their parents lived on in them. By internalizing aspects of the parents they loved and admired, they could feel their parents were still with them.

Even sisters who don't feel this obligation to their parents often want to resolve their sister conflicts, especially as they grow older. Most people feel they lose a part of themselves when they lose the people who were important in their lives. When we are children, our parents are usually our primary witnesses in life—they give us a sense of continuity. Later in life, it's usually partners and children who do that. But our sister is often the only person who is with us all our lives. Sharing memories with her is also a way to feel connected to our parents after they are gone.

We can always have memories on our own, of course. But memories become relatively lifeless when there's no one to share them with, no one to remind us of details we've forgotten. Having someone who shares them makes our memories more real because they have an independent existence.

Sisters also help us reinterpret or reconstruct the past, which is something we do throughout life. As we age, our accumulated experiences often lead us to reassess our view of the past. In this continuous process of trying to remember and to reinterpret, it helps to have someone else who was there and who saw things from a slightly different perspective. If you have brothers, they were present, too, but sisters, being the same gender, tend to have more of a common experience.

Two Sisters Who Loved Their Father

Julie Rubin was born five years after her sister, Sherry. One of Julie's earliest memories is when Sherry's appendix burst and her father brought her back from the hospital: "My sister was all wrapped in my mother's fur coat and my father carried her up-stairs, and she got lots of dolls. I wanted to wear my mother's fur coat, too. I always thought Sherry was his favorite, and she thought I was his favorite."

The image of her beloved father tenderly carrying her sister, dressed in her mother's fur coat, which she and her sister ordinar-ily weren't allowed to touch, is a sweet reminder of Julie's love for her father and his tenderness toward his daughters. He was a well-liked pharmacist in their small Boston suburb, and he doted on his two girls, as they did on him. In contrast, Julie had never been wild about her mother, who appeared to be selfish and cold.

Julie's sister, Sherry, was the "perfect" child—sweet, agreeable, a straight-A student who always avoided conflict—while Julie was rebellious and "trouble." The girls shared a room until Sherry left for college, when Julie was thirteen. Around this time, her mother developed rheumatoid arthritis and took to her bed. After that she was depressed and complained all the time.

Sherry married an optician and remained in the same town as their parents. According to Julie, her sister was the Earth Mother who had four children and "who took everyone to her bosom." In contrast, Julie moved into the city where she became a successful businesswoman after she married her boss, a wealthy manufac-turer who was ten years older and who made it possible for Julie to have an exciting life. While her sister was a full-time mother, Julie had a live-in maid from the day her son was born.

Sherry lived close to their parents, but Julie returned every Saturday and Sunday for eight years to visit them, mainly because she wanted to help their father, who was totally devoted to their mother's care. When their mother reluctantly moved into a nursing home, their father became a volunteer at the home so he could be with his wife all day.

Sharing the burden of caring for their parents and becoming parents themselves is what really brought the sisters close together. Sharing a past is very powerful, but we can't just live in the past. Sherry and Julie cared for their parents and valued one another's children because they had learned about family devotion from the father they adored. Unfortunately, both of their husbands slightly resented how close the sisters were to each other and how much time they spent taking care of their parents. Maybe their husbands resented their closeness not only because it was a competing relationship, but because their bond was connected to their father. They might have felt that Julie and Sherry could never love them as much as they loved their father. Their husbands also hadn't shared their childhood.

Julie laughs when she thinks about it.

My brother-in-law is paranoid—"What are they whispering about?" he always wants to know. My sister is totally different when we're alone—we'll giggle and have a much better time. When our husbands were around, we always had to take care of them. My husband was jealous of my girlfriends and my sister, because men don't have close relationships of their own.

Julie's husband was always ill. He had a stroke the day after their son was born, and Sherry came and lived with her while Julie's husband was in the hospital. Julie has never forgotten her sister's loyalty and kindness through this ordeal. She was very young when her husband died, and on her own for a while. But now Julie lives in Boston with a new partner—a lawyer who specializes in litigation and has "an overwhelming personality." Her sister and brother-in-law felt intimidated by the sophisticated crowd Julie moved in with her first husband. Now they're turned off by her new partner's aggressiveness. Julie feels her partner is just accustomed to acting like a lawyer in a trial, even when he's with friends. She thinks he really has the sweetness she saw in her father. "I told him, 'You have to let someone else talk.'" She knows her sister will get to like him, because he makes her happy.

After all these years, Julie has come to appreciate her brother-in-law, because she can plainly see he's made her sister happy and he's been a loving father. He was also good to Julie when her husband suddenly died. "I'm more respectful and kinder as I'm older, because I see he is what he is. He'll repeat stories four times. He's tight with money and a nervous wreck. But he's a good father and a wonderful grandfather."

They've become close to each other's children. Julie's children adore their aunt Sherry, and Julie looked after her niece when she moved to Boston and feels very close to her. One of Sherry's children has a chronic illness, and Julie says it's a comfort for Sherry to know that Julie would always take care of her.

Until her father died, Julie was never involved with her Jewish religion, unlike her parents and sister and brother-in-law. But after her father died of a heart attack, she started to go to synagogue, at first to say the prayers for the dead. And this was something she always did with her sister. Their bond had always revolved around their adoration for their father and now it centered around remembering him. "I would always go with my sister to say Kaddish for my father, and on the anniversaries of his death. If I hear someone say *Ohmain* [Amen in Yiddish] I feel that he's right there."

Keeping a Promise to Your Mother

Maria Acosta is the woman who moved to the United States from Colombia. In chapter 9, I told of how she didn't get to say good-bye before her mother lapsed into a coma because her older sister was orchestrating her mother's final hours. Maria has a younger sister, too—a sister she detested in childhood.

Her elder sister was eleven years older than Maria, so Maria felt like the only (and favored) child until Donna was born seven years after she was. This last child was totally unexpected and not welcomed by Maria:

Suddenly I had a little sister. I was put aside and I didn't like it. My parents doted on her like grandparents, and she was a spoiled brat. My father was richer by then, and more flexible, so she had more material things and freedom than I had. She was disciplined less. If she saw new shoes that she wanted, she'd get them right away, when I'd had to wait. She had tantrums and everything was given to her whenever she demanded attention.

When people came to visit, she'd ask if they wanted to hear her act or sing, and everyone hushed and had to listen to her. She was the center. She and I were not close at all—we were very distant.

When I came to the United States at age thirty-five, after living in Venezuela and Brazil, Donna was already here and going through a rough time with her marriage. She was all alone. My mother wanted me to help her. I didn't like her at the time, but she was my sister, and out of love and respect for my mother I took the obligation seriously.

Latin families are close. In general, you take care of each other. She had been so spoiled and now I saw her suffering so much. She adored her husband and he left her with two small children. I didn't think she'd make it; I took over the mother role and we talked twice a day.

Then she married a second guy who was a total jerk. He tried to isolate her from everyone else and was very controlling. He didn't like us to speak Spanish with each other. She wouldn't leave him, but she'd call me every time they had a fight. I told my sister, "It's your life, do what you want, but I wouldn't put up with it." On Mother's Day he hit her and threw her out of the house.

I helped her get divorced and away from him. I told her she had a place in my house, she was my family—she wouldn't have to live under a bridge. Seeing her hurt, I saw a different person. Now she married a third guy who treats her so nice. I love her, and now we're very close.

To honor my parents I would do a lot to have a good relationship with my brothers and sisters. We had the same mother and father, and if you can't get along with your sister, how can you get along with strangers?

My parents told us that no matter what happens to them, we needed to be close with our sisters and brothers.

Something else happened that allowed her to move beyond simply keeping her promise. When Maria was seven, she was the one who felt abandoned and rejected when her baby sister pushed her from the center of their parents' attention. But now it was her sister who was abandoned and rejected, while Maria had a happy marriage. Maria was the adult who could give care and comfort to her sister. Seeing her sister so hurt and so powerless altered her view. Acting as her mother would have made Maria feel closer to her mother. Seeing her sister in a new light also allowed them to evolve into friends and equals.

Losing a Sister Is Losing Yourself

Pearl and her sister Dorothy, who was two years older, grew up on a farm in Nebraska. There were no other children within miles of their home, so they played with each other. Pearl adored her older sister, who could mistreat her, and once Dorothy egged her on to climb too high in a tree (by calling her a baby) and Pearl fell and hurt herself.

When their mother gave Dorothy an unprecedented spanking, Pearl felt worse than her sister. "I was so upset that my mother was spanking my sister that I took my favorite doll and slammed it on the floor and broke its head. My parents didn't replace it."

> We did certain things that were special to us. The Big Lady Look—we'd play mommies or adults by putting on cupid bow lipstick and we'd dress up and prance around. She was the leader and had such an imagination. Sometimes she was mean to me, but in later years she apologized to me so many times.

She remembers Dorothy's kindness to her over an incident with their father that was so hurtful it affected her for years.

My father was a stickler for grammar. He was always pointing out someone's grammatical errors. Once we were sitting around the table, talking about something our minister had said in a sermon, and my father made a grammatical error. I asked him why he said it that way when it sounded better another way.

"Who are you to criticize me?" he said. I was devastated by his tone of voice. He made me feel worthless, and this was from someone who was supposed to make me feel great.

For a long time after that, Pearl, who was a very obedient child, acted very gingerly around her father. That one rebuke had changed her entire demeanor.

My sister helped me to see that you can't take one incident and make it into a life-forming thing. She reminded me of how proud my father was of me. I was twelve or thirteen at the time.

When Dorothy was fifty she was diagnosed with a slow-growing cancer in her salivary gland, which had already spread to her lungs. For four years Pearl did all she could to find the best doctors and treatments for her sister and alternated with their elderly parents in taking care of Dorothy at the end. Toward the end, Pearl had gone back home, and got a call from Dorothy's son. He said, "Mom wants to talk with you."

She could hardly speak. Every word was such a big effort. She took long pauses between every breath. I thought it was a strain, and that she needed some rest, so I told her I loved her and that I'd talk to her soon. The phone rang a few minutes later. Her daughter told me that Dorothy wasn't done talking yet. I sat on the phone with her for forty-five minutes. She wanted to remember something, and we said good-bye. She died a couple of days later.

You have to cherish that special thing you share. When Dorothy died, I lost a lot of things I remembered. Our dolls and what we called them. Our Big Lady Look. What it was like to be a little girl on that farm, and that time we spent as children. That's something you share only with a sibling who's close to your age. My younger sister, who was born when I was fifteen, never lived on a farm. My folks had a lot more money when she was born, and she didn't have younger siblings. Her memories are not the same as mine.

No one else remembers your childhood in the same way as a sister who was almost your age. You need to cherish that. You need to be able to count on your family and you need to be able to be counted on. Who else would care as much and give you moral support and kindness and physical help when you need it?

———

ONE OF THE GREATEST PLEASURES I had was meeting sisters who had reached a point in life where they understood what really mattered. Perhaps their brother-in-law, who once annoyed them because he was anxious or repeated his stories, now looked a lot better for having shown his loyalty and devotion to his family over the years. Raising children, losing people they loved, made them look at life a different way. Some learned these lessons earlier than others because they'd been lucky enough to have wise and loving parents and they remembered what their parents had taught them.

We all know how easy it is to get caught up in petty resentments or old hurts, and not see what we are missing. Some of the sisters in this book have suffered a lot because they tried to hold on to something they never really had—a wish or an illusion—like

Nora, the nearly blind child who was forced to cling to her selfish sister: Forty-five years later, she's still not ready to let go. There are some extreme cases where a sister might need to give up on a relationship. But these are very rare. Far more often, I saw sisters who loved each other but their unexamined expectations and assumptions kept getting in the way.

When we can't have the relationship we thought we wanted, we're frequently blind to the even better one that's in easy reach. I think of Nina's birth mother who, for twenty years, postponed the chance to meet her wonderful daughter. She lived her whole life in fear that the phone would ring and her secret would come out. As her other daughter recognized, she just couldn't imagine things could turn out so well—that she had something to gain, not everything to lose.

As every year comes to a close, movie versions of Charles Dickens's *A Christmas Carol* are always on television, and I never get tired of watching them. This is the story of Ebenezer Scrooge, who has persevered in the wrong path all his life, all because of an early disappointment. Just before Christmas, Scrooge is visited by three ghosts, who, in turn, force him to look at his past, his present, and his future. They have come to show him that he's followed a path that led him away from happiness. They remind him of people who were kind to him in the past (including his late sister) and the price he has paid by turning away from love and compassion. They give him a glimpse into his ghastly future.

Scrooge is already an old man when the spirits appear, but he learns there's still time to change his life. It's late, but he gets a second chance to express love and receive it, including from his good-natured nephew—the son of the sister whose loyalty and affection he'd forgotten. Scrooge is thoroughly shaken by what the ghosts of the past, present, and future have forced him to see. But he wakes up on Christmas Day with joy to discover he's still alive. Scrooge makes a vow, which he keeps, that he won't forget the lessons the three ghosts have taught him. And of all things, he's most grateful he still has time before him to make amends.

I've been saying all along that we need to understand the past but live in the present. I think of the sisters in this book as being like those three spirits, holding up their lights to our past and present, but also to our future, to help us if we, too, need to make amends.

Epilogue

I want to offer some references on earlier sibling studies and discuss how they relate to my research. An excellent source for an overview of what has been done by social scientists is *Sibling Relationships Across the Life Span* by Victor G. Cicirelli (New York: Plenum, 1995). In this volume the author reviews the research done up to 1995 from a wide range of disciplines and perspectives and notes that most of the studies have focused either on childhood and adolescence or sibling support in old age. One of Cicirelli's conclusions is that we need to develop theories that explain sibling attachment, sibling behavior, and changes in relationships over the entire course of siblings' lives. I share that view, which is why I asked women to think about their relationships with their sisters starting from their early childhood to the present.

One conclusion I reached in my research is that it's unlikely there will be any single theory that explains all sister relationships—they are too diverse and have such widely different meanings. I also concluded that sister relationships are often embedded in a complex web of attachments and identifications that involve relationships with mothers. I also concluded that just as daughters relate to different images of their mothers (some realistic, some shaped by fantasy or emotion, some constructed by the culture) so do sisters relate to multiple images of their sisters—and not all of these images are consciously recognized. I found that sister relationships are initially shaped by the larger family context and parent-child relationship. But those relationships don't necessarily remain fixed: Sisters who had little affection or contact in childhood might become close friends in adulthood or vice versa.

In his review of research findings Cicirelli also makes the point that we need to develop concepts that help to explain why siblings are close or distant and why their relationships change. I think these are also the questions that matter most to the people who are trying to understand their relationships and resolve their conflicts. For this reason, I chose a method of gathering data and reporting my findings that would go the very heart of these issues. In an open-ended way, I asked my informants to describe their relationships with their sisters, starting with their early years growing up in their family and continuing through their lives to the present. I also asked them to tell me about the events that were especially important or memorable to them. I used this approach to move the interviews toward the issues that held the greatest emotional importance for my informants. I believe the use of narratives gives us an opportunity to get close to the emotional experiences and meanings of sisterhood.

One of the major problems in the research summarized by Cicirelli is that the studies typically investigated siblings rather than sisters or brothers or cross-sibling pairs. In recent years gender has come to the forefront of the way we look at intimate relationships. From the recent gender-specific findings that appear in the sibling studies, it's clear that we can't group together all sibling relationships as if sisterhood, brotherhood, and cross-sibling ties are equivalent. A consistent finding on surveys is that sisters, taken as a group, have more frequent contact and are closer to one another than are brothers or sister-brother pairs. For example, Shelley Eriksen and Naomi Gerstel found that women were more likely than men to discuss personal concerns with siblings and more likely to provide siblings with childcare and help when someone is sick (*Journal of Family Issues*, vol. 23, no. 7, October 2002).

Gender differences in assuming the caretaking role appears early in life: Cicirelli and others have noted that parents ask older sisters, but not older brothers, to take care of their younger siblings. In her review of research on the kinds of sibling support that appear at different stages of life, Ann Goetting also noted that older daughters may assume considerable caretaking responsibilities and the bonds between sisters in old age are stronger than ties between other combinations of siblings (*Journal of Marriage and the Family*, vol. 48, November 1986). Goetting also found there's more sibling interaction among those who are widowed, divorced, single, or childless—sibling relationships assume a greater importance when other family ties are absent. Considering that women are much more likely than men to spend major portions of their lives without a partner, this also suggests why many women attach a great value to having a close sister as they reach middle age. But I want to stress that it would be a mistake to ignore the great variation within gender-specific dyads. There are brothers who are extremely close and sisters who rarely speak.

The Sibling Bond by Stephen Bank and Michael Kahn (New York: Basic Books, 1982) was one of the early attempts to investigate whether or not siblings influence personality development and how that influence is affected by insufficient parental attention.

Unfortunately, their consideration of gender was limited to just a few pages and their investigation didn't examine sisterhood per se. I agree with these authors that siblings may play a large role in identity formation, and I also share their assumption that the original sibling bond must be understood within the context of the broader family dynamics. But in 2004 it strikes me that gender must be a central concern when thinking about identity formation.

Judy Dunn and a number of her colleagues have published several interesting studies based on their direct observation of young children and their mothers. Dunn's book, *Sisters and Brothers* (Cambridge: Harvard University, 1985) gives an overview of some of this interesting research. In this body of work one may find many touching descriptions of how infants become very attached to their older siblings when their mothers aren't present and how older children interpret the communications made by infants and infer what the babies are feeling or trying to say. Dunn and her colleagues also document the impact of supportive or critical behavior from older siblings on the adjustment of the younger child.

For readers who are interested in studies of sisters in literature and film, I would recommend the following books: Eva Rueschmann's *Sisters on Screen: Siblings in Contemporary Cinema* (Philadelphia: Temple University Press, 2000) and Lucy Fischer's essay, "Sisters: The Divided Self", in *Shot/Countershot: Film Tradition and Women's Cinema* (Princeton: Princeton University Press, 1989). These books were interesting to me because they explore many of the psychological issues that appear so prominently in the stories I heard—the construction of "good" and "bad" sisters; sisters as mirrors reflecting sameness and difference; the connection between sisterhood and parent-child bonds.

Many people like to speculate about the impact of birth order, and an older body of research tried to find some connection be-

tween birth order and individual characteristics such as personality types. Most current researchers find little evidence for any in-
trinsic differences according to birth order, but instead they are
trying to examine the complex effects of occupying a different
birth position in the family structure or history.

Finally, I want to recommend Barrie Thorne's *Gender Play: Girls
and Boys in School* (Piscataway, NJ: Rutgers University Press,
1993). Although it's not specifically about siblings, it provides a
brilliant portrait of how children construct their own shared
worlds and meanings in their play and games—a separate world
that isn't sufficiently appreciated by adults. I often thought about
Thorne's book when I heard the frequent and memorable accounts of how young sisters created elaborate make-believe worlds
in their hours of play and their nightly whispering after the lights
were turned out.

Acknowledgments

I am deeply grateful to Jane Isay, my editor at Harcourt, for her wisdom and guidance throughout this project. Her responses to the interviews were penetrating and illuminating. She saved me from drowning in a sea of papers and files with her thoughtful suggestions about how to organize and use the massive amounts of material I had collected. I also want to thank Jane for her constant enthusiasm, responsiveness, and friendship.

David Hough was a superb reader and editor in the later stages of the project. I thank him profoundly for his unfailing patience, warmth, and good humor and for improving nearly every paragraph of the manuscript. I'm indebted to Jenna Johnson for her remarkable skill, energy, and dedication in guiding the book through every step of its publication. And finally, at Harcourt, I thank Rachel Myers and Susan Amster for their very careful and sensitive readings of the manuscript. *The Perfect Sister* is far better for having passed through the hands of all these generous and talented experts, and they made it a genuine pleasure to write the book at Harcourt.

As always, I'm greatly indebted to Sandra Dijkstra, my brilliant and indefatigable agent, for her terrific vision and direction since day one of this project. I also want to thank Babette Sparr and Elisabeth James of the Sandra Dijkstra Literary Agency for their enormous contributions and kindness over the years.

I am grateful to the University of California at Santa Cruz for allowing me to take time off from teaching so I could do the research for this project and have the focus required for writing the book. In particular, I want to thank Craig Reinarman, Donna Hagler, and Lorraine Meusel of the Sociology Department at UCSC for their generosity and efforts when they were already under so much pressure to cover the curriculum.

Nancy Adler, Naomi Bushman, Charlie Haas, Carol Hill, Steve Kornetsy, B. K. Moran, and Michael Schaffer have made countless contributions to this work. I thank them for all their insights, suggestions, and generosity in helping me think through a great many issues and problems.

I want to thank my sister, Sandra Resnick, for being the big sister I looked up to and adored and for all those years during our childhood when she allowed me to tag along after her. She was my first playmate, my ally and teacher. Many of my happiest memories from childhood are inseparable from her. It means more than I can say to have had my sister then and to have her now, and to have my sister throughout my entire life.

Wayne A. Myers has been an inspiration throughout this project. His insights and ideas about families and relationships appear in every chapter and page of this book. He has the patience and generosity of a saint, and, fortunately, he's a saint with a wonderful sense of humor.

Finally, I am deeply grateful to all the women who allowed me to interview them for this project and who generously and courageously shared their feelings and experiences. I regret I'm unable to thank them by name, for their stories have given this book its life.